Essentials of Psychological Tele-Assessment

Essentials of Psychological Assessment Series
Series Editors, Alan S. Kaufman and Nadeen L. Kaufman

Essentials

of Psychological

Tele-Assessment

A. Jordan Wright
Susan Engi Raiford

WILEY

This edition first published 2021
© 2021 John Wiley & Sons, Inc.

The right of A. Jordan Wright and Susan Engi Raiford to be identified as the author(s) of this work has been asserted in accordance with law.

Registered Office(s)
John Wiley & Sons, Inc., 111 River Street, Hoboken, NJ 07030, USA

Editorial Office
111 River Street, Hoboken, NJ 07030, USA

For details of our global editorial offices, customer services, and more information about Wiley products visit us at www.wiley.com.

Wiley also publishes its books in a variety of electronic formats and by print-on-demand. Some content that appears in standard print versions of this book may not be available in other formats.

Library of Congress Cataloging-in-Publication Data
Names: Wright, A. Jordan, author. | Raiford, Susan Engi, author.
Title: Essentials of psychological tele-assessment / A. Jordan Wright, Susan Engi Raiford.
Description: Hoboken, NJ : John Wiley & Sons, [2021] | Includes bibliographical references and index.
Identifiers: LCCN 2020037412 (print) | LCCN 2020037413 (ebook) | ISBN 9781119771883 (paperback) | ISBN 9781119771906 (pdf) | ISBN 9781119771890 (epub)
Subjects: LCSH: Psychological tests. | Telecommunication in medicine.
Classification: LCC BF176 .W73 2021 (print) | LCC BF176 (ebook) | DDC 150.28/7—dc23
LC record available at https://lccn.loc.gov/2020037412
LC ebook record available at https://lccn.loc.gov/2020037413

Cover image: © Greg Kuchik/Getty Images
Cover design by Wiley

Set in 10.5/13pt Adobe Garamond Pro by Integra Software Services Pvt. Ltd, Pondicherry, India

SKY10024318_012221

CONTENTS

I n the Essentials of Psychological Assessment series, we have attempted to provide the reader with books that will deliver key practical information in the most efficient and accessible style. The series features instruments in a variety of domains, such as cognition, personality, education, and neuropsychology. For the experienced clinician, books in the series offer a concise yet thorough way to master use of the continuously evolving supply of new and revised instruments as well as a convenient method for keeping up-to-date on the tried-and-true measures. The novice will find here a prioritized assembly of all the information and techniques that must be at one's fingertips to begin the complicated process of individual psychological diagnosis.

Whenever feasible, visual shortcuts to highlight key points are used alongside systematic, step-by-step guidelines. Chapters are focused and succinct. Topics are targeted for an easy understanding of the essentials of administration, scoring, interpretation, and clinical application. Theory and research are continually woven into the fabric of each book, always to enhance clinical inference, never to sidetrack or overwhelm. We have long been advocates of "intelligent" testing— the notion that a profile of test scores is meaningless unless it is brought to life by the clinical observations and astute detective work of knowledgeable examiners. Test profiles must be used to make a difference in the child's or adult's life, or why bother to test? We want this series to help our readers become the best intelligent testers they can be.

In *Essentials of Psychological Tele-Assessment*, a timely and invaluable book meant to provide concrete answers to abstract dilemmas posed by the pandemic, A. Jordan Wright and Susie Engi Raiford—both international experts in educational and psychological assessment—balance the very real-world need of clients with the limitations of the current state of the science. Between exhaustive reviews of the current literature and extremely practical tips for doing the actual work of tele-assessment, they have grounded their guidance in an ethical framework to ensure the valid and useful assessment of individuals in this mode that is new to most of the profession. They bring experience in research and development, but perhaps more importantly grounded in the real-world practice of conducting assessments in a tele-assessment context.

The book covers the different layers necessary for conducting tele-assessment, from high-level research on equivalence, to concrete strategies for adapting interpretation of data that emerge from tele-assessment measures, to extremely specific information on how to administer, adapt, and interpret scores from some of the most widely used performance-based cognitive and academic achievement tests. Psychologists new to tele-assessment will want to familiarize themselves with the ethical, practical, and interpretation concerns presented throughout the book. Psychologists who are actively engaging in psychological tele-assessment will find the practical and test-specific information useful as reminders. Psychological assessment already requires a great deal of juggling (both cognitive and often hands-on, when tests come with many physical components). Tele-assessment adds a few more balls in the air to the already complex procedures, and Wright and Raiford have provided in this book several extra pairs of hands to keep all the balls in the air.

Alan S. Kaufman, PhD, and Nadeen L. Kaufman, EdD, Series Editors
Yale Child Study Center, Yale University School of Medicine

One

THE LANDSCAPE OF PSYCHOLOGICAL TELE-ASSESSMENT

The COVID-19 pandemic has changed the landscape of health and mental healthcare across the globe. And it seems that it has changed the landscape forever. While the psychotherapy functions of psychologists and other mental health professionals have relatively easily transitioned to an online modality, one which has had significant empirical inquiry and support (Batastini, King, Morgan, & McDaniel, 2016; Bolton & Dorstyn, 2015; Reese, Slone, Soares, & Sprang, 2015; Varker, Brand, Ward, Terhaag, & Phelps, 2019), the psychological assessment functions of psychologists have had to rapidly adapt within a context of significantly less empirical support. The requirements for some, especially performance-based, tests—using manipulatives and physical stimuli—have placed a disproportionate burden on psychological assessment to figure out ways to adapt to a remote, online environment.

Many clinicians chose to pause their assessment services, expecting the world to resume its in-person engagement capabilities relatively soon. However, it is becoming clearer that while a vaccine will likely emerge at some point, COVID-19 may permanently alter health and mental health practices. Thus, clinicians need to consider how they can adapt and continue to deliver essential assessment services to clients, whether in a tele-assessment or somehow physically distanced format.

While psychological tele-assessment has certainly garnered a great deal of attention lately, some researchers have been working toward an evidence base for it for many years. The impetus for such research agendas seems originally to be related more to equity and access, ensuring that those in remote or rural areas have access to needed assessments. This reasoning also accounts for why so much of the research to date evaluating tele-assessment has focused on older adults,

Essentials of Psychological Tele-Assessment, First Edition.
A. Jordan Wright and Susan Engi Raiford
© 2021 John Wiley & Sons, Inc. Published 2021 by John Wiley & Sons, Inc.

neuropsychological assessment, and specifically assessment of cognition (e.g., dementia evaluations). While it seems somewhat counterintuitive that this population would naturally gravitate toward technology, these older adults are also more likely to be home-bound and have difficulty getting to appointments (Qiu et al., 2010). Because of these lines of research, we are lucky to at least have some empirical evidence base for remote, online tele-assessments (in contrast to assessments conducted with social distancing measures, such as masks, plexiglass partitions, greater distance between assessor and client, etc., which have no empirical inquiry). Our research evidence base is young and imperfect, but it allows for some confidence in some measures administered in this way.

STATE OF THE RESEARCH

The research landscape focused on psychological tele-assessment has amassed a modest, though compelling, body of evidence for the reliability, validity, and utility of tele-assessment procedures in collecting psychological data. First, as a primary measurement tool in psychological assessment, the evidence that *clinical interviews* conducted through tele-assessment procedures are generally equivalent to traditional, in-person procedures is quite strong (Garb, 2007; Hyler, Gangure, & Batchelder, 2005; Luxton, Pruitt, & Osenbach, 2014; Schopp, Johnstone, & Merrell, 2000; Singh, Arya, & Peters, 2007). The Society for Personality Assessment's (COVID-19 Task Force to Support Personality Assessment, 2020) guidance on tele-assessment of personality and psychopathology notes that this is likely related to the fact that clinical interview data accuracy is heavily related to the quality of the therapeutic alliance and relationship, which has been shown to be quite strong in telehealth in general (Bouchard et al., 2000; Germain, Marchand, Bouchard, Guay, & Drouin, 2010; Morgan, Patrick, & Magaletta, 2008; Simpson, 2001). The equal quality of data elicited through tele-assessment and in-person procedures seems especially true for more structured clinical interviews (Grady et al., 2011; Hyler et al., 2005; Ruskin et al., 1998; Shore, Savin, Orton, Beals, & Manson, 2007), and has even been supported in forensic evaluations (Lexcen, Hawk, Herrick, & Blank, 2006; Manguno-Mire et al., 2007). There is similarly relatively strong evidence that *self-report questionnaire measures* are generally equivalent (Garb, 2007; Luxton et al., 2014), especially if specific steps are taken to ensure the integrity of the self-report tests (Corey & Ben-Porath, 2020).

As stated previously, a great deal of the literature on equivalence between psychological tele-assessment and traditional, in-person psychological assessment administration of measures is found on *neuropsychological tests*. Research has evaluated the equivalency of specific, performance-based neuropsychological tasks and built a significant evidence base for tele-neuropsychological testing. Most of this work has included older adult populations and a variety of tasks. These tasks include broader, multitask and multi-construct measures like the Mini-Mental State Examination (MMSE; Folstein, Folstein, & McHugh, 1975) and the Repeatable Battery for the Assessment of Neuropsychological Status (RBANS; Randolph, 1998), both of which include verbal and nonverbal components. Also evaluated are select tests and subtests that evaluate single neuropsychological constructs, like the Boston Naming Test (Kaplan, Goodglass, & Weintraub, 1976), Digit Span, Matrix Reasoning, and Vocabulary subtests of the Wechsler Adult Intelligence Scale (WAIS; Wechsler, 2008), and drawing tasks like clock drawing and the Beery Visual-Motor Integration, Fourth Edition (VMI-I; Beery, 2004). The literature has shown that in general these performance-based, tele-neuropsychological assessment techniques are effective at evaluating older adults, both with and without cognitive impairment, and discriminating impaired from non-impaired individuals equally as well as in-person neuropsychological procedures (Cullum, Weiner, Gehrmann, & Hynan, 2006; Galusha-Glasscock, Horton, Weiner, & Cullum, 2016; Grosch, Weiner, Hynan, Shore, & Cullum, 2015; Harrell, Wilkins, Connor, & Chodosh, 2014; Loh, Donaldson, Flicker, Majer, & Goldswain, 2007; Luxton et al., 2014; Temple, Drummond, Valiquette, & Jozsvai, 2010; Tukstra, Quinn-Padron, Johnson, Workinger, & Antoniotti, 2012; Wadsworth et al., 2018).

In a systematic review and meta-analysis of neuropsychological tele-assessment test administration with adults, Brearly and colleagues (2017) identified several themes, including overall findings that videoconferencing administration did not yield any significant change in test scores when compared to in-person assessment, with a very small effect size noted for administration procedure. They noted an average of 1/33rd of a standard deviation lower scores elicited by tele-assessment procedures than by in-person ones. They did note in their analyses that while verbally mediated, synchronous tests (those that require in-the-moment interaction and scoring) were unaffected by the different administration modalities, those tests with both verbal and visual stimuli did have significantly lower scores in tele-assessment conditions. However, the effect size of these differences, even though significant, was small, and scores were about 1/10th of a standard deviation lower in the tele-assessment condition. It should be noted that most equivalence research on neuropsychological tests has taken a task-based (rather than full measure-based) approach.

Rapid References 1.1 and 1.2 summarize the major studies that have attempted to determine equivalence between traditional in-person methods and tele-assessment methods of test administration (to date). In addition to study details, a study rating column is provided to rate the strength of each study. The studies are rated on a three-point scale, with 1 indicating the strongest study qualities (and thus the most convincing evidence) and 3 indicating less strength. To receive a study rating of "1," a study must (a) be peer reviewed, (b) possess a convincing sample size, and (c) provide a strong research design (e.g., random assignment to groups) and statistical results (e.g., not merely a correlation or interrater reliability) that allow equivalence to be examined. If any one of these three criteria were not met, the study received a rating of 2. If two of these three criteria were not met, the study received a rating of 3 (studies that did not meet any of these criteria were not included). The Rating Reason column provides the area deemed problematic (i.e., a, b, or c in the aforementioned description) that resulted in the Study Rating being downgraded.

While not nearly as much has been accomplished in areas other than neuropsychological tele-assessment, there has been some effort to evaluate equivalence between traditional and tele-assessment administration procedures for *cognitive/ intellectual ability tests*. While some of the neuropsychological tele-assessment literature specifically looked at subcomponents of cognitive tests like the WAIS and similar tasks (Brearly et al., 2017; Temple, Drummond, Valiquette, & Jozsvai, 2010), only a few studies have been completed looking at equivalence between full cognitive ability and academic achievement measures in tele-assessment and traditional assessment contexts. Hodge and colleagues (2019) conducted a relatively small field study to determine agreement between scoring on traditional administration and tele-assessment administration of the Wechsler Intelligence Scale for Children, Fifth Edition (WISC-V; Wechsler, 2014) with students with learning disabilities. They found extremely high correlations for the different WISC-V primary index scores (ranging from .981 to .997), with the Full Scale IQ correlated at .991.

In larger studies, Wright (2018a, 2018b, 2020b) found similar evidence of (mostly) no significant impact of tele-assessment versus in-person methodology

Rapid Reference 1.1

Tele-Assessment Mode Equivalence Studies for Neuropsychological Tasks

Reference	Population	Study Rating	Rating Reason	N	Ages	Measures/Tasks	Software	Data	Results
Barcellos, Bellesis, Shen, Shao, & Chinn et al. 2018	Multiple sclerosis	1	n/a	270	18–69	California Verbal Learning Test-II	n/a (Telephonic)	Mean for 5 trials	Equivalent
Brearly et al., 2017	Meta-analysis of healthy, medical, psychiatric, substance use, dementia, and mild cognitive impairment (MCI)	1	n/a	497, 12 studies	Adult	Numerous but multiple studies aggregated for: – Boston Naming Test – Semantic fluency – Clock Drawing – List learning (total) – MMSE – Phonemic fluency	Videoconference	Hedges' g (standardized mean difference)	– Equivalent overall – Of 12 accepted studies, one with significant mode effect, and two with Hedges' g ≥ 20 (criteria for small effect) – Boston Naming Test had significant mode effect – No task-specific analyses, age, or population-specific analyses yielded Hedges' g ≥ 20
Cullum et al. 2006	Neurocognitive (MCI, Alzheimer's)	2	b	33	51–84	– MMSE – Hopkins Verbal Learning Test – Clock Drawing Test – Digit Span – Category Fluency – Letter Fluency – Boston Naming Test (short form)	Videoconference	– Task-level means – Correlations between modes	All equivalent except Hopkins Verbal Learning Test retention percentage and Clock Drawing – Correlations ranged from .54–.88

(continued)

Reference	Population	Study Rating	Rating Reason	N	Ages	Measures/Tasks	Software	Data	Results
Cullum, Hynan, Grosch, Parikh, & Weiner, 2014	Mixed (MCI, Alzheimer's, healthy)	1	n/a	202	46–90	– MMSE – Hopkins Verbal Learning Test–Revised – Digit Span forward and backward – Boston Naming Test (short form) – Letter Fluency – Category Fluency – Clock Drawing	Videoconference	– Task-level means – Correlations between modes	– Means statistically equivalent except Clock Drawing Test and Hopkins Verbal Learning Test-R, but differences deemed clinically negligible (BNT = 2; HVLT = .9) – Correlations ranged from .55–.91 with mean of .74
Dekhtyar, Braun, Billot, Foo, & Kiran, 2020	Aphasia	2	b	20	26–75	Western Aphasia Battery–Revised (WAB-R)	Teleconferencing (consumer grade)	Composite means, interrater reliability, and intercorrelations across modes	Equivalent
Galusha-Glasscock et al., 2016	Mixed (MCI, Alzheimer's, healthy)	2	b	18	58–84	RBANS index scores: – Immediate Memory – Visuospatial/Construc-tional – Language – Attention – Delayed Memory – Total Scale	Videoconference	– Index score means – Correlations between modes	– Means statistically equivalent – Correlations ranged from .59–.90 with mean of .80; all significant
Grosch et al., 2015	Psychiatric outpatient	2	b	8	67–85	– MMSE – Clock Drawing Test – Digit Span	Videoconference	– Task means – Correlations between modes	– Means statistically equivalent – Correlations ranged from .42–.72

Hildebrand, Chow, Williams, Nelson, & Wass, 2004	Healthy	2	b	29	60 +	Rey Auditory Verbal Learning Test Controlled Word Association Test WAIS-III and WASI Vocabulary WAIS-III and WASI Matrix Reasoning Brief Test of Attention Clock Drawing	Videoconference	– Task means – Correlations between modes	Equivalent except Clock Drawing Test
Jacobsen, Sprenger, Andersson, & Krogstad, 2003	Healthy	2	b	32	Mean: 35	Benton Visual Retention Test Digit Span Grooved Pegboard Symbol Digit Motor Test Seashore Rhythm Test Visual Object and Space Perception Battery Silhouettes WAIS Vocabulary and Digit Span (Norwegian) Wechsler Memory Scale (WMS) Logical Memory	Videophone	– Task means – Correlations between modes	– Equivalent except WMS Logical Memory I and Seashore Rhythm Test (auditory attention) – Correlations ranged from .37–.86 with median of .74

(continued)

Reference	Population	Study Rating	Rating Reason	N	Ages	Measures/Tasks	Software	Data	Results
Stain et al, 2011	Psychosis	2	b	11	14–27	– Wechsler Test of Adult Reading – WMS Logical Memory – WAIS-III Digit Span – Controlled Oral Word Association Test (verbal fluency)	Videoconferencing	– Task means – Correlations between modes	– Equivalent except Wechsler Test of Adult Reading – Correlations ranged from .59–.96 with average of .84
Sutherland 2017	Language impairment and SLD	3	b, c	23	8–12	CELF-4 subtests and composites: – Concepts and Following Directions – Word Structure – Recalling Sentences – Formulated Sentences – Word Classes – Core Language Score – Receptive – Expressive	Telehealth application National Information Communications Technology Australia (NICTA)	– Composite interrater correlations between modes	– Correlations ranged from .96–1.0
Turkstra et al, 2012	Traumatic brain injury (moderate to severe)	2	b	20	21–69	– Mediated Discourse Elicitation Protocol – AphasiaBank discourse tasks	PC-based Polycom encrypted videoconferencing or iChat and iSight on Mac Powerbooks	– Task means – Correlations between modes	– Equivalent – Overall correlation was .92

| Vahia et al., 2015 | Older rural Latino adults with suspected cognitive impairment | 2 | b | 22 | 65 + | – MMSE
– Hopkins Verbal Learning Test
– EIWA-III Digit Span
– Letter Fluency
– Category Fluency
– Clock Drawing
– Brief Visuospatial Memory Test
– PontonSatz Spanish Naming Test
– Standardized measure of overall cognitive functioning | Videoconferencing Remotely controlled Pan Tilt and Zoom cameras | – Task means
– Overall cognitive functioning mean | – Equivalent |
| Vestal, Smith-Olinde, Hicks, Hutton, & Hart, 2006 | Alzheimer's | 2 | b | 10 | 68–78 | – Picture Description (Boston Diagnostic Aphasia Examination)
– Boston Naming Test
– Token Test (Multilingual Aphasia Examination)
– Aural Comprehension of Words and Phrases (Benton)
– Controlled Oral Word Association Test (Benton) | Polycom videoconferencing | Task means | Equivalent |

(continued)

Reference	Population	Study Rating	Rating Reason	N	Ages	Measures/Tasks	Software	Data	Results
Wadsworth et al., 2018	Cognitively impaired and nonclinical	1	n/a	197	Means: 66 healthy 73 impaired	- MMSE - Hopkins Verbal Learning Test - Letter Fluency - Category Fluency - Boston Naming Test - Digit Span forward and backward - Clock Drawing Test	Polycom videoconferencing	Task means	Equivalent except Category Fluency (small effect not deemed clinically meaningful)
Waite, Theodoros, Russell, & Cahill, 2010	Language impairment or difficulties	3	b, c	25	5–9	CELF-4: Concepts and Following Directions Word Structure Recalling Sentences Formulated Sentences	Videoconferencing Scanned stimuli Stimulus video recordings	Intra- and interrater reliability	Equivalent

WAB-R subtests: Conversational Questions, Picture Description, Yes/No Questions, Auditory Word Recognition, Sequential Commands, Object Naming, Word Fluency, Sentence Completion, Responsive Speech, Reading Comprehension of Sentences, Reading Commands, Written Word–Object Choice Matching, Written Word-Picture Choice Matching, Picture-Written Word Choice Matching, Spoken Word-Written Word Choice Matching, Spelled Word Recognition, Spelling, Writing Upon Request, Writing Output, Writing to Dictation, Writing Dictated Words, Alphabet and Numbers, Dictated Letters and Numbers, Copying a Sentence, Drawing, Block Design, Calculation, Raven's Coloured Progressive Matrices; Writing Irregular Words to Dictation, Writing Nonwords to Dictation, Reading Irregular Words, Reading Nonwords. Composites: Aphasia Quotient, Language Quotient, Cortical Quotient.

RBANS subtests: List Learning, Story Memory, Figure Copy, Line Orientation, Picture Naming, Semantic Fluency, Digit Span, Coding, List Recall, List Recognition, Story Recall, and Figure Recall.

in the administration of three other cognitive tests, the Woodcock–Johnson IV Tests of Cognitive Ability (WJ-IV-Cog; Schrank, McGrew, & Mather, 2014), the Reynolds Intellectual Assessment Scales, Second Edition (RIAS-2; Reynolds & Kamphaus, 2015), and the WISC-V. In each similarly designed study, clients (children/students) were recruited, matched on demographic characteristics (at least age and gender), then randomly assigned to either the control (traditional, in-person administration) or experimental (tele-assessment) condition. In the WJ-IV-Cog study, clients were also administered the Cognitive Abilities Test (CogAT; Lohman & Hagen, 2001), all in the same format, as a randomization check. For the WISC-V study, clients were administered the Kaufman Brief Intelligence Test, Second Edition (KBIT-2; Kaufman & Kaufman, 2004) in traditional format for the same purpose. The WJ-IV and the RIAS-2 studies reported both significance (p) and effect sizes, and both found negligible to small effects (<.20), all non-significant, for administration method. The WISC-V study utilized a different approach to equivalence testing that is well known across many industries (see Chapter 4), reporting confidence intervals for the subtest and composite score differences. This study also supported equivalence on all scores, except for one secondary subtest that exceeded the predetermined criteria for a small effect (<.30). While some have identified that, despite revealing no statistical differences, the samples did exhibit actual score differences (especially on the RIAS-2; Farmer et al., 2020), this ignores the purpose of evaluating the statistical equivalence of the methods. Of course, there will be sample variations in actual scores obtained, but the statistical equivalence between the two methods takes into account error in measurement and non-identical samples (see Chapter 4 for further discussion on equivalency).

To date, only one equivalency study of tele-assessment and traditional assessment of *academic achievement tests* was identified. Wright's (2018b) study of tele-assessment procedures for the Woodcock–Johnson IV Tests of Achievement (WJ-IV-Ach; Schrank et al., 2014) similarly found no statistical significance or notable effect sizes (all were well below .20) for assessment procedure. Like the study of the WJ-IV-Cog, the WJ-IV-Ach study included a relatively large sample size (240 students in total, split across conditions), a design to ensure equivalence between groups (case control matching on age and gender), and randomization (matched pairs were randomly assigned to condition, and a randomization check utilizing the CogAT measure was utilized). This study begins a foundation for establishing that academic achievement tests can be given through tele-assessment procedures, maintaining their reliability, validity, and utility.

It must be noted that the overwhelming majority of the research on equivalence between tele-assessment and traditional, in-person procedures for specific test administration has been conducted in highly controlled environments and most often with the use of a proctor or helper of some sort on the client's side of the assessment. That is, very few of the studies anticipated the need for individuals to be assessed in their homes without the ability to dispatch some sort of (even non-psychologist) helper. Additionally, there are only studies on a few very specific measures.

However, these studies provide a foundation to support the conclusion that results derived from tasks with previously studied input and output requirements—and thus the psychological, cognitive, behavioral, and interpersonal processes that the tasks engage—are not significantly altered when administered in a tele-assessment format. For example, an auditory digit span task (which has shown to be equivalent across multiple studies and sample types) requires an auditory verbal stimulus and an auditory verbal response. Other measures that require these inputs and outputs (and especially those evaluating the construct of working memory) have indirect evidence of equivalence. Similarly, a writing task exhibiting equivalence on the WJ-IV-Ach should indirectly support a similar writing task on another test, as the inputs, construct-relevant processes evaluated, and outputs are extremely similar. Rapid Reference 1.2 summarizes the existing tele-assessment mode equivalence studies that have been conducted on cognitive, achievement, and neuropsychological tests to date.

> **DON'T FORGET**
> ······································
> Existing equivalence studies support the conclusion that results derived from tasks with previously studied input and output requirements are not significantly altered when administered in a tele-assessment format.

The two areas of general psychological assessment practice that (at the time of writing this book) have extremely limited guidance and support, either in the research or from professional organizations, are forensic assessment and developmental—specifically autism-spectrum disorder (ASD)—assessment. Specifically for *forensic assessment*, Drogin (2020) highlights that courts have not yet truly engaged in the discussion of tele-assessment and its use in forensic settings, but they are likely going to have to quite soon. He also notes, though, that it is very likely that attorneys on both sides will soon become extremely good at both defending and criticizing tele-assessment work. A great deal of forensic assessment does not include formal performance-based testing, and structured and semi-structured forensic interviews have some support (Lexcen et al., 2006; Manguno-Mire et al., 2007), but the field will need to reconcile this specific difficulty relatively quickly and soon.

Rapid Reference 1.2

Tele-Assessment Mode Equivalence Studies for Cognitive and Academic Measures

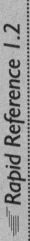

Reference	Population	Study Rating	Rating Reason	N	Ages	Measures/Tasks	Software	Data	Results
Hodge et al., 2019	Specific learning disorder (SLD)	3	b, c	33	8–12	WISC-V primary index scores and Full Scale IQ	Coviu	– Composite inter-rater correlations between modes	– Correlations ranged from .98–.99
Temple et al., 2010	Intellectual disability	2	b	19	23–63	– Beery-Buktenica Developmental Test of VMI WASI composites: – VIQ – PIQ – FSIQ	Polycom encrypted videoconferencing	– Composite means – VMI mean – Correlations between modes	– Mean differences ranged from 0.6–2.1 standard score points – VIQ significantly different at .05 level – Correlations ranged from .92–98
Wright, 2018a	General	2	a	104	3–19	RIAS2 (8 subtests and all composites)	PresenceLearning	Subtest and composite means	Equivalent except Speeded Naming Task (equivalent at ages 7–19 only) and Speeded Processing Index

(continued)

Reference	Population	Study Rating	Rating Reason	N	Ages	Measures/Tasks	Software	Data	Results
Wright, 2018b	General	1	n/a	240	5–16	WJ IV Cog tests and composites (10 subtests) WJ IV Ach tests and composites (11 subtests)	PresenceLearning	Test and composite means	Equivalent
Wright, 2020b	General	1	n/a	256	6–16	WISC-V (10 primary and 6 secondary subtests) WISC-V primary index scores and FSIQ	PresenceLearning	– Subtest and composite means – Subtest and composite intercorrelations within and between modes	Equivalent except Letter–Number Sequencing

RIAS-2 subtests: Guess What, Odd-Item Out, Verbal Reasoning, What's Missing, Verbal Memory, Nonverbal Memory, Speeded Naming, and Speeded Picture Search. Composites: Verbal Intelligence Index, Nonverbal Intelligence Index, Composite Intelligence Index, Composite Memory Index, Speeded Processing Index.

WISC-V primary subtests: Similarities, Vocabulary, Block Design, Visual Puzzles, Matrix Reasoning, Figure Weights, Digit Span, Picture Span, Coding, Symbol Search. Secondary subtests: Information, Comprehension, Picture Concepts, Arithmetic, Letter–Number Sequencing, Cancellation. Primary index scores: Verbal Comprehension Index, Visual Spatial Index, Fluid Reasoning Index, Working Memory Index, Processing Speed Index.

WJ-IV-Cog tests: Oral Vocabulary, Number Series, Verbal Attention, Letter–Pattern Matching, Phonological Processing, Story Recall, Visualization, General Information, Concept Formation, Numbers Reversed. Composites: General Intellectual Ability, Gf-Gc, Comp-Knowledge, Fluid Reasoning, Short-term Working Memory, Cognitive Efficiency.

WJ-IV-Ach tests: Letter-Word Identification, Applied Problems, Spelling, Passage Comprehension, Calculation, Writing Samples, Word Attack, Oral Reading, Sentence Reading Fluency, Math Facts Fluency, Sentence Writing Fluency. Composites: Broad Reading, Broad Mathematics, Broad Writing.

When it comes to *ASD assessments*, no professional organization has yet (as of the time of writing this book) made a statement or offered guidance on developmental tele-assessment. This is especially notable as the Autism Diagnostic Observation Schedule, Second Edition (ADOS-2; Lord et al., 2012) is widely accepted as a gold-standard assessment of ASD, and it includes so many physical toys and manipulatives and so much specific interaction that it is nearly impossible to complete via tele-assessment procedures (with the possible exception of some of the interview prompts in Module 4, for older clients). While the ADOS-2 is the most widely used performance-based measure to evaluate ASD, there are certainly many other tests, including interview measures (that primarily focus on parent/caregiver report) and holistic clinician rating measures (that are meant to account for amassed evidence from different sources). Chapter 8 of this book discusses some of these measures in detail.

CURRENT PROFESSIONAL GUIDANCE

As of the writing of this book, only a handful of professional organizations have provided specific guidance documents related to conducting psychological assessment in a telehealth modality. The guidance offered by these professional organizations forms the basis of the recommendations used throughout this book. However, much of it is vague and aspirational. Presently, several organizations have emerged with specific guidance related to the practice of tele-assessment (Table 1.3). The American Psychological Association (APA)—in addition to their general guidelines for the practice of telepsychology (Joint Task Force for the Development of Telepsychology Guidelines for Psychologists, 2013)—has published guidance for tele-assessment in general (Wright, Mihura, Pade, & McCord, 2020), as well as specific guidance for tele-assessment with children (Banks & Butcher, 2020), pain evaluations (Brown & Bruns, 2020), and presurgical evaluations (Block, Bradford, Butt, & Marek, 2020). The Inter Organizational Practice Committee (IOPC, 2020a, 2020b) has produced two separate documents related to the practice of neuropsychological tele-assessment. The National Association of School Psychologists (NASP) developed and published a general guidance document in 2017 and offered a specific update related to the COVID-19 crisis (NASP, 2020). The Society for Personality Assessment (SPA) published guidance on tele-assessment of personality and psychopathology (COVID-19 Task Force to Support Personality Assessment, 2020). Although there have been no professional guidance documents related to forensic work, the California Commission on Peace Officer Standards and Training (2020) disseminated guidance on pre-employment tele-assessment for police officers (see Rapid Reference 1.3).

≋ Rapid Reference 1.3

Professional Guidance and Recommendation Documents for Psychological Tele-Assessment

APA General Guidance on Tele-Assessment: https://www.apaservices.org/practice/reimbursement/health-codes/testing/tele-assessment-covid-19

IOPC Guidance for Teleneuropsychology: https://static1.squarespace.com/static/50a3e393e4b07025e1a4f0d0/t/5ed7d6c58ec40f3dce143b40/1591203525610/IOPC+Models+of+Care+During+COVID-19+Pandemic.pdf

NASP Guidance for Delivery of School Psychological Telehealth Services: http://www.nasponline.org/assets/documents/Guidance_Telehealth_Virtual_Service_%20Delivery_Final%20(2).pdf

NASP Guidance on Virtual Service Delivery: https://www.nasponline.org/resources-and-publications/resources-and-podcasts/school-climate-safety-and-crisis/health-crisis-resources/virtual-service-delivery-in-response-to-covid-19-disruptions

SPA Guidance on Tele-Assessment of Personality and Psychopathology: https://resources.personality.org/www.personality.org/General/pdf/SPA_Personality_Tele-Assessment-Guidance_6.10.20.pdf

APA Guidance on Tele-Assessment of Children: https://www.apaservices.org/practice/legal/technology/telehealth-testing-children-covid-1erican

APA Guidance on Tele-Assessment for Presurgical Evaluations: https://www.apaservices.org/practice/news/presurgical-psychological-evaluations-covid-19?_ga=2.116775942.169813268.1591026574-1626901323.1573678255

APA Guidance on Tele-Assessment for Chronic Pain Evaluations: https://www.apaservices.org/practice/news/chronic-pain-covid-19

California Commission on Peace Officer Standards and Training Guidance on Tele-Assessment with POST Selection Standards: https://post.ca.gov/Portals/0/post_docs/bulletin/2020-18.pdf

Most of these professional guidance documents offer overlapping advice, though some are much more specific than others. Generally, they acknowledge the limitations of the current literature and evidence base for tele-assessment mode equivalence with traditional in-person administration. They also tend to acknowledge that psychologists have many resources available to them to conduct assessments, including multiple methods, early support for administration mode equivalence, and the ability to adjust interpretations appropriately, utilizing clinical and professional judgment, training, and experience.

While they do not outright say this, by acknowledging that tele-assessment can be a viable procedure for collecting psychological data, they imply that imperfect data can still be good, useful data. While bad data is worse than no data at all, data collected through tele-assessment procedures can be imperfect but good, usable data.

> **DON'T FORGET**
>
> Imperfect data can still be good, useful data. Data collected through tele-assessment procedures can be imperfect but good, usable data.

MEASURES WITH LONGSTANDING TELE-ASSESSMENT ADMINISTRATION PROCEDURES

Many psychological assessment measures have a significant history of tele-assessment administration. The most obvious of these are collateral report questionnaires and surveys. While many of these began as physical, pencil-and-paper questionnaires often sent home with clients to give to knowledgeable others to fill out, more recently, most of these have adapted to a remote, online administration procedure. Surveys for parents and teachers, for example, to fill out are widely administered in this fashion. A link is sent out to the respondent, who fills out the survey online wherever they are and whenever they want, and the report is generated for the clinician. There are even some self-report inventories that have been developed and utilized in this way, without very much concern for test security or integrity. It is important to note that these measures constitute a part of an assessment that carries with it *absolutely no change at all* in the "new" landscape of tele-assessment. The conversation about psychological tele-assessment should always acknowledge that at least some of the "traditional" work we have been doing has included methodologies that can be accomplished entirely unaltered.

MEASURES DEVELOPED FOR ONLINE ADMINISTRATION

While much of the focus in psychological tele-assessment is on how to adapt traditionally developed in-person measures to an online, virtual procedure, there have been some (and will likely continue to be more) measures that were specifically developed, standardized, and normed for online use. Aside from questionnaires and surveys, several cognitive and neuropsychological measures have been developed for online use and may prove useful, though each has some significant drawbacks, mostly in terms of the state of the supportive empirical evidence. However, each of these represents some promising moves in the field that are likely to improve our tools in the future.

One promising general measure of cognitive ability for ages 6 through adult is the Mezure instrument (mezureschools.com). Built around measures of crystallized (Gc) and fluid (Gf) intelligence, it includes online tasks for these constructs as well as processing speed, memory with distractions, social perception, and (for adults) stress tolerance. The development of the test is impressive, as are the data security features and graphical and auditory stimuli, and many of the tasks do seem to tap what they are intended to measure. The clinical manual (Mezure, n.d.) provides solid test development information, including reliability and some validity information, such as an exploratory factor analysis. The standardization sample is adequately large at 4184 individuals, though they break down the numbers by age band for children, but not adults (and it is unclear if or how they standardized for older adults). The biggest weakness for the Mezure as it currently stands is in its presentation of validity information. The criterion-related validity (only concurrent) is limited to a correlation between the overall score of the Mezure (based on the seven core subtests) and the WISC-III (Wechsler, 1991) Full Scale IQ, Verbal IQ, and Performance IQ. The three major flaws with this are that: 1) the WISC-III is obviously quite outdated (and there is no indication of when this study was performed); 2) this study only addresses validity for children aged 6 to 16, with no evidence of validity for use with adults, which the Mezure claims to work for as well; and 3) the relationships between subtests of the Mezure and similar constructs on other tests are not reported, even though presumably the data exist from the WISC-III study. Similarly, the supplemental subtests (processing speed, social perception, distractibility) lack reported validity evidence. Further, internal validity is only asserted through the use of subtest correlations, rather than a confirmatory factor analysis. Until these data are provided, it is recommended that the Mezure be used with extreme caution.

Another measure entirely developed and standardized online to evaluate general cognitive ability for individuals age 7 through adult is the Cognifit measure (cognifit.com). This measure reportedly evaluates individuals on focus, distractibility, processing speed, spatial perception, inhibition, and a host of other cognitive abilities, all organized into perception, coordination, attention, memory, and reasoning. Most of the subtests are generally quite technologically elegant and seem to measure what they purport to measure. There are two significant drawbacks to this program, though. First, the report generated is extremely difficult for psychologists who understand psychometrics to interpret. Specifically, the program has developed an odd scoring system (it is unclear if this is even a standard score) with a maximum of 800, making it extremely difficult to interpret. Additionally, the algorithms used to derive scores on indices are somewhat obtuse and not well explained in any materials (individual subtests contribute partially to multiple different index scores). The second and more troubling problem with the measure is its description of psychometrics (CogniFit, 2020). The only psychometric information provided in the clinical manual is measures of reliability (which it calls validity), both internal consistency and test-retest. While the reliability findings are adequate, they are reported for the tasks (not the derived index scores at all), and no validity information has been provided. There is no information on the internal structure of the test itself, nor is there evidence of concurrent or predictive criterion-related validity. As such, this measure is not yet ready to be used by professionals (and indeed seems to be marketed more to lay people and medical professionals).

Finally, the CNS Vital Signs measure (cnsvs.com) offers another online-developed and standardized instrument of cognitive functioning for individuals aged 7 to 90. The measure reportedly evaluates memory, fine motor functioning, attention and concentration, processing speed, and mental flexibility. The measure does not purport to evaluate general cognitive functioning or intelligence, but rather employs some commonly used neuropsychological techniques to evaluate discrete neuropsychological and cognitive abilities. While research (summarized in Gualtieri & Johnson, 2006) has established adequate reliability, the normative sample is quite small (25 children under 10 years old) and not very racially or ethnically diverse. The validity data are generally adequate but based again on quite small sample sizes, especially related to discrimination ability with certain neurocognitive disorders (e.g., 52 participants in a dementia discrimination study). In all, there are fewer concerns with a measure like the CNS Vital Signs than the other measures, as it does not purport to measure broader general cognitive abilities, but rather discrete skills that are reasonably well established in neuropsychological and tele-neuropsychological assessment, though caution should be taken especially with children.

CONCLUSION

The current landscape of psychological tele-assessment is either promising but young at the moment or young but promising at the moment, depending on perspective. While imperfect, in general the professional organizations that organize health service psychologists (school, clinical, counseling, and related fields) have encouraged careful and considered practice when engaging in tele-assessment. And the research seems to support this—some tests have direct evidence supporting their equivalence and thus use for tele-assessment, and many more can use indirect evidence from the necessary inputs (stimuli) and outputs (client responses) that have been evaluated to support their use as well. Further, while currently none of the measures is ideal for use yet, several cognitive measures have been developed and standardized entirely online, and this sets the stage for an exciting future of psychological tele-assessment and further development of fully online measures.

Two

ETHICAL CONSIDERATIONS IN PSYCHOLOGICAL TELE-ASSESSMENT

Certainly, the most crucial consideration (and criticism) when conducting psychological tele-assessment is whether or not it is ethical to do so. The ethics surrounding tele-assessment are complex and nuanced, and there are a number of factors at play. Perhaps the most obvious is that psychologists conducting psychological tele-assessment must maintain all the ethical and legal integrity that they would in their in-person services (IOPC, 2020b; NASP, 2020b; Wright, Mihura, Pade, & McCord, 2020). This guidance is obvious, though vague. Balancing the best interest of clients with humility about the limitations of our techniques requires deliberate consideration. The information in this chapter raises some, though likely not all, of the ethical challenges to engaging in tele-assessment practice.

More concrete are issues around legal, jurisdictional, and licensing concerns. For example, at the time of the writing of this book, the permanent licensing laws dictate that psychologists need to be licensed in the state where the client is physically located (these laws were temporarily relaxed in some states due to the COVID-19 pandemic and the needs that arose because of it, but this was just temporary). Additionally, there is currently an extremely popular petition calling for national, inter-state reciprocity in tele-practice, such that tele-health providers could freely practice across state lines. (This is a complicated issue, and one that would be difficult for state licensing boards to enact, however.) You must always confirm the most current laws for what is legally permissible in practice. You should also confirm with your liability insurance what is covered. Some (again, at the writing of this book) explicitly will not cover claims related to tele-assessment services; others have stated that they will.

Related to legal issues is whether or not psychological tele-assessment results will be "admissible" to whatever organization needs the data. For example, some

Essentials of Psychological Tele-Assessment, First Edition.
A. Jordan Wright and Susan Engi Raiford
© 2021 John Wiley & Sons, Inc. Published 2021 by John Wiley & Sons, Inc.

school districts have been using and accepting tele-assessment data for years, whereas others have stated outright that they will not accept evaluations conducted through tele-assessment procedures (see the section later in this chapter on social justice for a discussion on this topic). Similarly, if you are doing testing for accommodation on specific tests (like the SAT or ACT), you need to confirm with those respective organizations that they will accept data collected through tele-assessment procedures. It would certainly not be beneficial (and may be specifically harmful) to a client to have them undergo an entire assessment that will ultimately not be accepted by the decision-making body (this is different than a client being turned down for accommodations because they do not meet criteria—we can of course never guarantee that they will meet criteria and receive accommodations, but we can ensure that our methods will be accepted).

As of the time of writing this book, while there have been individual opinions in the literature and widely online, no professional organization dedicated to forensic psychology has made a clear statement or provided guidance on the use of psychological tele-assessment for forensic work. While professional organization guidance would be both welcomed and extremely helpful, forensic psychologists should certainly be conservative in the use of tele-assessment services, especially if their work is likely to be cross-examined. While the use of tele-assessment is certainly defensible, the empirical evidence is extremely young (and mostly not yet replicated). As is discussed in Chapter 5, psychologists do not use individual test scores as if they are perfect; data are contextualized and integrated with a great many other pieces of information before making conclusions. However, in legal matters, the precision and validity of even small pieces of data within a larger picture can be scrutinized and used to "poke holes" in psychologists' conclusions. Thus, forensic psychologists should take caution with tele-assessment work. However, a great deal of the work of forensic psychologists does not utilize cognitive and other performance-based measures; much of forensic work is based on interviews, records reviews, and collecting collateral information/data. This work can absolutely be accomplished—in a highly defensible way—through tele-assessment procedures.

While legal, licensing, and other such issues can provide easy guidance on whether or not to engage in psychological tele-assessment, once those more concrete issues are reconciled, psychologists need to engage in critical

> **DON'T FORGET**
> ....
> Some immediate, concrete issues that inform the decision to engage (or not) in tele-assessment:
> - Legal issues
> - Licensing and jurisdiction issues
> - Policies and acceptance of tele-assessment of the body receiving the report
> - Forensic nature of the evaluation

thinking around the other myriad ethical issues inherent in doing this type of work, at this point in history, with all its current (especially empirical) limitations. This includes really understanding the limits of your own competency (and how to mitigate those limits), understanding which clients may and may not be appropriate for these kinds of services, and truly trying to balance clients' needs with the limitations of our current evidence base.

YOUR OWN COMPETENCY

The APA's (2017) current ethical guidelines mandate that those providing services that are unfamiliar to them—including new technologies—engage in relevant educational activities to ensure competency. These activities may include courses, professional development trainings, consultation, or (vaguely described in the ethical guidelines) study of some sort. Similarly, the American Educational Research Association (AERA), APA, and National Council on Measurement in Education (NCME) (2014) standards for testing require specific training and expertise on measures in order to use them. It can certainly be argued that a test given through tele-assessment is significantly different enough relative to the original to warrant additional specific training. The APA's *Guidelines for the Practice of Telepsychology* (2013) similarly argue that psychologists are responsible for monitoring their own technical and clinical competencies throughout any tele-psychological work.

When beginning to think about engaging in psychological tele-assessment, it is not enough to be fully trained on tests and measures in their in-person format and to be fully trained on videoconferencing technology, separately. You need to be fully trained, comfortable, and competent at administering whatever measures you will administer on tele-assessment platforms, as well as fully competent in understanding the data and their limitations when they are collected in this format (Joint Task Force for the Development of Telepsychology Guidelines for Psychologists, 2013). Some have urged clinicians to get specific training and professional development in tele-assessment procedures (NASP, 2017, 2020). Others recommend systematically and repeatedly practicing the entire workflow of tele-assessment, from beginning to end (California Commission on Peace Officer Standards and Training, 2020). Still others recommend being extremely liberal and exhaustive in seeking consultation (Wright et al., 2020).

In ensuring your own competency, and being able to defend it, it is strongly recommended that you do all three of these things. Find any and all trainings on specific tests and giving them through tele-assessment procedures, practice thoroughly—over and over—with every aspect of the tele-assessment, and consult

DON'T FORGET

....

Before you begin conducting psychological tele-assessments:
- Attend trainings on tele-assessment, including broad trainings and those on specific tests
- Practice thoroughly—over and over—with every aspect of tele-assessment
- Consult liberally and thoroughly, both before and during tele-assessment cases

liberally and thoroughly, both before and during tele-assessment cases. Make no assumptions about your ability to conduct tele-assessments, no matter how comfortable you are with traditional in-person assessments. Just like when you were first learning how to administer some of our most widely used measures, it can take quite a bit of hands-on practice before you are comfortable, confident, and ultimately competent to administer tests via tele-assessment.

DECIDING WHEN AND WHEN NOT TO CONDUCT TELE-ASSESSMENT

The decision to conduct a psychological tele-assessment or not, as with in-personal assessments, should always rest on the client's best interest (IOPC, 2020a; NASP, 2020). In actuality, though, a more prudent way to determine whether or not to proceed is to try to balance the client's needs with the current evidence base of our tools (Luxton, Pruitt, & Jenkins-Guarnieri, 2015; Luxton, Pruitt, & Osenbach, 2014). Proceed with the understanding that there are some clients in circumstances who have no other recourse than to engage in a psychological tele-assessment and others in situations for which tele-assessment is not at all necessary or imminently needed; however, there are a host of clients in situations that fall in between these two poles. Certainly, in the cases that do not need tele-assessment for any tangible reason, you should consider conducting it in person, postponing the assessment, or referring to someone who can conduct it in person (Banks & Butcher, 2020; Block, Bradford, Butt, & Marek, 2020; IOPC, 2020a; Wright et al., 2020). However, if the client's need outweighs the reticence due to the limited tele-assessment evidence base, you should also consider how appropriate the particular client is for psychological tele-assessment.

DON'T FORGET

....

Balance the client's needs with the current evidence base of our tools when deciding to engage in tele-assessment, to postpone the assessment, or to refer.

There is no current rigorous empirical study of what kinds of clients are and are not appropriate for psychological tele-assessment services, though lack of empirical evidence is not the same as evidence against. That is, just because there is no study saying a particular type of client is appropriate for tele-assessment does not mean that they are not (Joint Task Force for the Development of Telepsychology Guidelines for Psychologists, 2013). However, there is guidance and wisdom about client factors to consider when determining if they are a good fit for tele-assessment services. Notably, most professional guidance on psychological tele-assessment urges psychologists to think carefully about which clients are appropriate for tele-assessment services and which are not (APA, 2020; Banks & Butcher, 2020; HGAPS, n.d.; IOPC, 2020a; Luxton et al., 2014, 2015; NASP, 2017, 2020b; Wright et al., 2020).

The first consideration is whether the client is a *high-risk client* (HGAPS, n.d.; Joint Task Force for the Development of Telepsychology Guidelines for Psychologists, 2013). High risk can mean many different things. In general, if a client is a potential danger to themselves or others, tele-assessment may not be appropriate. However, you should also consider their access to alternatives. That is, if a client is an imminent risk to themselves and has no options other than tele-assessment, the client should of course be evaluated and potentially referred for emergency care. This evaluation will likely not be a full psychological tele-assessment, but may just involve interview-based risk assessment or using collaborative measures like the CAMS approach (Jobes, 2016). Still, because of the logistical difficulties in coordinating emergency procedures at a distance (discussed further in Chapter 3), high-risk clients may not be ideal candidates for full psychological tele-assessments.

While a great deal of the research supporting psychological tele-assessment has been conducted on children and older adults (e.g., Wadsworth et al., 2018; Wright, 2018b), some have still raised the concern that psychological tele-assessment may be less appropriate for these populations (IOPC, 2020b). Thus, you may want to consider *age of the client* when determining if they are likely appropriate for tele-assessment. Certainly, children,

> **CAUTION**
>
> If a client is a potential danger to themselves or others, tele-assessment may not be appropriate. However, you should also consider their access to alternatives. If a client is an imminent risk to themselves and has no options other than tele-assessment, evaluate and potentially refer for emergency care.

especially young children, are likely to have less impulse control when being asked to sit in front of a screen for an extended time period as compared with adults. This may require intervention from a proctor of some sort, including a parent/guardian/caregiver if the client is being tested in their home. Getting young children—and perhaps especially those presenting for assessments because of some behavioral difficulties—to stay seated at the computer, follow instructions, and remain engaged in a focused manner for hours at a time can be extremely challenging, even in person. When it comes to older adults, it is likely that age is simply a proxy for their likelihood of being literate and comfortable with technology, which is a consideration when asking them to engage with it so much in a tele-assessment.

More direct than age in determining appropriateness for psychological tele-assessment is the client's *level of literacy and comfort with technology* (APA, 2020; HGAPS, n.d.; IOPC, 2020a; Wright et al., 2020). Some have considered proxies other than age to approximate computer literacy and comfort, including culture (Luxton et al., 2015) and socioeconomic status (Wright et al., 2020), though the latter is also intertwined with technology access. However you decide to determine this, it is important to ascertain just how comfortable and literate (at least to the degree needed to engage in the tele-assessments) the client is with the necessary technology. Technology comfort and literacy can be concrete, such as the skills to turn on the computer, run programs, and interact with stimuli using a mouse, as well as more nuanced and abstract, such as not understanding where the camera is embedded in the monitor, forgetting that they can be seen when logged into the videoconferencing software, or just generally being somewhat uncomfortable interacting with others in this way. Any of these variables can interact with a client's performance on tasks delivered in a tele-assessment, and so they should be considered ahead of time.

Related to issues of class, race, and socioeconomic status, it is important to ensure that clients have *access to the necessary technological and environmental resources* they need to engage in a tele-assessment. Several organizations have highlighted this equity and social justice issue (NASP, 2020; Wright et al., 2020). This of course is not an issue if the client is coming into an office equipped for tele-assessment, but it is crucial if they are being tested in their own home. Clients engaging in psychological tele-assessment need to have access to a physical environment that is quiet, comfortable, and free from distractions (APA, 2020; Wright et al., 2020). Further, they must have the necessary technology resources to engage, including consistent and reliable internet connectivity (broadband/Wi-Fi) and an appropriate device (computer, laptop, or tablet) with a large enough screen (typically, 13 inches is seen as a minimum), a webcam, and enough power and memory to run the videoconferencing and any other software required (APA, 2020; Banks & Butcher, 2020; California Commission on Peace Officer Standards and Training, 2020; IOPC, 2020b; NASP, 2017; Wright et al., 2020). Certainly, equity issues are salient when it comes to access to such resources, and (as discussed in the social justice section in this chapter) psychologists should think carefully not just about avoiding engaging in tele-assessment services with those who do not have reliable access to these resources but about ways to meet their needs otherwise.

Once a client is determined to be, at least in theory, appropriate (or at least acceptable) for tele-assessment services, there are two other primary areas you should evaluate before continuing. First, you should evaluate the client's *level of acceptance of tele-assessment methodologies.* There is no perfect way to capture this variable, but clients need to generally accept the process, including the videoconferencing methodology and all of tele-assessment's limitations, in order to fully and earnestly engage in it (Luxton et al., 2014). The acceptance level will vary from client to client, and may vary from culture to culture as well (Luxton et al., 2015; Shore & Manson, 2004). Tactics that may increase an individual's acceptance of and confidence in tele-assessment include the assessor being confident in their work, being transparent about the process and its limitations, and taking a stance of partnering with the client in the assessment process (Finn, Fischer, & Handler, 2012; Riddle, Byers, & Grimesey, 2002).

> **CAUTION**
>
> Psychologists should avoid tele-assessment with clients who do not have reliable access to the necessary resources *and* should find ways to meet their needs otherwise.

Finally, you should determine if an individual client is appropriate *in the moment* for psychological tele-assessment services (Rapid Reference 2.1). Evaluate the *clinical and cognitive status of the client* to determine if there are any factors that may interfere with their interaction with you via a tele-assessment platform (APA, 2020; Luxton et al., 2014). Make it your goal to determine if they can and will actively participate in the process at that moment, knowing that both clinical and cognitive factors can interfere with this ability. Cognitive or sensory deficits can preclude clients from fully engaging with the technology required for tele-assessment, though technological aids and testing adaptations can sometimes mitigate the effects of these (Luxton et al., 2014). Some clinical factors can also interfere, such as extreme paranoia related to technology (e.g., believing they are being spied on constantly through their devices), disorganization (such that they cannot follow the additional instructions needed in a tele-assessment), or catatonia related to depression. Each of these would affect any assessment, even under in-person circumstances, but their effects may be amplified in a tele-assessment situation.

⬟ *Rapid Reference 2.1*

Determining Client Appropriateness for Tele-Assessment

- Are they a high-risk client?
- Will the client's age affect their interaction with technology?
- What is their level of technology literacy and comfort?
- Do they have access to the necessary technology and environmental resources?
- How accepting are they of this modality for assessment?
- Are there any clinical or cognitive status factors that could interfere with their interaction with the necessary technology?

DOING NO HARM

Of course, the number one, most important ethical rule for psychologists is to do no harm. This should always be a guiding principle when conducing psychological tele-assessments, as well. The most important component of tele-assessments that relate to not doing harm is the validity of results. That is, *you of course never want to report or make clinical decisions based on test scores that are not valid, or that do not actually represent the functioning, traits, or abilities of the person you are assessing.* This issue is discussed further in Chapter 5. As presented in Chapters 6 through 8, there is some, but not much, direct and indirect evidence of the reliability and validity (typically evaluated through equivalency studies) of many of our most widely used psychological tests when administered in tele-assessment mode. However, this research is admittedly young, not well enough replicated, and somewhat limited to highly specific and controlled situations (Farmer et al., 2020). This allows for the possibility that individual test scores are less accurate when obtained through tele-assessment.

Psychologists are urged to remember that there is a difference between testing and assessment, though (Meyer et al., 2001). Testing relates to administering, scoring, and interpreting individual tests. Assessment involves utilizing data (from testing, as well as many other places) in an integrative, sophisticated way to inform conclusions (such as diagnosis) and decisions (such as recommendations). Valid test data are indeed a foundation of ethical assessment, but an assessment—utilizing

CAUTION

Do not make clinical decisions based on test scores that are not valid or that do not actually represent the functioning, traits, or abilities of the person you are assessing.

the psychologist's clinical and professional judgment—can continue, even when some individual test results do not provide a valid representation of the client. This occurs frequently in traditional in-person assessments, when a test, scale, or score is determined to be an invalid representation of the client. While this affects a psychologist's ability to make precise conclusions and definitive decisions, it typically does not require the entire process to be aborted. The invalidity of the data, in fact, often serves as additional clinical data.

In the end, the psychologist has to determine whether or not the data elicited from any test (and in this case a test given in a tele-assessment method) is likely a valid representation of a given client's functioning, traits, or abilities. There are several safeguards for you to enlist to make these kinds of decisions, many of which are discussed in Chapter 5. When psychologists decide that the test data themselves should be making decisions for clients, then we need to be extremely conservative in the use of alternative and not yet fully proven methods, like tele-assessment. However, when we have alternate data sources—including interviews, records reviews, observations, collateral measures, and tests that likely are not significantly affected by tele-assessment procedures, among others—to inform and contextualize any specific test result, our clinical judgment becomes much more important in decision-making for clients. This assumes, of course, a high level of competency to understand and contextualize all these data, including reconciling discrepancies.

While validity is likely the primary concern about potentially doing harm to a client, there are some other, more concrete risks of doing harm in a psychological tele-assessment context. For example, you need to be extremely vigilant (as much as you can be) about online privacy and security, as interactions online are much easier to "hack" than those in your office (California Commission on Peace Officer Standards and Training, 2020; Joint Task Force for the Development of Telepsychology Guidelines for Psychologists, 2013; NASP, 2017). In fact, there are many risks to privacy and security in a telehealth environment (Hall & McGraw, 2014). Most of us are not IT experts, but there are very concrete steps you can take to protect a client's information online. HIPAA and FERPA compliance of videoconferencing platforms is discussed in Chapter 3, but how you use those platforms can be more or less secure. For example, you should be using a private Wi-Fi or broadband connection, rather than a public Wi-Fi source (as should your client, ideally). Additionally, you should always enable a waiting room in the online meeting and require a password. This makes it much more difficult for hackers to jump into your online session. Your Business Associate Agreement (BAA, discussed further in Chapter 3) should also be explicit about where any recordings will be housed (e.g., in the host's cloud versus only on the psychologist's computer) and what will happen if any data are leaked by the videoconferencing platform somehow.

Watzlaf and colleagues (2017) reviewed literature on ensuring privacy and security of your tele-assessment system (including the videoconferencing technology). Included in a number of studies for consideration are use of an online meeting password, private (password protected) internet access, and storage and record-keeping (being especially wary of cloud services). In addition, they highlight encryption issues, multifactor authentication, inactivity time-out functions, and security and antivirus software on both devices (psychologist and client). While we can take many obvious steps to ensure privacy and security of our clients and their data, it is always helpful to consult with IT security experts to ensure your setup is as protective as it can be (Rapid Reference 2.2).

Where doing no harm is concerned, one more important consideration is to ensure that clients are keenly aware when tele-assessment is suboptimal and they may need to engage in further or repeated testing after the tele-assessment is completed. Ensure that clients (or other stakeholders), who reasonably assume they are getting a full, useful assessment via tele-assessment procedures, are aware

≋ Rapid Reference 2.2

A Non-Exhaustive Checklist for Videoconferencing Privacy and Security

While these are good basic measures, you should consider consulting with an IT security expert to ensure your systems are as protective as they can be.

- HIPAA- and/or FERPA-compliant videoconferencing system
  - Encryption of information, including video and audio
  - BAA in place
    - Where are any recordings stored (be wary of cloud storage, especially of an outside company)?
    - What happens in the event of any data breaches?
  - Inactivity time-out functions
- Private, password protected internet connection
  - On client's side as well, when possible
- Enable a virtual waiting room
- Password required to enter meeting
  - Multifactor authentication, whenever possible
- Security and antivirus software on your computer
  - On client's side as well, when possible
- Consult an IT security expert

that if key parts cannot be completed, further testing may be necessary immediately after the first assessment is completed. If they are informed of this ahead of time, then it is not a potential harm.

For example, consider a school district that requires the use of an Autism Diagnostic Observation Schedule, Second Edition (ADOS-2; Lord et al., 2012) for identification of an autism spectrum disorder (ASD). If a parent does not know that a tele-assessment will not include this measure, which is required by the district for identification, and you engage in the tele-assessment anyway, this is a kind of bait-and-switch situation. If the client believes they will receive a service, and that service cannot be provided through tele-assessment, informing them only after the fact that they need to engage in further assessment is potentially harmful. The key to combating this situation is clear communication, and ensuring consent is fully and explicitly informed.

ENSURE CONSENT IS *FULLY* INFORMED

Consent is a process, not a form. While clear, complete consent forms often ensure that we engage in this process with our clients, too often clinicians present consent forms to clients who sign them, perhaps without reading or understanding all the details in them. With newer procedures, like tele-assessment, we must be extra vigilant to ensure that clients know and understand what the process entails, what factors may impede it (like technology problems), and what its limitations are. These are above and beyond all other information that is relatively standard in consent, like limits to confidentiality (Block et al., 2020; California Commission on Peace Officer Standards and Training, 2020; HGAPS, n.d.; IOPC, 2020a, 2020b; Luxton et al., 2014, 2015; NASP, 2017, 2020b; Wright et al., 2020).

As has already been discussed, there are some limitations to tele-assessment, and these should be clearly laid out for clients. Some are purely practical, such as not being able to see entire bodies on videoconferencing platforms. Some are clinical, such as not being able to administer certain tests, measures, or tasks. Others relate to performance-based test data being less precise using tele-assessment procedures. *You must be transparent about these limitations* (California Commission on Peace Officer Standards and Training, 2020; IOPC, 2020a, 2020b; Wright et al., 2020)!

For these reasons, it is likely more important in tele-assessment services than traditional, in-person services to make consent a discussion, even with clients estimated to be of very high intelligence. Because clients are generally unaware of all the processes and data that go into a full assessment, they are likely also uninformed about the potential for technology to interrupt and disrupt tele-assessment. As such, you should explain each point clearly and ensure that clients understand.

DON'T FORGET

You must be transparent about the limitations of tele-assessment!

Remember, if clients are aware that they may have to engage in further assessment after the entire tele-assessment process is completed, they may decide to wait for in-person assessment and forego tele-assessment. However, they should know of this possibility ahead of time to allow them to make a fully informed decision. You should discuss with them what further evaluation may need to look like—in some cases, it may be adding one or two additional in-person tests at a later date; in other cases, it may require starting from scratch with a new assessment provider. You need to be clear and transparent about this from the beginning, so that clients are unlikely to feel "duped" if tele-assessment findings are not fully conclusive or definitive (Rapid Reference 2.3).

≡ Rapid Reference 2.3

Sample language for tele-assessment consent to supplement a typical consent form, which also outlines limits to confidentiality and so on:

I _____ hereby consent to engage in a tele-assessment with [provider/organization]. Tele-assessment is a form of psychological assessment and evaluation service provided via internet technology, which can include interviews, surveys, and other interactive tasks using interactive audio, visual, or data communications. I also understand that tele-assessment involves the communication of my medical/mental health information, both orally and/or visually.

Tele-assessment has the same purpose or intention as psychological, educational, or neuropsychological assessment sessions that are conducted in person. However, due to the nature of the technology used, I understand that tele-assessment may be experienced somewhat differently than face-to-face, in-person assessment sessions.

I also understand that some measures used in tele-assessment may not be as precise or accurate as they would be in face-to-face, in-person assessment sessions. This is because some measures used in tele-assessment are being administered in a way that they were not specifically developed to be administered. I further understand that the assessor knows and understands these issues and will use the data in a way that maximizes their accuracy and work with any unsure circumstances. This may include adding more measures to evaluate areas that are unclear, and it may result in the assessor being unable to make as specific conclusions, decisions, or recommendations as would be possible in face-to-face, in-person assessment services.

I understand that I have the following rights with respect to tele-assessment:

Client's Rights, Risks, and Responsibilities

1. I, the client, need to be a resident of [state where services take place]. (This is a legal requirement for mental health professionals practicing in this state under a [state] license.)
2. I, the client, have the right to withhold or withdraw consent at any time without affecting my right to future care or treatment.
3. The laws that protect the confidentiality of my medical information also apply to tele-assessment. As such, I understand that the information I disclose during the course of my assessment or consultation is generally confidential. However, there are both mandatory and permissive exceptions to confidentiality, which are described in the general consent form I received.
4. I understand that there are risks and consequences of participating in tele-assessment, including, but not limited to, the possibility, despite best efforts to ensure high encryption and secure technology on the part of my assessor, that: the transmission of my information could be disrupted or distorted by technical failures; the transmission of my information could be interrupted by unauthorized persons; and/or the electronic storage of my medical information could be accessed by unauthorized persons.
5. There is a risk that services could be disrupted or distorted by unforeseen technical problems.
6. In addition, I understand that tele-assessment-based services and care may not be as complete as face-to-face services. I also understand that if my assessor believes I would be better served by another form of assessment services (e.g., face-to-face services), I will be referred to a professional who can provide such services in my area.
7. I understand that I may benefit from tele-assessment, but that results cannot be guaranteed or assured. I understand that there are potential risks and benefits associated with any form of psychological assessment, and that despite my efforts and the efforts of my assessor, my condition may not improve, and in some cases may even get worse.
8. I accept that tele-assessment does not provide emergency services. If I am experiencing an emergency situation, I understand that I can call 911 or proceed to the nearest hospital emergency room for help. If I am having suicidal thoughts or making plans to harm myself, I can call the National Suicide Prevention Lifeline at 1.800.273.TALK (8255) for a free 24-hour hotline support. Clients who are actively at risk of harm to self or others are not suitable for tele-assessment services. If this is the case or becomes the case in future, my assessor will recommend more appropriate services.
9. I understand that there is a risk of being overheard by anyone near me if I am not in a private room while participating in tele-assessment. I am responsible for (1) providing the necessary computer, telecommunications equipment, and internet access for my tele-assessment sessions, and (2) arranging a location with sufficient lighting and privacy that is free from distractions or intrusions for my tele-assessment sessions. It is the responsibility of the assessor to do the same on their end.

I have read, understand, and agree to the information provided above regarding tele-assessment services with [provider/organization].

TEST SECURITY

The APA (2017) ethical code requires psychologists to take reasonable steps to ensure the security and integrity of tests, including test stimulus materials, questions, manuals, record forms, and other materials. While we have never been able to maintain 100% control over test materials (and certainly there are ways to find a great number of stimuli and test items on the internet), when it comes to tele-assessment, you need to take *reasonable* steps toward maintaining test security and integrity (Block et al., 2020; IOPC, 2020b; Wright et al., 2020). If the client is located in a testing office, remain vigilant to keep test materials secure with help from the onsite professional. Protocols for keeping stimulus materials and response forms (that you need to mail to clients) secure when clients are participating in tele-assessments from home are discussed in Chapter 3.

There are two test security and integrity layers to consider when conducting tele-assessment. The first layer is the technology, which, as previously discussed, should be encrypted, requiring a password to access, and so on. The second layer relates to user practices (further discussed in Chapter 3). These include instructing clients that no part of any session may be recorded or screen-grabbed; establishing protocols for providing materials to the onsite professional (or the client, if direct-to-home) that involve opening mailed materials on camera during a session and sealing them back in provided envelopes when completed; and using headphones throughout sessions, so that passers-by cannot hear verbal stimuli.

Another consideration regarding test integrity and security in psychological tele-assessment (also discussed in Chapter 3) is ensuring that the person being tested is in fact the client (California Commission on Peace Officer Standards and Training, 2020; Corey & Ben-Porath, 2020; Wright et al., 2020). Videoconferencing technology helps a great deal, as we can actually see, face-to-face, the client with whom we are interacting. However, there are some components of tele-assessment during which it is easy for the psychologist to become complacent and not remain engaged. For example, when a client is taking a relatively long self-report inventory, it is tempting for the psychologist to turn their camera off, disengage from the video, and do other work. Checking in throughout administration, though, can ensure that the client is the one completing the inventory. Additionally, watching a client respond to self-report inventories can help ensure that they are not copying down individual questions, doing internet searches on items, or doing something else that might jeopardize test security or accuracy. Although somewhat tedious and boring, it is important to remain engaged, on video whenever possible, with clients as they engage with our psychological measures in tele-assessment.

DOCUMENTATION AND REPORTING

Just as you did in the consent process, it is important in any documentation and reporting (including feedback sessions, assessment reports, and any other deliverables from a psychological tele-assessment) to be entirely transparent about any alterations to standard administration procedures, clear about where different data came from, and specific about any and all limitations of the tele-assessment process (California Commission on Peace Officer Standards and Training, 2020; IOPC, 2020a, 2020b; Wright et al., 2020). These statements should be clear and repeated. That is, you may include a specific "Notes on Testing" section in the report that discusses the necessary alterations made for the tele-assessment process. You may then also place an asterisk (*) next to any test listed in the measures administered section of your report, with yet another note that these included administration procedures that needed to be altered for the tele-assessment process. Additionally, you may include a note at the bottom of any table that lists test results, whether in an appendix or within the report, clarifying altered administration procedures. While this conveys humility about the meaning of any single data point, it also conveys expertise on the part of the psychologist, noting that they took into account these alterations and the potential impact they had on test data when aggregating, integrating, and interpreting data.

SOCIAL JUSTICE

When discussing ethical responsibilities of psychologists, the issue of social justice needs addressing. While inequities are rampant in our society, disasters like the COVID-19 crisis and other situations that have brought psychological tele-assessment to the forefront of professional conversation have highlighted and even exacerbated these inequities, with vulnerable populations having the least access to the services they need (van

> ### DON'T FORGET
>
> *Balance humility and expertise.* Acknowledge limitations of individual test data points (especially those that emerge from tele-assessment procedures) and convey that you accounted for any test result uncertainties in the integration of data and development of conclusions.

Dorn, Cooney, & Sabin, 2020; Yun, Lurie, & Hyde, 2010). The required access to safe, secure environments and the technology necessary for a psychological tele-assessment will further highlight this inequitable societal divide. There are likely to be very real barriers to conducting psychological tele-assessment with some clients, especially those from the most vulnerable populations. This does not mean we should halt all services to those who do have access to the necessary resources, but we must be cognizant of reinforcing some of these inequities, as well as steps we might be able to take to ameliorate them.

One example is access to reliable, high-speed internet, which many do not have. For potential psychological tele-assessment clients who have the proper hardware (device) but not the high-speed internet connection, consider connecting them with organizations that can help them gain even temporary access to broadband or high-speed Wi-Fi. This has been accomplished successfully by some training clinics that have secured reliable, high-speed internet at least for a month, during which the assessment took place. While this is inadequate on a broader scale (and the clients had to negotiate with non-profit organizations to get continued access after the month was over), it at least allowed them to receive the tele-assessment services they needed and (in these cases) get the educational accommodations and interventions from their school district that they required to succeed. As another example, one organization providing school assessments worked with a school district to have them provide students temporary access to a laptop computer and a Wi-Fi hotspot for the purposes of tele-assessment. Some psychologists have purchased headphones to give to clients, and even an inexpensive yet adequate laptop (kept clean of any sensitive information, of course) to loan to clients who need access for tele-assessment.

Understanding that inequities in access to psychological tele-assessment are also emblematic of a racial and social issue, psychologists are encouraged to harness their expertise and the power inherent within their roles (as well as their identities, especially for white, cisgender, straight, upper-middle class psychologists) to act as advocates (Burney, Celeste, Johnson, Klein, Nordal, & Portnoy, 2009; Garrison, DeLeon, & Smedley, 2017; Shriberg, 2016). One of the areas that may be extremely important at the moment, especially with knee-jerk reactions from many school districts and other decision-making bodies against tele-assessment services, may be to advocate with organizations for the acceptance of psychological tele-assessments for the purposes of accommodations and interventions. This will likely require psychologists to assert their expertise and educate school districts and other decision-makers in the state of the research behind tele-assessments (as well as remind them of the importance of multi-method assessment and the integration of information by a professional, rather than an overreliance on individual test scores, when making decisions).

You of course should never misrepresent the nascent state of the empirical literature on tele-assessment testing. However, if individuals are not receiving the accommodations, interventions, or other services that they require because tele-assessments are not accepted and they have no access to in-person options, you should begin to assert the advocacy side of yourself and fight for those individuals. While many psychologists are often too busy and overwhelmed with their practice to engage in advocacy efforts, fighting for clients' access to services via utilization of tele-assessment helps distinguish assessment broadly as an essential service, as well as further bettering the lives of those we assess.

CONCLUSION

There is an adage that bad data are worse than no data at all, and this is certainly true when it comes to psychological tele-assessment. However, what constitutes "bad data" requires more than a glib proverb. That is, while bad data can be harmful, imperfect data can still be good data. And good data are better than no data at all. As should have always been the case, even with traditional in-person assessment, we need to balance humility in our individual measures with our own expertise. That is, we need to be explicit and honest about the limitations of our test measures (which we always should have been) and their ability to reflect true, underlying psychological constructs. At the same time, we need to reassert our own expertise and authority in integrating data from multiple (imperfect) sources, including reconciling discrepant data, to inform conclusions and clinical decisions. Above all else, we need to be deliberate and explicit in our consideration of ethics in the work we do in psychological tele-assessment.

Three

PRACTICAL CONSIDERATIONS IN PSYCHOLOGICAL TELE-ASSESSMENT

Once you have determined that a client and a referral question are appropriate for psychological tele-assessment, there are a host of practical decisions to be made and preparations to attend to. The "nuts and bolts" of psychological tele-assessment can get quite complicated, and practicing the entire process from beginning to end, multiple times, is key. A psychologist fumbling with test materials, including the technology used to deliver them, can undermine a client's comfort and confidence in the process. As such, psychologists need to be fluid, confident, and nimble in their use of test materials remotely, and they need some contingency plans for if and when the technology falters or fails.

> **DON'T FORGET**
> ....
> Make sure you practice every aspect of psychological tele-assessment, multiple times, before attempting to conduct it with real clients.

GENERAL CONSIDERATIONS

There are several considerations about the process overall that need to be made ahead of time, even before creating the appropriate environments to conduct psychological tele-assessments. While some advocate for finding ways to simplify psychological assessment, either relying only on clinical interviews (IOPC, 2020a) or relying only on self-report measures (Brown & Bruns, 2020), you may certainly decide that, ethically, it is not only acceptable but better for you to continue conducting tele-assessments with multiple measures, including performance-based ones. In order to conduct ethically- and validity-defensible tele-assessments, you should understand the limitations of

Essentials of Psychological Tele-Assessment, First Edition.
A. Jordan Wright and Susan Engi Raiford
© 2021 John Wiley & Sons, Inc. Published 2021 by John Wiley & Sons, Inc.

the evidence base (discussed further in Chapter 5), and make practical decisions from there.

Some tests have direct evidence of equivalence in tele-assessment and traditional assessment formats (i.e., that the method of administration does not introduce significant alteration in the data elicited, and as such the norms and validity data from the original measure can be utilized in tele-assessment), though even these have only limited empirical support (i.e., lacking in replication studies, etc.). Other tests have indirect evidence of equivalence, such as academic achievement tests that are extremely similar to the WJ-IV (Schrank, McGrew, & Mather, 2014), which do have direct evidence (Wright, 2018b). Regardless of whether a test has direct or indirect empirical support of equivalence, the ultimate goal is to try to replicate, as closely as possible, the conditions of traditional in-person test administration, but in the remote, tele-assessment environment (Banks & Butcher, 2020; Block, Bradford, Butt, & Marek, 2020; California Commission on Peace Officer Standards and Training, 2020; IOPC, 2020a; Wright, Mihura, Pade, & McCord, 2020). Much of the preparation guidance throughout this chapter is aimed at helping you do just that, ensuring that technology and other issues that diverge from typical, standardized practice do not significantly interfere.

In actuality, there are going to be some tasks that are impossible to give and replicate with even a semblance of fidelity the traditional in-person administration processes. Some measures, like the ADOS-2 (Lord et al., 2012), simply require too much physical interaction between psychologist, client, and physically manipulated stimuli (manipulatives) to be able to even approximate administration. Similarly, widely used tasks like Block Design from the WISC-V (Wechsler, 2014) include components that pose significant challenges for even approximation (in this case, physical blocks that need manipulating by both the psychologist and the client). In these cases, you need to know either how to conduct the tele-assessment without that specific information, if possible, or if there are ways to substitute other tasks for these (Wright et al., 2020). That is, when the construct being evaluated by a task that cannot be administered is clearly understood and has alternative ways to measure it that can be administered, substitute in these tasks. If there are no comparable ways to assess the construct in a tele-assessment context, you need to determine if you can competently and completely assess the client without that information. If you cannot, you may need to postpone the assessment or refer out. Once you have determined that you will move forward and what tests, measures, and tasks you will administer, there are a number of practical considerations to think about.

TELE-ASSESSMENT PLATFORMS

There are now many varied options for telemedicine, telehealth, teleconferencing, and other tele-whatever platforms that can be used for psychological tele-assessment. Several sources have undertaken comparisons of some of the most widely used ones for telepsychology purposes (e.g., HGAPS, n.d.; Owings-Fonner, 2019), however, none to date have focused exclusively on tele-assessment utility of platforms. In order to aid in selecting the right platform for you, here are some of the major areas you should consider (Rapid Reference 3.1).

One of the first major considerations to make is the *cost of the platform*. While most likely you will have to incur some costs, it is important to note where there may be hidden costs or upcharges for some of the features that will be discussed here. While some, even HIPAA-compliant, platforms may be free, in order to access some of the features that will be necessary for tele-assessment (such as screen sharing), a premium version of the platform must be purchased. When considering cost of the platform, be sure to understand if there are usage limits (e.g., limited numbers of sessions per month), limitations for different practice types (e.g., one subscription for a clinic or group practice versus requiring a separate subscription by individual clinician), and what you are getting for the cost (e.g., amount and quality of customer support). The old adage—"you get what you pay for"—may be an important one to bear in mind, as it may ultimately be worth spending a bit more money for a higher quality product.

≡ Rapid Reference 3.1

Things to consider when deciding on a tele-assessment videoconferencing platform:

- Cost of the platform
- HIPAA- and/or FERPA-compliance/BAA
- Noted problems with connectivity
- Level of intuitiveness
- Device battery draining
- Problems with specific operating systems
- Customer service/tech support
- Compatibility with our psychological tests
- Psychologist control
- Extra features

Another major concern for psychological tele-assessment platforms is their level of *HIPAA and/or FERPA compliance*. Information communicated during a psychological assessment is extremely private and sensitive (and much of it constitutes protected health information), so protection of client data and information should be a top priority. Many platforms have HIPAA-compliant options (some at a much higher price point), but psychologists should be aware that because platforms are necessarily outside entities (vendors that can and will have access to clients' protected health information), they need to ensure that there is a *Business Associate Agreement* (BAA) in place. A BAA is a contract between a healthcare provider (the psychologist) and the platform company that ensures proper handling of protected health information and protects the psychologist if somehow the platform itself breaches confidentiality. At a minimum, a BAA should include:

- Parameters for permitted disclosures of protected health information
- Requirements for the platform to safeguard protected health information
- Requirements for the platform to immediately report any breaches of confidentiality to the psychologist
- Requirements for the platform to release protected health information at the request of the psychologist or client
- Requirements for the platform to return or destroy all protected health information at the end of the business relationship with the psychologist

BAAs can also include other requirements, such as where and how platforms can and cannot store information (e.g., whether or not the platform is allowed to store its recordings in its own cloud system). Again, because platforms are outside venders or contractors with access to client information, *do not use a platform for psychological tele-assessment if you do not have a BAA in place*. This protects you legally.

DON'T FORGET

....

Do *not* use a platform for psychological tele-assessment if you do not have a BAA in place!

Another consideration when evaluating tele-assessment platforms is the issue of any *noted problems with connectivity*. Obviously, having consistency in the connection between the psychologist and the client is extremely important in psychological assessment, as "blips" in connection or poor sound quality can significantly affect the client's perception of stimuli presented to them. While internet connection is not specifically a platform-related issue, there are several platform-related factors that can affect connectivity. Some platforms are cloud-based, and some are peer-to-peer service-based. *Cloud-based platforms tend to perform better (more consistently) when internet connection is weaker.* If there is a concern about a client's (or a psychologist's) internet strength, a cloud-based platform may be a better choice, in order to minimize technological interruptions. Additionally, some platforms suggest that in order to improve connection, you should opt for lower resolution in the picture/video transmission. While this may be a viable option for psychotherapy and counseling (and parts of psychological assessment, like clinical interviews and feedback sessions), lowering resolution may significantly impact the quality of stimuli presented to clients. If lowering the resolution makes stimuli grainy, fuzzy, or in any way less easily perceived, this can systematically affect the data collected by these measures. Therefore, it is important to research platforms that can maintain decent, consistent connectivity between psychologist and client without sacrificing quality of picture or sound.

One consideration that many people appreciate in the comparison of platforms is the *level of intuitiveness* in their use. While this may be important to you, it may also be secondary, as once you get used to a platform and its functioning, you may be perfectly comfortable with it, even if it was not inherently intuitive at the beginning of use. However, it should still be a consideration, especially if and when you are contingency planning and troubleshooting. That is, while the primary features of many platforms are relatively similar and intuitive, there are many ancillary functions within each that may be needed throughout an assessment that you may not have needed previously or even explored thoroughly. How intuitive the platform is to navigate through quickly, if and when needed, should at least be on your radar when selecting a system for psychological tele-assessment.

Similar to issues with connectivity, many reviews also include information on the level of *device battery draining* of different platforms. Some systems simply deplete the batteries of laptops and other devices extremely quickly and work better if all devices (on both sides, client and psychologist) are continually plugged in during use. This may or may not be prohibitive in your practice, depending on your personal environment and the typical environments of the clients you work with. Many situations will absolutely allow for all devices to be plugged in constantly during sessions (especially if you and clients are working at desks). However, there may be times when it is either preferable or only possible for a client to physically be somewhere that they cannot plug their device in. If this may be the case, then opt for one of the platforms that does not tend to drain the battery of devices as much.

While this is becoming less the case, there are still some platforms that have *problems with specific operating systems.* Some platforms require clients to download their system to their device, while others work completely through web browsers. When a platform requires download, there is always a possibility that its functionality may be limited on different operating systems (i.e., Windows versus Mac) or on different devices (e.g., tablets). While it is most often advisable to have a client use a computer or laptop for the primary tele-assessment device, there may be instances in which they only have access to a tablet. You should ensure that whatever platform you choose is compatible with the operating systems and devices available to both you and your client population.

Because there is a large set of variables (technological), which we generally do not have to worry much about in traditional in-office assessment, that are out of our control in tele-assessment, perhaps one of the most important things to consider when selecting a platforms is the speed, quality, and access to *customer service/ tech support*. If there are platform-related problems that occur in the middle of tele-assessment sessions, it can be extremely important to be able to access, and quickly, a live person to help you troubleshoot. Most of us are not experts in IT, and likely even fewer of us are experts in the back ends of these platforms. As such, we have to rely on customer service and technology support professionals in the case of platform-related problems, and we certainly do not want to have to abort sessions entirely when we can help it. If we can get rapid, high-quality tech support in the moment, while we may lose a few minutes of assessment time, we can most often get back to the tasks at hand once problems are fixed (how to handle the data that are affected by such problems is a different issue, addressed in Chapter 5).

At a minimum, we need to ensure that the platform we select has adequate *compatibility with our psychological tests*. As noted earlier, some functions like screen sharing are crucial for many of the tests we administer. Additionally, some tests benefit from (or require) remote control of your computer. For example, there are some self-report measures that have not yet been set up to allow for a link to be sent out for clients to complete the tests. In these cases, typically, clients would be sitting in your office at your computer entering in their responses. In order to replicate this for tele-assessment, you can open the survey form on your computer, share your screen with the client, and give them remote control over your screen so that they can fill it out as if they were sitting in your office (it is important to note some security issues this practice may bring up, noted later in this chapter). Additionally, make sure that all of your stimulus materials can be displayed adequately through the system, and if you are using document cameras, that those can be housed and used within the system as well. These are often considerations that are not addressed in reviews of platforms for telepsychology in general, as they are generally less necessary for psychotherapy or counseling. But, they are extremely important features to have for psychological tele-assessment.

Another area that is often not as necessary in psychotherapy or counseling is the level of *psychologist control* over the client's experience of the session. That is, most platforms allow each user to toggle through different views, deciding which they would prefer to see. These may be a large view of the speaker (the psychologist) with a minimized (or eliminated) view of themselves; a gallery view in which the psychologist and client are the same size, side-by-side; or some other view. Most often, when a psychologist is sharing their screen, this restricts what clients can do (they see whatever the psychologist is presenting very large, and themselves and the psychologist very small). However, when there are no visual stimuli (via screen sharing), most platforms let the client control their view. It may be important for some tasks for the clients not to see themselves, or to see the psychologist as large as possible (as if they were in close proximity in an office). Thus, it may be important and useful for a platform to allow the psychologist to assert more control over the client's experience, rather than allowing them to control their own views.

Finally, one consideration you may want to make, which is more like "the icing on the cake," is related to the *extra features* that often come packaged with telehealth platforms. For example, some of the widely used telehealth platforms are tied to electronic health records (EHRs) or electronic medical records (EMRs), so that psychologists do not have to juggle multiple systems between the actual videoconferencing and charting and noting. Some have scheduling features attached, and some allow for secure (HIPAA-compliant) messaging between psychologists and clients and between trainees and supervisors. None of these extra features is likely to bear significantly on the quality of data collected via tele-assessment, so these considerations should likely not sway you toward or away from any one platform. However, they can be nice conveniences in our busy lives!

DOCUMENT CAMERAS

Document cameras are typically high-resolution webcams used to present high-quality images (often to large groups originally, though they work extremely well for the one-on-one transmission of visual information in tele-assessment!). They are useful in many ways, and can be connected to devices and signed in to most videoconferencing platforms. If the client will be physically located in a testing room used for tele-assessment, in which you can leave the setup intact or store equipment for an onsite professional (e.g., teacher, counselor, psychometrist) to set up, you should provide a document camera there. While it may not be feasible to supply a document camera in the client's home for a psychological tele-assessment, when possible, having a document camera trained down at the client's workspace can allow a psychologist to see what is happening, in real time, with very high quality. This can be important for tasks that require writing or drawing, for example. Certainly, at times, it may be necessary to find a workaround, such as using a smartphone logged into the tele-assessment system and pointed down at the workspace; however, the quality of the video may not be good enough to see exactly what is going on. A document camera allows for the psychologist to see clearly what the client is doing in their workspace without sacrificing the primary view of the client (generally shoulders up). Most videoconferencing platforms allow the document camera to be selected as a spotlighted or pinned view on the psychologist's screen, which results in an enlarged view of the client's workspace and progress. This is helpful if the psychologist is required to provide feedback based on performance or code information in the moment.

On the psychologist's side, a document camera can be extremely useful for presenting stimuli to clients. The high-quality nature of document cameras allows the visual of stimulus materials to be relatively uncompromised when projected to clients over the tele-assessment platform. It should be noted that many stimulus materials are available from test publishers online in PDF (or similar) format, which allows for them to be utilized without needing a camera trained on a physical stimulus book in the psychologist's office. But when this is not available, stimuli are projected mostly intact when using a document camera on the psychologist's side of the assessment. It is important to check with the test publisher to ensure that the kit purchasing agreement permits the psychologist to display stimulus materials on a document camera (many do not).

It should be noted that document cameras have a very large range of cost associated with them, with basic ones being relatively inexpensive. Some come with a lot of bells and whistles, such as video captures, remote controls, split screen capabilities, and other such extras that simply are not necessary in the context of psychological tele-assessment. As long as you ensure that it has an optical zoom lens (which most do) that can allow you to zero in on details, if needed, even a basic document camera should work (on both sides of the assessment). While there are several costs associated with adapting to tele-assessment, this should not be one to spend a great deal on!

PREPARATION: THE PSYCHOLOGIST ENVIRONMENT

Before your session, make sure to *practice with the technology and the tests yourself.* You do not want to be fumbling around either with the technology or the test materials themselves (just as you would not want to be clumsy with test materials in traditional, in-person assessments), and no amount of watching videos or demonstrations can replace actual, hands-on practice. Find test-secure ways to practice full administrations, when and if possible. This may include enlisting another psychologist to spend time online with you (via your tele-assessment platform) doing mock administrations. That way, you can not only administer actual items (as they are qualified to see them), but you can also get in-the-moment feedback about what exactly they are seeing on their screens, so you can be sure you understand the client's experience.

When determining what tests you are going to give, make sure you *know and understand the literature base* behind them (reviewed in Chapters 6–8), the constructs they purport to measure (and with which populations this seems to be accurate) and how they measure them, and ultimately how any altered administration procedures are likely to affect the data collected by them. There may be some tests or subtests that you decide to abandon entirely, either for practical reasons (they simply cannot be accomplished logistically through tele-assessment procedures) or empirical reasons (the data that emerge from the altered administration mode is likely so affected by method that they no longer accurately represent the client and their functioning). In these cases, if the data are necessary, you should be thoughtful about *test and subtest substitutions*, whenever feasible. Ultimately, the goal (especially when there is only indirect support for tele-assessment alteration of a measure) is to try to *approximate as closely as possible standardized administration procedures*. When using a measure that has standardized procedures that cannot even be approximated, it is important to plan your assessment battery around this.

There are multiple areas technologically that require specific preparation before tele-assessments can happen effectively. Perhaps most foundational, you need to *ensure that your connectivity is consistent*. Some psychologists live or even work in places that do not have reliable internet access, and this can undermine the ability to engage in the process entirely. When determining the reliability of your internet connection, make sure that both your video and audio quality is consistent and clear. While you may not be able to control the adequacy of internet connection on the client's side, you don't want technological hitches to be due to *your* poor or unreliable internet connection.

Something that does not present itself as an issue in traditional in-person services but can significantly affect tele-assessment (and telepsychology) services is *eye gaze angle*. When using a webcam that's integrated into a laptop or monitor, most often videoconferencing platforms have accounted for this issue, such that the platform corrects for eye gaze when you are looking at generally the middle of the screen (usually where the image of a client would be). However, if you are using an independent webcam, you need to make sure that wherever you will generally be looking on your monitor/screen does not look awkward or uncomfortable on the client's side. Again, this is something that can be evaluated through practicing with a colleague (or a friend or family member), so that you are not assuming it is fine when it is not, as well as not having to correct it in a session with a client somehow.

There are two plans that need to be developed before embarking on a psychological tele-assessment. First, you should *prepare a contingency plan for technological glitches.* During some parts of the assessment, a contingency plan may be changing to a different device or modality. For example, you may determine that, if there are technological problems during a clinical interview, you may want to switch to a phone call to finish collecting those data. Or you may want to access your tele-assessment platform through your smartphone instead of your computer or tablet, if those are the problem. These contingency plans, however, likely will not be useful if you are in the middle of a cognitive assessment, for example. You may determine that, at certain points during a tele-assessment, the only contingency plan is to abort the session and continue at another time. This may mean throwing out some bad data or supplementing your assessment battery with another test looking at the same construct as the one that was potentially ruined. Make sure, though, that you have clearly thought through a plan, and even communicated this to the client.

The next pre-psychological tele-assessment preparation to accomplish is to *develop a safety plan* (Joint Task Force for the Development of Telepsychology Guidelines for Psychologists, 2013). While you may be in the same state, city, or even office as a client, the logistics around safety are quite different in a tele-assessment context than they are in traditional, in-person work. Ideally, during the tele-assessment the client will be located in a testing room or clinic office with a professional (e.g., teacher, counselor, psychometrist) nearby who is knowledgeable about local resources and accessible by cell phone. Ensure that the onsite professional is fully oriented to the possibility that they may need to be involved in this aspect of the session in the event that a safety need arises, as well as specifically what the plan is.

However, if the client cannot be located in a testing room during the tele-assessment, the safety logistics are amplified. First and foremost, you should know what resources are available near wherever the client is. If the client is a child, adolescent, or adult who requires a caregiver or other assistance, you should also know exactly where a parent, guardian, or caregiver will be during each assessment session, as well as having their contact information (such as their cell phone number) in case of emergency. Be mindful of confidentiality and of what consent is needed to involve them in tele-assessment, as an adult's caregiver may not hold medical power of attorney or be a legal guardian; the adult with a caregiver may still hold their own medical power of attorney and thus confidentiality. Even for adults who are independent, know what emergency resources are available near them. And make sure you always have the phone number and address of wherever the client is during your sessions, just in case!

Once you know what resources are available, think through procedures. Psychologists should be very familiar with typical procedures related to hospitalization, starting with encouraging voluntary agreement and compliance and, if not agreed to, working with local emergency or law enforcement agencies to get clients to a hospital. This is generally done (most often) in an office context, as a psychologist has evaluated that a client is somehow a danger to self or others and needs immediate higher-level care. In the tele-world, keeping a client engaged through this process may be more difficult, as it is so easy for them to simply disconnect from the session. You should "play it out" ahead of time, thinking through all the different ways a situation could progress. Knowing information about mobile crisis units or local mental health safety check organizations can be invaluable in these instances. Whatever your procedures, make sure they are clearly thought through ahead of time.

Once you have thought through all the above issues, and just before you begin a session, there are two more areas to prepare. In terms of technology, you need to *prepare your own computer* for optimal tele-assessment services. You should clear your browser history and make sure all other programs on your computer are closed all the way (not even running in the background, if possible). Additionally, you should turn off all programs that have notifications, such as email and messaging. You do not want any of those programs or systems to interrupt you during your tele-assessment sessions. If you are going to be using screen share and allowing the client remote control over your computer, *you should set up a separate login/profile that has none of your files or programs on it, other than the ones needed for the assessment itself.* That is, your computer likely has many files on it from other clients, your own notes, and many other things clients should not have access to. While very unlikely, a client having remote control over your computer does allow them to snoop through your computer (obviously, you will be there and seeing it all, and you can hopefully quickly and easily disable the remote control). Do not even leave a little bit of risk for clients to access data they should not be privy to. Setting up a separate login (a separate profile when your computer boots up) that you only use during tele-assessment can ensure that even if a client goes rogue and starts snooping through your computer, they will not have access to anything private.

In addition to setting up your computer, you should also *set up your physical space.* You should ensure that your physical space is relatively quiet and free from distractions, and will continue to be throughout any and all tele-assessment sessions. Think about what the client can see in your immediately surrounding environment. You may want to remove any distracting personal items, artwork, or other things that may pull attention during the assessment. Some videoconferencing platforms have the ability for people to use virtual backgrounds. These can be useful to create a neutral background palate (though colleagues have been known to use intergalactic and cartoon-based backgrounds during meetings). However, even the neutral virtual backgrounds can also be somewhat distracting, as they are often imperfect and the space right around your head can look odd, especially when you move. So, be careful about using these virtual backgrounds.

Further, make sure that you are very well lit from the front. While a room may be bright, if the majority of light is coming from behind your head, it will cast you in a severe shadow online. One option is to use a specific monitor light for video conferencing, one that clips onto a monitor or a laptop and shines directly into your face to ensure you are well lit.

Finally, *ensure that all testing materials are set up and ready to use* on your side of the tele-assessment. Any stimulus materials that you will be using physically (with a document camera) should be easily accessible. Any stimulus materials that you will be using online (with a screen share) should be open on your computer but minimized. Additionally, even though you may have planned to give only a certain test or measure in a given session, you should have at the ready alternative options, should you for some reason need to abort giving one measure and replace it with another. This can happen for all the same reasons as in a traditional in-person session, such as a client struggling with a type of task or becoming upset; it can also happen, though, for technology reasons, such as a task not cooperating on a certain day for some reason (e.g., bandwidth issues due to bad weather may require tasks that do not need heavy video use).

PREPARATION: THE CLIENT ENVIRONMENT

In many ways, you have much less control over the client's physical and technological environment than you do over your own, and much less than you would in a traditional in-person assessment. As stated repeatedly throughout this book, the ultimate goal is to try to replicate standardized and typical assessment practices as closely as possible, and as such clients require preparation for the process. You should *discuss with the client (or parents/guardians/caregivers) exactly what to expect* throughout the psychological tele-assessment process. Much like you

Checklist for Psychological Tele-Assessment Preparation: Psychologist's Side

- Practice with the technology and the tests yourself
- Know and understand the literature base
  - Consider test and subtest substitutions
  - Approximate as closely as possible standardized administration procedures
- Ensure that your connectivity is consistent
- Prepare and test your eye gaze angle
- Prepare a contingency plan for technological glitches
- Develop a safety plan
  - Client's phone number during sessions: _____
  - Client's address during sessions: _____
  - Emergency resources near the client: _____
  - If a child:
    - parent/guardian whereabouts during session: _____
    - parent/guardian cell phone during session: _____
- Prepare your own computer
  - Clear browser history
  - Close all other programs, even ones running in the background
  - Turn off all notifications, such as from email and messaging programs
  - If using remote control, set up a separate login/profile
- Set up your physical space
  - Ensure that it is quiet and relatively free from distractions
  - Remove any distracting personal items or artwork that will be in the client's view
  - Consider a virtual background, but be careful that it is not itself distracting
  - Ensure you are very well lit from the front
- Ensure that all testing materials are set up and ready to use
  - Physical stimulus materials are out and within reach
  - Virtual stimulus materials (such as PDFs for screen sharing) are open and minimized on your computer
  - Prepare backup/alternate tests for administration, in case needed

probably would in a typical assessment, you should describe the difference between what a clinical interview will look like in a tele-assessment and what tests and other measures will require of them (and their children, if applicable). As stated in Chapter 2, this is part of informed consent, ensuring that clients (or parents/guardians/caregivers) understand what the process will look like.

If it is your first time using a testing room at a new location, considerable attention must be paid to preparing the client's physical environment; a clinic or school room may not meet the requirements for tele-assessment without some planning and intervention on your part. All of the considerations outlined in the subsequent paragraphs are also considerations for a testing room you are using for the first time. Do not assume that a teacher, counselor, or other assistant will know how to set up the client's environment.

Ideally, if the client will be located in a testing room, you will be able to ship or store materials at that location and instruct the onsite professional to prepare the necessary materials. However, if the client is not located in a testing room (such as when they need to be tested in their own home), you may need to *send materials to the client*. For example, if you are doing educational testing, you may need to send them response booklets with math problems or writing prompts in them, in addition to an addressed, stamped envelope for them to return them once used. When you send materials, make sure that clients or parents/guardians know the rules and parameters for those materials. This may include instructing them *not to open them* before the session in which they will be used (we will elaborate further on instructing the use of materials throughout sessions). It is possible you may choose to send other types of stimulus materials (within the bounds of test security), and clients or parents/guardians/caregivers should know exactly what and what not to do with these before sessions.

If the tele-assessment takes place in an environment other than a testing room, when it comes time to orient clients or parents/guardians/caregivers to the actual assessment sessions, there are a number of things to communicate to them ahead of the sessions. First, *instruct them on their physical environment*. This will include how to set up the physical space around them in order to minimize distraction and maximize focus on the tasks at hand. In addition to minimizing distraction, the physical environment on the client's side should be comfortable and private. You should organize with clients to ensure that whatever times you choose to conduct the tele-assessment are likely to be relatively free of distraction. Some clients may have only small pockets of time when this is the case—try to capitalize on these times whenever possible. Additionally, it is best practice to instruct clients to use headphones throughout the process. Headphones not only reduce distraction in the immediate environment, but they also protect privacy and test security. Remember, people tend to speak much louder through videoconferencing platforms than they do in person, so at least eliminating half of the conversation from potential on-listeners (the psychologist's side of the conversation, including verbally-presented stimuli, will only be heard in the headphones) is better than not.

Always make it absolutely clear (and repeat as necessary) that there should be *no recording of sessions* on the client's side. Whether the client is in a testing room or at home, smartphones (which have cameras and can capture video) should be powered off and placed in a secure area until the session concludes. Clients should not have access to the test materials presented to them indefinitely. They are presented for a short amount of time for many reasons, including test security and usability (so that they cannot study the items and retake the test having somehow prepared). You may be recording sessions on your side (in fact, this can truly aid the psychological tele-assessment process, as you can go back and look for behavioral observations, without the burden of juggling all the technology and test materials in the moment), but clients should not be recording. Audio recordings, photos, or videos you capture may have to be stored as part of the client's protocol or electronic health record in some areas, so be mindful of this possibility and consult appropriate guidelines.

Just before sessions, you should *communicate clearly to the onsite professional, the client, or parents/guardians/caregivers what will happen if technology fails* during a session. The contingency plans that you created for each session (described earlier) should include concrete actions for what will happen in the (hopefully rare) case that technology causes problems. This may include a follow-up phone call (be clear who will call whom) to regroup and plan, it may include the use of a secondary tele-assessment platform, or it may include some other plan altogether. Whatever the plan is, make it clear to the client, so that no session is ever abandoned. Even if the plan is to abort the session in the case that something goes wrong, make sure that you have communicated a way to "close the loop" on that plan, such as a quick phone call to say that you will end the session and meet another day.

Additionally, *help onsite professionals, clients, or parents/guardians/caregivers prepare their own technology for optimal functioning.* First, it is important that the client's side of the session has sufficient technology, including a monitor of adequate screen size (there is no consensus on adequate screen size, but many point to a minimum of a 13-inch monitor). Before sessions, the onsite professional or the client themself should close every other program running, even in the background, on their computer. This minimizes not only distraction but also competing Wi-Fi/bandwidth use. Like you have done with your computer, you may instruct them to turn off any notifications or messaging they get as pop-ups on their computer, such as from their email. Any other potential technological distractions or internet competition should also be addressed before the session, in order to maximize connection in the session. You can verify that this was accomplished by having the onsite professional or client share their entire screen through the teleconferencing platform before testing begins, ensuring the task bar does not indicate any active programs, and making sure that "off" is selected within the notifications setting.

When applicable, you should *instruct the onsite professional, client, or parent/ guardian/caregiver to prepare any necessary materials* for the tele-assessment session. These may include response booklets (still in sealed envelopes), paper, pencils without erasers, or any other materials. You may also instruct them to have water nearby and handy, or even a snack, depending on the time of day and the tasks for that session. Think through the entire session and try to anticipate any and every physical material the client may possibly need, and ensure these are at the ready.

Finally, if you are using a parent/guardian/caregiver (or other individual) as a proctor or facilitator at all throughout the session, make sure to *coach them very specifically on what they should and should not do during sessions.* If they are going to be in the room with the client, if at all possible, ask them to sit behind and to the side of the client (as far back as possible), so that they are themselves not distractions and can be easily seen on camera by you throughout the process. This may not always be possible, given physical room constraints, but try to figure out a way to replicate this even if you have to get creative (e.g., if they are far off to the side, off camera, you may have them join the session on their phone so that you can monitor them visually, but make sure the client cannot see them on their view of the tele-assessment platform; you may need to have them on a different platform going to a different device on your side, such as your smartphone).

Onsite professionals', in a testing room scenario, or parents/guardians/caregivers' interaction with the assessment will vary based on the specific measures being given; you should be clear with them when and how they should help out. This may include "delivering" a response booklet to the client at specific moments during the session, for example. You should also be clear about when and how they should *not* intervene in the session, such as when a client is struggling to respond to a cognitive or academic prompt. One way to be absolutely clear is to instruct them not to participate or intervene unless and until you specifically address them. An empathic way to convey this to parents/guardians/caregivers can include understanding that it can be very tempting to help a client out when they are struggling, especially if you know they know something but are not demonstrating it. But reassure them that this is the process, and you want to get the most accurate "snapshot" of the client as possible, which will require them not to intervene unless asked to. Detailed guidance on how to coach facilitators is provided by Taylor and Wright (2020).

Checklist for Psychological Tele-Assessment Preparation: Client's Side

- Discuss with the onsite professional, client, or parents/guardians/caregivers exactly what to expect
- Supply materials at the client's location
  - Include response booklets and similar materials
  - Include an addressed, stamped envelope for returning materials
  - Discuss with the onsite professional, client, or parents/guardians/caregivers) the rules and parameters for those materials (such as not opening them until instructed)
- Instruct the onsite professional, client, or parents/guardians/caregivers) on the physical environment
  - Relatively free from distraction
  - Comfortable and private
  - Times for sessions when there are likely to be few distractions
  - Use headphones
- Instruct the onsite professional, client, or parents/guardians/caregivers that there should be no recording of sessions
- Communicate clearly to the onsite professional, clients, or parents/guardians/ caregivers what will happen if technology fails
- Help onsite professionals, clients, or parents/guardians/caregivers prepare the client's side technology for optimal use
  - Ensure an adequately-sized monitor (at least 13 inches)
  - Ensure all other programs are closed, even ones running in the background
  - Ensure all notifications are turned off, such as from email and messaging programs
- Instruct onsite professional, client, or parent/guardian/caregiver to prepare any necessary materials for the client's side
  - Testing materials (such as response booklets, still in sealed envelopes, paper, pencils without erasers, etc.)
  - Water nearby and handy
  - Snack nearby and handy, if appropriate
- If an onsite professional or parent/guardian/caregiver is being used during a session:
  - Coach on what they should or should not do during sessions
  - Specify where they should be seated during sessions
  - Instruct them about what kinds of interactions are ok and not ok
  - Warn them when it may be tempting to intervene
  - Let them know exactly what kinds of tasks they will be asked to do

SESSION CONSIDERATIONS

Now that you are fully prepared and beginning your actual sessions, there are a host of considerations that are important to note as you progress through the actual psychological tele-assessment (Rapid Reference 3.2). First of all, while this may be straightforward in most cases, it is important to *verify the identity of the client* at the beginning of the process. This is probably not practiced widely enough even in in-person assessment. However, when assessments are conducted 100% in tele-assessment format, it is always a possibility that the person on the other side of the technology is not the person we think we are assessing. This may be selectively true with different types of tasks in the assessment. For example, if a client is motivated to emerge from a tele-assessment with a specific finding, they may enlist someone else to respond to certain self-report measures on their behalf. Similarly, if a child were being evaluated for placement in a gifted and talented program, a parent/guardian may be motivated to respond to cognitive or academic prompts for the client. While hopefully this is an extremely low base rate occurrence, the psychologist should verify that the person being assessed is who they think it is.

Throughout the assessment sessions, it is extremely important to *continuously monitor the client's physical environment*. You should be mindful of the myriad distractions that can present themselves, whether a client is participating in the psychological tele-assessment from a testing room or from home. These can include other people directly or indirectly interacting with the client (often at inopportune times!), noises and movements happening from outside windows, or many other things outside your and their control. It is important to note moments during tasks that these outside distractions occur, in order to

≡ Rapid Reference 3.2

In-session considerations include:

- Verify the identity of the client
- Continuously monitor the client's physical environment
- Be explicit and specific about how clients should use materials
- Shorten sessions
- Monitor fatigue
- Be ready to abort sessions, if needed
- Be ready to access tech support in the middle of sessions
- Test the limits and follow up, as necessary and appropriate

cross-reference them with any responses that may have been affected by them. As stated previously, it can be helpful to record sessions and rewatch them with a specific eye toward possible distractions. If an onsite professional or parent/guardian/caregiver is in the room with the client, be particularly mindful of their interactions and potential distractions during the process. It is best to make sure you can see them at all times (either on the primary camera, behind and to the side of the client, or on a separate video feed somehow) so that you can ensure they are not interfering with the assessment in inappropriate ways.

Throughout sessions that require the use of physical materials on the client's side, *be explicit and specific about how clients should use materials*. For example, if response booklets have been sent to the client's location for a specific test, and the onsite professional or client has been instructed not to open the envelope until told, during the session it will be important to instruct them and then *watch them* open the envelope and take out the response booklets. Once the testing is complete for that session, again both instruct them and watch them put the response booklets into the addressed, stamped envelope and seal it to return to you. This is even important if the client is located in a testing room, because materials could be misplaced or altered. This practice also protects test security by minimizing opportunities to copy the actual items from the response booklets in some way. It does not make it impossible, but it is a *reasonable* step toward maintaining test security (APA, 2017).

Regarding the sessions themselves, psychologists should be prepared to *shorten sessions* throughout the tele-assessment, relying on more, shorter sessions, rather than fewer, longer ones. In general, between not having the in-person interaction to keep a client engaged, not having as much recourse to observe body language (below the shoulders), and what is known about eye strain and fatigue in videoconferencing (Mouzourakis, 1996), it is safer to err on the side of shorter sessions. Of course, consistent with standardized practice, you do not want to stop sessions in the middle of tests (or worse, subtests), but consider administering fewer measures in any given session, in order to mitigate fatigue.

Related to shortening sessions, it is important to *monitor fatigue* throughout sessions, especially ones with tests being administered. Signs of tele-assessment fatigue can include more frequent glances away from the monitor, neck stretches, sighs, and of course clients saying that they are tired! Additionally, keep track of clients asking repeatedly how much longer a given task is. While this is generally pretty common, even in traditional, in-person assessments, on tasks like continuous performance tests (which are quite long and boring, on purpose), more frequent questions about time left in a session can be a sign of actual fatigue.

Relatedly, psychologists should always *be ready to abort sessions, if needed.* Fatigue is one reason psychologists might choose to abort a session, and another is when there is significant and justified frustration with the technology being used. That is, if there are constant interruptions to the connection on the platform, or audio keeps cutting in and out, clients (and psychologists) can get justifiably frustrated. When this is the case, it is often best to cut your losses, abort the session, and come up with a contingency plan (meeting another day, utilizing a different platform, etc.). While sessions are cut short in traditional assessment from time to time, for varied reasons, the introduction of technology that, unfortunately, is often not reliable can require us to implement this strategy more often.

If necessary, *be ready to access tech support in the middle of sessions.* Make sure you have the contact information for the tech support of the tele-assessment platform you have chosen, as well as the best way to contact them (some respond faster using the chat option on their website; some respond faster with a phone call; etc.). Hitches in technology are often unavoidable, and most people know and understand this. Clients also most often realize that you did not design and do not run the tele-assessment platform you are using. That being said, be transparent throughout the process, letting them know that because of whatever is happening, you need to "pause" the session for a bit and contact the platform's tech support for help. This may be a moment to suggest that the client take a break, get some water, go to the bathroom, or otherwise just take a break from staring at a computer screen (assuming you do not need them present to fix whatever is happening on the platform). Hopefully, in most cases, tech support will be rapid and effective, and within a few minutes sessions can continue.

Because of your limited view of the client's body language, as well as limits to what has been validated or equated in a tele-assessment environment relative to a traditional, in-person one, psychologists should be ready to more liberally *test the limits and follow up* on specific constructs during the assessment. Luxton, Pruett, and Osenbach (2014) discuss how, even on brief, symptom-focused rating scales, it may be important and useful to follow up with more and varied specific questions related to the construct, as reporting biases are less well-understood in this context. When administering tests, it is best to do this *outside of the typical administration* of the measures; that is, for example, for a rating scale looking at depressive symptoms, it is best to allow the client to complete the scale in its entirety before following up with additional, probing questions. This holds true for other tests as well, such as self-report inventories and performance-based tasks. A review of results from a self-report inventory may prompt additional probing into certain areas of functioning, for example, when results strike the psychologist as different from what was expected (in either direction: pathology or non-pathology). Similarly, psychologists often "test the limits" on cognitive and other performance-based tasks, after the standardized procedures have been completed. On a subtest on which a client reaches their ceiling/discontinue, psychologists again may choose to be somewhat more liberal in the use of testing the limits—continuing to administer items, which will not contribute to the formal score—in order to determine if and how clients' functioning may not be quite as precisely reflected in the scores obtained from tele-assessment procedures. Even if not formally scored, data collected can contribute to the overall understanding of an individual being assessed.

THE IN-OFFICE TELE-ASSESSMENT SETUP

One way of mitigating the uncontrolled nature of the client's environment, while maximizing the benefits of the contactless tele-assessment setup, is by creating an in-office tele-assessment setup. In general, it looks nearly identical to the ideal setup of a psychological tele-assessment that utilizes a client's home as their side of the assessment, but it uses two offices (ideally adjoining, especially if using bluetooth-enabled technologies for certain test administrations), one for the psychologist and another for the client. The psychologist's office includes a computer or laptop, a tablet (if using tests that are administered in such a way), and a document camera (if using physical stimulus materials that are not available for screen sharing and need to be projected). The client's office includes a computer or laptop, a tablet (if using tests that are administered in such a way), a document camera, a packet of response booklets, and any other manipulatives needed, set to the side. Clients should be prepared ahead of time for what they should expect to see and interact with in this setup, as it can be jarring to walk into an office and be instructed to go to an empty (of other people) room set up with a great deal of technology. Clients can feel like they are research participants in mid-century psychological experiments being spied on!

This setup has many benefits, most notably the ability to better control the client's environment. It also allows you to use some manipulatives and stimulus materials that may not otherwise be feasible (as we typically do not mail or deliver test materials to clients' homes). Some clients, especially those who have been screened and who present as intellectually average or better, can be instructed how to interact with stimulus materials and perform some of the functions that you typically carry out. However, the cost of this setup can also be prohibitive. Not only is there a great deal of equipment required, but it requires twice the real estate, as each session is occupying two offices. Additionally, with so much technology and test material alone in a room with a client, we cannot maintain control over any destructive behavior that may occur, even as we watch from next door, somewhat helplessly. This may be especially true for children, but all clients have the potential to, accidentally or on purpose, ruin or destroy technology or test materials. Finally, if tele-assessment is occurring to keep you or the client safe from potential illness, a specific procedure for disinfecting materials both before and after client sessions should be carried out, so that you both can feel secure that the materials are safe to use.

CONCLUSION

Psychological testing and assessment already have a great deal of minutiae to consider and wrestle with under normal circumstances. Psychological tele-assessment adds another host of considerations and details to engage with, many that can be frustrating and seem outside the realm of why we went to graduate school. However, it is important to be methodical in our preparation and implementation of materials and procedures in psychological tele-assessment to try to ensure the best possible data emerges from it. Clients and other stakeholders are placing a great deal of trust in us to deliver them useful conclusions, and often recommendations, and so we want to ensure that even seemingly minor issues do not get in the way of us doing so.

ADDITIONAL RESOURCES

https://www.apaservices.org/practice/reimbursement/health-codes/testing/
    tele-assessment-covid-19
https://www.apa.org/practice/programs/dmhi/research-information/
    telepsychological-services-checklist
https://en.wikiversity.org/wiki/Helping_Give_Away_Psychological_Science/
    Telepsychology
https://www.presencelearning.com/Cognitive-and-Academic-Tele-Assessment-
    APractical-Guide

Four

NORMS, EQUIVALENCE, AND EQUATING

One of the first questions asked by psychologists considering tele-assessment is, "Are new norms needed for tele-assessment?" To answer this question, it is important to understand three distinct but inter-related concepts: norms, equivalence, and equating. A nomothetic, normative approach to psychological assessment has been the hallmark of valid, defensible, and scientific study of human functioning within the field of psychology. The idea that many (perhaps most) of the variables that we study in individual psychological assessment (and especially skills and abilities) are roughly normally distributed in the population allows for individuals to be compared to norms to describe how they are functioning compared to others their age, their academic grade-level, in the general population, or in some other special subpopulation.

Developing tests and measures to be compared in this way has required strict standardization of administration, coding, and scoring of them; that is, if we are collecting data to compare to a bunch of other people, we want to make sure we are collecting the data in roughly the same way for each of them, so that it is an "apples-to-apples" comparison. If we veer from standardized practice, we need to understand what method effects exist. We also need to know if and how changing the way we have administered, coded, or scored a measure affects the data that are collected. Only by understanding if and how much the scores derived from altered methods are influenced by the changes in method, as opposed to the construct-relevant (what we want to know) variables, can we continue to assert our typical interpretations of those data.

Essentials of Psychological Tele-Assessment, First Edition.
A. Jordan Wright and Susan Engi Raiford
© 2021 John Wiley & Sons, Inc. Published 2021 by John Wiley & Sons, Inc.

NORMS

Norms are sets of scores that allow us to compare an examinee's score against those of a specified population. Collecting a representative sample from this predefined population is paramount to accurate norms. Normative samples should also be generally representative of the socio-demographic features of the population, especially on variables that are important to predicting performance on a construct of interest.

For many types of tests, norms are provided separately by variables known to strongly affect performance. For example, intelligence tests generally provide norms separately by age. When determining the general ability of a 6-year-old child, it is important to compare to other 6-year-old children. Comparing a 6-year-old to everyone in the population on, for example, a vocabulary test would not accurately describe their intellectual ability (pretty much every 6-year-old would come out with extremely low IQ if compared to children and adults together!). Similarly, many tests collect and present different norms for different subgroups of a population. For example, a personality measure used in pre-screening law enforcement officers may have specific norms for law enforcement, so that a psychologist can decide to compare personality traits to the general population or to others in that specific profession.

In other situations, norms are not presented separately based on subgroups or other variables. For example, although gender explains some variability in cognitive test scores, the average differences are not considered practically meaningful enough that separate norms are necessary. In this case, the differences are smaller than the standard error of measurement (Chen, Zhang, Raiford, Zhu, & Weiss, 2015; Kaufman, Raiford, & Coalson, 2016; Reynolds, Keith, Ridley, & Patel, 2008), and factorial invariance on gender has been generally supported for cognitive tests (e.g., Chen et al., 2015; Chen & Zhu, 2012, Reynolds et al., 2008). Ultimately, understanding how the norms were developed informs the psychologist about exactly whom they are comparing their examinee to, which is extremely important to understand.

When Are New Norms Needed?

Psychologists who are considering tele-assessment frequently ask if new norms are needed. They are trained that in the event of any type of change to the original test specifications after a measure is standardized, the continued applicability of score comparisons to the original normative information is a primary concern

(*Standards for Educational and Psychological Testing* [*Standards*]; AERA, APA, & NCME, 2014).

Many current behavior and personality tests were standardized in digital format, and sometimes normative data were collected using remote administration. However, almost all performance-based measures (typically cognitive, achievement, and neuropsychological tests) that psychologists commonly administer were standardized using a face-to-face administration mode and a paper-and-pencil format. Therefore, administering tests via tele-assessment is often a change to standardized administration. Scores obtained in a tele-assessment mode therefore require special consideration and review of validity studies that have examined the impact of a mode change.

When mode is altered, studies can be conducted to examine the impact of the change and to provide information about how well scores obtained across the two modes or formats correspond. These correspondence studies help to determine if adjustments are required and/or if new norms are needed. The study designs for these purposes may be unfamiliar to psychologists, who are unaccustomed to evaluating the differences across test formats or modes. If the differences are not practically meaningful, new norms are not needed.

TYPES OF CORRESPONDENCE STUDY DESIGNS

Examining sets of psychological test scores to determine the extent to which they correspond is not a new endeavor. A century ago, Thorndike (1922) discussed the practical need to compare scores across two intelligence tests for World War I United States Army recruits, the Alpha (for those who could read) and Beta (for those who could not).

> **DON'T FORGET**
> ....
> New norms are not needed for a change from face-to-face to tele-assessment if the differences are not practically meaningful.

In this newer tele-assessment context, some test users have asked if a study investigating the correspondence of the newer mode should involve examinees taking both the face-to-face and the tele-assessment mode of a test to compare the scores obtained. This question describes (to some extent) a common type of study used to examine the relations between two tests. It has limitations when examining test mode changes for various reasons. A brief overview of these types of studies, their purposes, and their features can help clarify the questions addressed by different study designs in the event of a mode change.

Dual Mode Administration

One option for score correspondence studies is to administer a test in both modes to each examinee. This yields a direct comparison and correlation between the two modes, which provides information about the extent to which they yield similar results.

Almost every commercially available test manual—especially those for tests that are updates from previous versions—provides these types of validity studies with other measures of the same construct to investigate their comparability. For example, the WISC-V (Wechsler, 2014) provides a score comparison study with the prior edition, the WISC-IV (Wechsler, 2003). Similarly, the manual for the Millon Clinical Multiaxial Inventory, Fourth Edition (MCMI-IV; Millon, 2015) provides a score comparison study with its prior edition, the MCMI-III (Millon, 1994). In each of these, scores are correlated between individuals who took the tests in both modes.

Many such studies are designed to provide analyses beyond correlations between the two tests (e.g., mean comparisons). For these, often the testing order is *counterbalanced*. This means that both tests are administered to every examinee, and the entire sample is split across two orders. Examinees are randomly assigned to one of two testing orders, in which half are administered the first test then the second test, and the other half are administered the second test followed by the first. Counterbalanced studies are typically used to examine concurrent validity either across two similar tests or to examine a new edition of a test to determine if it produces results that are consistent with the prior edition. To the extent that it does, the research base from the prior edition can be applied more readily to the new one.

Psychologists are aware that if they administer a test too soon after another similar measure, the scores on the second test can be affected. This is especially true for cognitive measures, in which practice can improve an examinee's performance. This is commonly observed in test–retest studies, where examinees take the same test twice within a few weeks. Counterbalanced studies assume that by counterbalancing the administration order, the carryover or practice effect in one testing order will cancel out the effect in the other testing order when data are aggregated (Coleman, 2018). To the extent that assumption is accurate, the mean differences can be examined.

Whether counterbalanced or not, there are limitations on studies that have examinees take both modes of a test. Taking the task multiple times may change how an examinee interacts with that task, simply because they have encountered it before. Repeated administration effects such as variation in examinee effort, item practice, and procedural learning may differ across the two orders (AERA, APA, & NCME, 2014).

For example, tele-assessment might be more distracting than face-to-face mode. If so, taking the test in face-to-face mode first may allow examinees to focus more intently, which could result in more learning as compared to examinees that took the test in tele-assessment mode first. In this case, one order's carryover effect would not cancel out the other's.

Furthermore, using data from this design to adjust the norms for any observed mode differences could be complicated due to this possibility (AERA, APA, & NCME, 2014), especially because there are reasons to suspect the order effects may vary. For similar reasons, the correlation may underestimate the relations in test mode equivalence studies that use this design.

Single Mode Administration

A second type of study design to investigate a mode change is to administer the test to two equivalent groups of examinees in one mode each. For *equivalent group* investigations, examinees are either randomly or nonrandomly assigned to take one of the two tests being studied (NRC, 1999; AERA, APA, & NCME, 2014). Random assignment helps to ensure that examinees in the two conditions are essentially the same on characteristics that involve random variation and could impact results. It also prevents selection bias, which occurs if the assigned condition is not random in an experiment and is a threat to the validity and generalizability of results. Furthermore, it avoids any change in the examinee's behavior as a result of having taken a task before. However, this method does not provide a direct estimate of the correlations between the scores obtained from the two modes. Therefore, alternate methods to investigate the extent to which the two modes measure the same construct may be necessary.

> **DON'T FORGET**
> ....
> Dual mode administration to investigate equivalence in different modes has limitations because examinees may respond differently to tasks on the second occasion as a result of having encountered them before, and because carryover effects may not cancel each other out across the two orders.

When studying equivalence of test scores across modes, it is important to ensure the groups are equivalent across variables known to be highly related with the test scores. For example, cognitive test scores are known to be related to age, socioeconomic status, ethnicity, and gender (Kaufman et al., 2016; Raiford, Coalson, & Engi, 2014). When groups are not generally equivalent on such important characteristics, the researcher might reach erroneous conclusions (Coleman, 2018).

To ensure that examinees are randomly assigned to take one test but that the two groups are roughly equivalent on important characteristics, pairs of examinees can be matched on these characteristics and then randomly assigned to one condition or another. This is termed a *matched pairs* or *case control matching* strategy. An equivalent group design that randomly assigns matched pairs to take the test in one of the two modes avoids the aforementioned carryover problems with counterbalanced studies. It also controls for potential confounding variables. If participants are paired on gender, for example, then randomly assigned to one of the two conditions, it controls for the possibility that gender may interact with the variable of interest (in this case mode of testing). It is efficient, clean, and interpretable.

In addition, equivalent group designs lend themselves to a remedy if scores from the two modes are not found to be interchangeable. Briefly, the data can be used to adjust norms for the new modes statistically in using a process called equating (or a related one called scaling). This process is discussed later in this chapter.

DON'T FORGET

An equivalent group design that randomly assigns matched pairs to take the test in one of the two modes is efficient and interpretable. It also avoids differential carryover effects, controls for potentially confounding variables, and allows the data to be used to equate or scale the two modes statistically.

Rapid Reference 4.1 reviews common types of test score correspondence studies, their purposes, and their features, as well as issues that may arise. In reality, perhaps the most informative study may be one that combines the two study designs and uses all of the information obtained, but this may not be the best use of the limited resources available to study tele-assessment mode equivalence in performance-based psychological tests.

WHAT IS EQUIVALENCE?

When a test mode change is considered, to inform interpretation psychologists need to evaluate the extent to which the resulting scores have been established as *equivalent*, or interchangeable, with those that result from the original mode. In the case of studies that compare face-to-face with tele-assessment modes, if equivalence is achieved, the scores obtained in either mode are interchangeable, and the normative information collected in the face-to-face mode can be applied to the tele-assessment mode. The existing equivalence evidence should be considered during interpretation, as discussed in Chapter 5.

≡ Rapid Reference 4.1

....

Score Correspondence Study Designs, Typical Purposes and Features, and Issues When Design Used for Mode Equivalence Purposes

Design	Typical Purposes and Features	Issues in Mode Equivalence Studies
Dual mode administration	• Directly examine concurrent validity • Determine correspondence of two different measures of same construct • Determine extent that prior edition's validity evidence can be applied to new edition • Predict scores of one measure from another measure • Every examinee takes both tests (modes) • Each examinee assigned to one of the two testing orders • Each examinee provides two scores or sets of scores • Direct, within-person correlation across modes obtained	• Inefficient use of resources • Longer testing time • Correlations could under-estimate relations due to differential mode order effect • Examinees' reaction to tasks may change after completing them the first time • Carryover (testing order) effects assumed to cancel out, but may not if there is differential mode order effect • Use of data to adjust scores for mode effects could be problematic if differential mode order effect
Single mode administration	• Examine interchangeability of scores • Determine correspondence of two different forms of the same test (e.g., paper/digital, face-to-face/tele-assessment) • Two equivalent groups of examinees take one each of two tests (modes) • Each examinee randomly assigned to which test (mode) is taken • Examinees often assigned to tests (mode) in pairs matched on variables known to impact scores (e.g., socioeconomic status, age, gender) • Each examinee provides one score • No direct, within-person correlation	• Avoids differential carryover that can occur in different formats or modes • No direct, within-person correlation • Alternate construct validity analyses

Equivalence Analyses

In one type of equivalence analysis, the two sample means elicited from each mode of assessment can be compared using a t-test. If the difference is not statistically significant, it suggests the scores from either mode are interchangeable. In this situation, if the p value is larger than α (usually $p > .05$), it suggests that there is no statistically significant difference between test scores across modes. If the p value is smaller than α, it suggests that there is a difference.

One issue with this approach is that one cannot claim there is no effect simply because the p value is larger than α. A simple solution to this issue was pioneered in the pharmacokinetics field to ensure quality when drugs shift from brand-name to generic (Little, 2015). Statistical procedures used in that industry are similar to another approach to studying equivalence in the field of psychology. Using these techniques, it is possible to determine if an effect is close enough to zero for practical purposes.

T-tests can be coupled with analyses examining standard differences (taking into account the variability in both samples) to obtain the effect size of the difference. If the effect size is lower than some preset criterion, it is concluded that the differences are small enough that the test scores across the two conditions are interchangeable. This set criterion is often around .2, as this is widely viewed as lower than even a small effect size (which is often cited as .3) and less than a single scaled score point. So, if the effect size of mode (tele-assessment vs. in-person) is less than .2, it can be said that mode does not have a meaningful effect on the scores elicited from individuals. There are several recent examples of this approach when investigating a test format or mode change (e.g., Daniel, Wahlstrom, & Zhang, 2014; Wright, 2018a, 2018b).

Another strategy for determining whether the mean differences between two modes is significant or not is using the *minimally detectable difference* (also known in the literature as minimally detectable change and minimally important difference; de Vet et al., 2006). This strategy uses a statistical calculation based on the standard error of measurement (*SEM*) of any task or measure to determine if there is a difference that is notable enough between two groups (or a group before and after an intervention) to be meaningful. Like using effect sizes, this adds a component of *practical or clinical meaningfulness*, beyond just statistical (as is the case with t-tests). However, also like effect sizes, this is a somewhat liberal measure of equivalence. The minimally detectable difference, as calculated, is usually not that small.

A common approach in the pharmacokinetics and other fields is to use two one-sided *t*-tests (TOST) to determine if the mean difference falls between an upper practical limit and lower practical limit, which are calculated using preselected acceptance criteria. The null hypothesis, in this approach, is the presence of a true effect, and the alternative hypothesis is the absence of an effect that is practically worthwhile. A difference across modes that falls within those preselected bounds is deemed too small to be practically meaningful (the smallest effect size of interest [SESOI]), and indicates equivalence (Lakens, 2017). Wright (2020b) utilized .3 standard deviation, reasoning that .3 is widely used to represent a small effect size and that it is smaller than the SEM for cognitive test scores.

> **CAUTION**
>
> One cannot claim there is no effect of mode simply because the *p* value is larger than α (not statistically significant).

When using this approach, standard scores (with means of 100 and standard deviations of 15), the 90% confidence interval (used for statistical purposes in a TOST test, rather than the 95% confidence interval) must fall between a lower limit of –4.5 and an upper limit of 4.5 to be considered equivalent (where α = .05). Scaled scores (with a mean of 10 and a standard deviation of 3) must fall between a lower limit of –.9 and an upper limit of .9 to be considered equivalent (Wright, 2020b).

As discussed, when two equivalent groups are assigned to take one test mode each, alternate methods to investigate the extent to which the two modes measure the same construct (rather than a correlation) are necessary. Other structural validity analyses could potentially be used to evaluate construct equivalence, for example, intercorrelations or establishing measurement invariance. A proposed tele-assessment equivalence research agenda for tele-assessment, which recommends these and other analyses, appears at the conclusion of this chapter.

> **DON'T FORGET**
>
> There are multiple analytic approaches for mode equivalence studies, but they usually involve a comparison of mean scores derived from each mode.

WHAT IS EQUATING?

The field of educational measurement uses research designs similar to those described in this chapter to compare and link scores on large-scale educational assessments for the purposes of examining student performance for state and national educational accountability standards (Berman, Haertel, & Pellegrino, 2020). The same field often uses equating to ensure that scores are interchangeable across formats (DePascale & Gong, 2020).

Equating is a common test score linking approach used to align scores from two forms or formats of a test (AERA, APA, & NCME, 2014); it involves adjusting scores from (usually) one test or task so that equal skill produces equal scores on the two measures. The process adjusts for slight difficulty differences across test forms to ensure examinees are not advantaged or penalized according to which form of the test is taken. For test formats or forms to be equated, a strict set of requirements is met, but the term equating is also used colloquially to refer to all test score linking methods. Another common approach to linking test scores that has less rigorous requirements is aligning/scaling (DePascale & Gong, 2020; NRC, 1999), which involves placing two comparable scores on the same scale.

Equating techniques have been used to adjust scores across modes or formats for large scale educational assessments. For example, college entrance exam scores are regularly equated across digital and paper delivery formats (Li, Yi, & Harris, 2016; Proctor, Chuah, Montgomery, & Way, 2019).

Two common equating methods are linear equating and equipercentile equating. *Linear equating* adjusts the mean and standard deviation of one distribution of scores to that of another. *Equipercentile equating* aligns one score distribution to a second score distribution by percentile, so that the raw scores that correspond to the same percentile are made to be equivalent by assigning them the same derived (e.g., scaled or standard) scores.

Future psychological test mode equivalence research may identify tasks or age groups for which normative information should be adjusted for tele-assessment. In this case, equating or scaling procedures can be applied to the data collected for equivalence studies to adjust scores so that the raw scores collected via tele-assessment result in different scaled or standard scores. That is, if a task given via tele-assessment ends up being slightly easier or harder than the same task given in person, equating can adjust how raw scores derived from tele-assessment are translated into standard scores, such that examinees of the same ability level end up with the same standard scores.

CONTEXT AND STATE OF MODE EQUIVALENCE RESEARCH

Comprehensive psychological tele-assessment was relatively uncommon prior to the spring of 2020. Most cognitive, academic, and neuropsychological testing took place in a face-to-face format, although on-screen (and less commonly, remote) administration of personality and behavior checklists was relatively common.

In large part, psychological tele-assessment was used to improve access for underserved populations. Some psychologists used tele-assessment to increase access to services for individuals in underserved areas who required evaluation, but for whom travel to the psychologist's location would be impractical or even prohibitive. Others engaged in tele-assessment for school districts with a shortage of school psychologists to make the assessment process more accessible and efficient for all. Still others engaged with homebound individuals who could not easily travel to a hospital or clinic setting.

Tele-assessment for performance-based measures was typically conducted by psychologists with special training, sometimes using proprietary platforms designed for tele-assessment, and often in partnership with a trained professional (e.g., counselor, teacher, technician) who was onsite with the examinee in a satellite school or clinic testing office set up specifically for this purpose.

Validity studies were designed and collected to support these procedures. Researchers from the neuropsychology field collected data on brief neuropsychological screening batteries administered remotely via teleconference, but not on many full comprehensive tests (Brearly et al., 2017). Several studies were completed on full school-age measures that were to be administered on proprietary tele-assessment platforms (Wright, 2018a, 2018b, 2020b). Meanwhile, behavior and personality measures were more well-researched (see Chapter 8 for a review).

In the spring of 2020, with the COVID-19 crisis severely limiting the ability for psychologists to conduct in-person assessments, much greater attention turned to remote tele-assessment. Fortunately, some prior validity evidence about tele-assessment was available. When accommodating examinees' health vulnerabilities through using tele-assessment, psychologists sought out those validity studies to gather information about how to take the new mode into account when interpreting test scores.

The available mode equivalence evidence on performance-based tasks was all collected prior to the COVID-19 crisis. A number of those studies produced evidence of mean score equivalence for tasks administered in tele-assessment and face-to-face modes for examinees with and without clinical conditions, with very few exceptions. That evidence does not yet suggest adjustments to norms are necessary for tele-assessment. However, the research base is limited.

A meta-analysis of tele-assessment equivalence studies provides support for telepractice and face-to-face mode equivalence across a variety of neuropsychological tasks with adults (Brearly et al., 2017). However, the literature does not span all psychological test performance-based task types, in every age range, with all clinical conditions. In general, these studies indicate similar results are obtained in tele-assessment mode compared with face-to-face administration of the tests.

It may be important to consider that studies published prior to 2014 did not always utilize high speed internet, which might increase correspondence between face-to-face and tele-assessment results. The equivalence studies for performance-based cognitive, achievement, and neuropsychological tests are discussed and summarized in Chapter 1.

Applying Mode Equivalence Research Using Cognitive Processing Demands Analysis

As the literature grows, it will be important to replicate the existing studies and to attend to task types, clinical conditions, and subpopulations that have not been evaluated. Conducting cognitive processing demands analyses of the tasks that have been evaluated is useful to yield information about their input and output demands. That information can then be applied to understand norm applicability for tasks with similar demands. Cognitive processing demands analysis relates to understanding all of the psychological, interpersonal, and behavioral demands (not just cognitive) that any task requires, both from the psychologist and the examinee. When administering a task, typically whatever stimulus is used is regarded as the *input demand*. These input demands can include verbal directions, visual stimuli, the use of manipulatives (like physical cards with inkblots or a pegboard), or audio recordings, for example. The *output demand* relates to how an examinee is required to respond, to have their responses recorded. These output demands can include verbal responses, pointing to multiple choices, performing a physical task, or writing something down, as examples.

As one example, various receptive vocabulary tasks are constructed with nearly identical input and output demands. For these tasks, the inputs are brief verbal directions and visual stimuli (pictures), and the required output is a brief oral response or a pointing motor response in a multiple-choice format. Similarly, various mathematical operations tasks are constructed with nearly identical input and output demands. These tasks include response booklets with math problems printed in them, perhaps with some vague verbal directions of where to start, as the input. The output is the examinee writing mathematical responses to the posed math problems directly in the response booklet.

Cognitive processing demands analysis can offer indirect evidence for equivalence, even if a test or task itself has not been directly evaluated in the research literature. That is, if one task of receptive vocabulary or mathematical operations has shown equivalence (and thus no effect of the mode on the data elicited), other tasks with nearly identical input and output demands (i.e., other tests of receptive vocabulary or mathematical operations built in nearly the exact same way) have indirect evidence that the mode (tele-assessment) should not have a significant effect on the data that emerge. Chapters 6 and 7 review the direct and indirect mode equivalence evidence by task and age range for many of the most frequently used performance-based cognitive and academic achievement tests according to recent practice surveys (Benson et al., 2019; Rabin, Paolillo, & Barr, 2016).

Tele-assessment involves the use of technology as well as viewing on-screen stimuli. For these reasons, studies that investigate clinical tests in digital versus traditional paper-and-pencil formats may also be informative. These data were not collected via remote administration. Still, they help to shed light on the broader question of the impact of viewing stimuli on-screen and the influence of technology in the assessment process. Several studies have also produced evidence of equivalence between traditional paper-and-pencil test administration and digital—though in-person—administration of tests (Daniel, 2012a, 2012b, 2013a, 2013b, 2013c; Daniel et al., 2014; Drozdick, Getz, Raiford, & Zhang, 2016). It should be noted that these studies only provided mean comparisons at the task level and not at the composite level.

Similarly, studies with children from special groups (intellectual disability, intellectual giftedness, specific learning disorder, ASD, ADHD) have investigated score differences in (in-person) digital versus traditional formats observed between these special groups and nonclinical examinees (Raiford, Drozdick, & Zhang, 2015, 2016; Raiford, Holdnack, Drozdick, & Zhang, 2014). These studies are also referenced—as further indirect evidence of mode equivalence—according to task in Chapters 6 and 7.

TEST STANDARDS FOR ACCOMMODATIONS

The *Standards* (AERA, APA, & NCME, 2014) do not provide explicit guidance for testing accommodations in the event of a global pandemic. However, they do provide guidance for changes to administration to allow tests to be given to individuals with disabilities or other special characteristics. Standard 9.9 reads:

> When a test user contemplates an alteration in test format, mode of administration, instructions […] the user should have a sound rationale and empirical evidence, when possible, for concluding that the reliability/precision of scores and the validity of interpretations based on the scores will not be compromised.
>
> (p. 144)

The *Standards* comment that in some instances, minor changes in format or administration mode might be expected to have negligible impact on scores, decisions made with them, or the appropriateness of norms. In other cases, the changes might be expected to have significant effects, alter the construct being measured, and potentially require new norms. If such an accommodation becomes widespread, evidence for validity should be gathered and, if necessary, new norms should be derived. In addition, the *Standards* describe several important considerations to maximize norms applicability in the event of a mode change.

Maintaining the Standards

According to the *Standards* (AERA, APA, & NCME, 2014), norms are most applicable when the original standardized testing parameters are maintained. The goal of tele-assessment should then be, in principle, to mirror as closely as possible the face-to-face experience. Replicating as closely as possible the experience an examinee has in a traditional, face-to-face assessment helps preserve the applicability of the norms when applied to the altered administration mode.

Prepare the Environment

The equivalence studies that provide the basis for tele-assessment and face-to-face equivalence were most often conducted in controlled environments (e.g., testing offices, school classrooms), and some testing—especially during the COVID-19 pandemic—may occur in examinees' homes. One way of replicating client experience is by preparing a client satellite testing office or instructing an examinee on how to prepare their environment to be similar to a testing office (as discussed in Chapter 3). Very little research has been done to determine the impact of remote assessment conducted with the examinee located in their home, although two known studies included administrations conducted in the examinees' homes (Wright, 2018a, 2020b), and Lana Harder's unpublished research (Stolwyk, Hammers, Harder, & Cullum, 2020) was based upon in-home administration and reportedly found no significant differences in scores across tele-assessment and face-to-face modes.

> **DON'T FORGET**
> ....
> Prepare the examinee's environment, by replicating a testing office environment as closely as possible, in order to maximize applicability of norms.

Gain Competency and Practice

The *Standards* (AERA, APA, & NCME, 2014) also indicate that norms are most applicable when psychologists maintain the standardized procedures. Most of the equivalence studies that support tele-assessment and face-to-face equivalence involve examiners gaining competency with the digital materials and video conferencing platform, as discussed in Chapter 3. All items and instructions of each task should be reviewed with an eye toward tele-assessment to become aware of any administration requirements that may differ in the new mode. For example, the examinee may need to point with a mouse instead of with a finger. Chapters 6 and 7 provide these considerations for the most widely used performance-based cognitive and achievement tests.

Prepare the Examinee, Onsite Professional, or Other Helpers
Studies that have established tele-assessment and face-to-face mode equivalence generally involve an onsite professional handling administrative and technological aspects of the session. Preliminary research conducted

> **DON'T FORGET**
> ....
> Before you administer any test, review every item and instruction of every task to be aware of any adjustments to administration requirements needed.

and described by Lana Harder (Stolwyk et al., 2020) with parents serving as in-home facilitators who managed audiovisual needs and response booklets found no significant differences in scores across tele-assessment and face-to-face modes. Psychologists should evaluate concerns such as threats to validity of conclusions and to test security, as well as any effects on the examinee's participation or communication between the examinee and examiner, yet none of these issues may be a reason to prohibit the third party's presence (Otto & Krauss, 2009).

Psychologists should consider involving a third party in the testing session if they conclude that that the third party's presence will result in more valid results than would otherwise be possible (Otto & Krauss, 2009). Psychologists engaging in tele-assessment may train facilitators to work with them on a regular basis in order to provide greater coverage to underserved populations (e.g., only two providers within a 500-mile radius, shortage of providers within a school district). Onsite professionals that are well trained and in a professional role can present manipulatives as well as adjust audiovisual equipment. There are subtests and even entire tests for which an onsite professional is a necessity, or tele-assessment is not recommended. Without an onsite professional, for example, some tasks with manipulatives cannot be administered correctly. In the presence of major alterations in administration procedures that considerably alter the construct measured, the existing normative information is less likely to apply.

It should be noted that *third party facilitators may not necessarily have to be trained professionals* (especially when they are not available). For example, in the study of tele-assessment administration of the WISC-V, Wright (2020b) noted that there were no tasks involved in the facilitation that required clinical training or experience, and the coaching of these facilitators generally took about 10 minutes before the assessment began.

TEST STANDARDS FOR TELE-ASSESSMENT VERSIONS OF TESTS

It is anticipated that the use of tele-assessment will increase in the future because it became widespread during the COVID-19 pandemic, and because psychologists and clients recognize its benefits. As such, test developers may eventually transition from making stimuli for the most commonly used performance-based tests digitally available to allow psychologists to accommodate for testing during COVID-19, to actually producing tests intended for tele-assessment that are supported as producing equivalent scores across modes, or that have norms developed in the tele-assessment mode. The *Standards* (AERA, APA, & NCME, 2014) indicate that in this case, associated documentation should be provided on the impact of mode differences on the validity of score interpretations, as well as on the precision and comparability of scores. Standard 4.5 reads:

> **DON'T FORGET**
> ....
> Psychologists should consider involving a third party in the testing session if they conclude that that the third party's presence will result in more valid results than would otherwise be possible.

> If the test developer indicates that the conditions of administration are permitted to vary from one test taker or group to another, permissible variation in conditions for administration should be identified. A rationale for permitting the different conditions and any requirements for permitting the different conditions should be documented.
>
> (p. 87)

As test publishers create formal tele-assessment versions of tests, additional validity studies may be required—depending on the adequacy of existing evidence—using some of the study designs and analyses outlined in this chapter. As examples, note some of the cognitive measures developed online presented in Chapter 1.

The Future Directions for Tele-Assessment Research section at the end of this chapter provides some recommendations for future empirical endeavors. These studies, however, require a portion of the data collection to be conducted under "normal" testing conditions. Therefore, much of it will have to wait until after the COVID-19 pandemic, because most psychologists who engage in face-to-face testing at present use many protective measures that also deviate from the conditions under which the test was standardized (e.g., masks, plexiglass barriers, gloves, face shields, etc.), and at present no validity evidence is available to evaluate the score impact of these protective measures.

FUTURE DIRECTIONS FOR TELE-ASSESSMENT RESEARCH

There are multiple general issues that would benefit from further evaluation in the new world of psychological tele-assessment. Some of the general issues that need more investigation involve special groups and populations, psychometric properties, alternate procedures and environments, malfunctions and interruptions, training and orientation efficacy, client satisfaction and engagement, and administration of full batteries commonly done in actual practice.

Special Groups and Populations

Within nonclinical populations of examinees, any identified mode differences should be further analyzed to determine if those differences are related to different demographic variables (e.g., socioeconomic status, ethnicity, and gender). Additionally, if mode differences are identified, it would be useful to have information about examinee familiarity and comfort with the technology that was used.

While there are a fair number of special group mode equivalence studies (e.g., individuals with dementia, MCI, language disorder, intellectual disability, specific learning disorders, traumatic brain injury; see the Rapid Reference 1.1 in Chapter 1 for a review of studies), more are needed to expand upon and replicate these studies and investigate both feasibility of the tele-assessment mode and results obtained by other special groups (e.g., those with ADHD, ASD, and giftedness) in tele-assessment mode. Studies with these special populations are important, because there may be interactions between the specific issues related to the populations and the technology use in tele-assessment.

It would be helpful if examinees with clinical conditions were screened with the same inclusion and exclusion criteria as those of previously published studies, to allow more direct comparison. Researchers should pay special attention to collecting information similar to the demographics in published test manuals. For example, typically parent (for children) or self (for adults) education level is used as the most stable variable to represent socioeconomic status, and published test manuals define how best to establish levels of education clearly. Test publishers often are able to provide demographically matched, nonclinical controls to researchers to bolster studies' interpretability and utility.

Psychometric Properties

A great number of the available studies have provided correlations between modes (see Rapid Reference 1.1. in Chapter). Another approach to providing structural validity involves providing intercorrelations among several tasks in each mode to demonstrate that the construct measured is similar across modes (Wright, 2020b).

Factor analytic studies would also be informative (Farmer et al., 2020), particularly factorial invariance studies. If two tasks are not found equivalent, it is also necessary to establish that reliability in the new mode is comparable prior to engaging in equating (DePascale & Gong, 2020).

Alternate Procedures and Environments

Chapter 3 outlines procedures to be used if the examinee is located somewhere other than a testing office (e.g., in their home). Specifically, these procedures indicate how to screen the available environment for appropriateness and prepare it for tele-assessment. It would be helpful to establish the extent to which the procedures for screening and preparing the examinee's environment are similarly effective across various types of living situations.

Similarly, Chapter 3 provides information about how to handle situations in which examinees or parents/guardians/caregivers, rather than onsite professionals (e.g., teachers, counselors, psychometrists, etc.), manage the necessary technology and testing materials (e.g., response booklets). Future studies should examine the effectiveness and equivalence of conditions established using these procedures.

Malfunctions and Interruptions

When psychologists have less control over the examinee's environment or must depend on technology during a testing session, malfunctions and interruptions can and often do occur. Chapter 3 outlines practical procedures designed to minimize such malfunctions and interruptions. Studies that employ these procedures should document the incidence of data loss and invalidation observed in different types of examinee environments (e.g., remote testing office, examinee's home). They should further document the rate of lost data due to technology malfunction so that psychologists are clearly aware of the risks and issues. One good example of such observational data appears in Waite, Theodoros, Russell, and Cahill (2010), who provided descriptions of each issue and the specific impact on assessments in both modes. The issues in the tele-assessment condition involved headset size, bandwidth, touchscreen sensitivity, screen glare, stimulus book positioning, low speech volume and intelligibility, audio breakup, and examinee restlessness.

Training and Orientation Efficacy

As tele-assessment has become more commonplace, various resources (e.g., written materials, recorded webinars, and live tutorials) have become available to gain training and competency. However, little is known about the efficacy of that training, and how a psychologist can be assured that they are well trained and proficient to administer tele-assessments with fidelity. Investigations are needed to determine the most effective methods to train psychologists embarking on tele-assessment, as well as the amount of training necessary to become competent in this mode.

Furthermore, more information is needed about the type and amount of orientation or training needed for onsite facilitators (professionals or non-professionals) at the examinee's location that facilitate the testing if needed. Although most of the existing studies involved some orientation or training, little detail is available; however, Taylor and Wright (2020) have offered insights based on Wright's research (2018a, 2018b, 2020b). It would also be useful to know how effective that training or orientation is when examinees or parents/guardians/caregivers are managing the technology and administrative tasks (e.g., opening response booklets).

Client Satisfaction and Engagement

Multiple studies indicate that client satisfaction with tele-assessment is generally positive (Hildebrand, Chow, Williams, Nelson, & Wass, 2004; Hodge et al., 2019; Stain et al., 2011; Turkstra, Quinn-Padron, Johnson, Workinger, & Antoniotti, 2012; Vestal, Smith-Olinde, Hicks, Hutton, & Hart, 2006). Additional research is needed to fully understand if there are populations or clinical conditions that may be less satisfied or engaged when tested in this mode.

Full Batteries

Particularly for adults, future investigations need to involve administration of full psychological tests with multiple subtests to allow examination of composite score differences across multiple tests. The composite score level of interpretation should be a focus because tele-assessment can introduce additional measurement error, to which composite scores are more resilient (see Chapter 5). As recommended in Chapter 3, it would be useful to divide up the testing across multiple sessions to avoid fatigue and eyestrain.

Challenging Tasks

Understandably, the research has focused on tasks that are generally not so challenging to administer. More investigations should focus on tasks that require an onsite professional or the examinee to manipulate materials and components with more complexity or to adjust camera angles are needed. Our search revealed only a small number of studies that included motor-related tasks requiring physical manipulatives other than response booklets (e.g., blocks, chips, pegboard, etc.). Hence, this is presently a great need.

Test Security and Dishonesty

Test security is a pressing concern for psychologists conducting tele-assessment. Even when the examinee is located in a satellite testing office, psychologists need to understand that audio stimuli may be recorded or pictures taken of stimuli. There are numerous measures that can be taken to protect test security during tele-assessment, as outlined in Chapters 2 and 3. Anecdotally, psychologists indicate that it is obvious during a tele-assessment session when someone is attempting to take screenshots or pictures of stimuli, audio record a session, or engage in dishonest behavior to improve performance (e.g., writing down digits or words they are asked to remember). These hypotheses can and should be tested.

Specific Issues by Age Range

Adults and Older Adults

Most of the existing equivalence studies for adults focus on neuropsychological screening batteries formed by extracting representative tasks from multiple tests, and many limit samples to older adults. These types of studies do not permit investigations of mode equivalence at the composite score level. Research is needed to establish the impact of a mode change at both the task and composite score levels.

School-Age Children

For school-age children, studies are needed to evaluate the use of consumer-grade and widely available videoconferencing software in tele-assessment. Most of the available tele-assessment studies with children were collected on proprietary platforms.

Preschool

There is a paucity of tele-assessment research on preschoolers from both non-clinical and clinical populations. A few studies have revealed that preschoolers do not always interact with technology in the expected manner, and that some tasks are not equivalent among preschoolers when placed in a digital format (Drozdick, Getz, Raiford, & Zhang, 2016; Krach, McCreery, Dennis, Guerard, & Harris, 2020). Due to the very limited nature of the equivalence data, additional caution should be exercised when using tele-assessment with preschoolers, particularly with very young children.

CONCLUSION

Psychologists should remain aware of the research-based evidence supporting equivalence to date. Although a great deal of additional research is necessary, the evidence to date does not yet suggest that normative adjustments or separate norms are necessary. However, this area of research is very new, and additional research will undoubtedly emerge over the coming years. Normative information collected in a traditional manner may need to be adjusted if future equivalence studies indicate this is necessary. The educational measurement field has used equating and scaling/linking techniques to make such adjustments in similar situations.

Besides consulting the equivalence research, psychologists considering tele-assessment should remain mindful of the information covered in Chapters 1, 2, 3, and 5 of this book. They should consult professional best practice recommendations, respective ethical codes, tele-assessment regulations, and legal requirements from federal, state, and local authorities, licensing boards, professional liability insurance providers, and payors. Psychologists should develop competence with tele-assessment through activities such as practicing, studying, consulting with other professionals, and engaging in professional development. Following these activities, psychologists should make an informed decision to determine if tele-assessment is appropriate for a given examinee, referral question, and situation, and that it is feasible and not contraindicated. It is important to weigh all these considerations against the potential benefits for each individual client.

Five

PRINCIPLES FOR PSYCHOLOGICAL TELE-ASSESSMENT INTERPRETATION OF DATA

While the research is still so nascent on data elicited through tele-assessment procedures, it can be assumed that psychologists need to be extremely deliberate and cautious when interpreting test data. Psychologists are reminded, though, that clinical decisions are not and should not be automatically based on test scores (AERA, APA, & NCME, 2014); even those who do believe test scores should be taken more seriously admit that it is best to contextualize them within other good, available data (Cizek, 1994). And when considering making clinical decisions, diagnoses, and recommendations in tele-assessment—*as is the case with all assessment*—psychologists need to remember that test data are imperfect and carry error in measurement (in addition to other possible errors, like response bias, etc.). Best practice is always to employ different methods, measures, and respondents when informing clinical decision making. This is the basis of an iterative, hypothesis-testing model of assessment (APA, 2020; see also Wright, 2020a).

YOUR PROFESSIONAL JUDGMENT AND CLINICAL EXPERTISE

Perhaps the most important first step for psychologists is to acknowledge the limitations of the underlying literature base for tests delivered in an online, tele-assessment format (Block, Bradford, Butt, & Marek, 2020; IOPC, 2020; NASP, 2017; Wright, Mihura, Pade, & McCord, 2020). As a psychologist, during your training, you inevitably focused at least somewhat on the theoretical, psychometric, and structural underpinnings of psychological tests (APA, 2020; APA Commission on Accreditation, 2017; NASP, 2020a). Because of this training,

Essentials of Psychological Tele-Assessment, First Edition.
A. Jordan Wright and Susan Engi Raiford
© 2021 John Wiley & Sons, Inc. Published 2021 by John Wiley & Sons, Inc.

you are well suited to make multiple critical decisions about the data you collect from tests in a non-standard, tele-assessment context. A reminder—you are a psychologist, with training, expertise, and credentialing to make informed, scholarly decisions about test data.

> ### DON'T FORGET
> You are a psychologist, with training, expertise, and credentialing to make informed, scholarly decisions about test data.

There are very real limitations to data that emerge via tele-assessment. For example, some have noted the disadvantages of not being able to see the client's full body when conducting an evaluation (Block et al., 2020). Indeed, you are generally limited to physical behavioral observations from about the shoulders up on most videoconferencing platforms, and for certain types of evaluations (and some would argue most all types of evaluations), this is a drawback. In reality, there are also other possible behaviors that can more easily be missed in tele-assessment than in traditional in-person assessment, though careful observation can detect and curtail most of these. Some that have been noted are clients somehow surreptitiously looking up answers to prompts online during the assessment or writing down stimuli from auditory working memory tasks. In fact, it would be extremely difficult to do either of these things undetected, even if you can only see a client's face. But there are some pieces of data that may be missing compared to in-person assessment, and some that are skewed because of the tele-assessment methodology. You, as the psychologist, must interpret data within the context of how they might be affected by the tele-assessment mode (Wright et al., 2020).

A separate issue that should be considered, which is not directly related to tele-assessment but is related to some of the reasons a tele-assessment may be necessary, is considering the data within the context of times of uncertainty, heightened anxiety, and stressful situations, both national and personal, such as pandemics and other national and global crises (Banks & Butcher, 2020; NASP, 2020b). Beyond the general mental health effects of global crises (e.g., Prime, Wade, & Browne, 2020; Rajkumar, 2020), issues like school closures (Golberstein, Wen, & Miller, 2020), home confinement (Xie et al., 2020), and many others affect mental health, cognitive capacities, and other psychological factors that can impact psychological assessments. Obviously, psychologists conducting assessments (tele-assessments or otherwise) need to understand the potential and likely effects of these large external factors on the individuals they are assessing. Again, as the psychologist, it is your responsibility to contextualize test results within all different factors, including tele-assessment alterations and what may be going on for the client being assessed.

Specific to tele-assessment, this chapter highlights some of the major areas to consider when interpreting data. In general, you should think about any test data that are likely to be affected by tele-assessment procedures (primarily performance-based measures, like cognitive and achievement measures; less so self-report measures) as having extra error (Wright et al., 2020). That is, consider measures that are meant to tap some underlying ability as somewhat less precise. Scores on a test of mathematical ability, for example, should still be heavily and primarily influenced by the actual math ability of the client being assessed. However, some of the construct-irrelevant variables (i.e., "noise") introduced by the alternative administration method of tele-assessment can add a layer of imprecision to the process. Just because the measure is slightly less precise than usual, though, does not mean that the data it elicits (about math ability) do not represent the client's actual functioning. Because of this slightly less precise measure of abilities and functioning, you should be even more deliberate than usual to confirm and triangulate tele-assessment test data with collateral informants' reports (Block et al., 2020), medical and other available records (Block et al., 2020; California Commission on Peace Officer Standards and Training, 2020), and behavioral observations (Banks & Butcher, 2020).

As the psychologist, and when considering all the potential variables listed later in this chapter and the context of collateral reports, records, and behavioral observations, you must determine if there is ever a point at which the data that emerge from a test, measure, or task via tele-assessment procedures are so skewed that they no longer represent a client's actual ability, traits, or functioning; when this is the case, *do not use bad data* (Wright et al., 2020). If you are unsure about the quality or representativeness of any particular piece of data (whether it come from a single subtest of a single measure, a particular task, or an entire psychological test), try to add in another, comparable measure of the same construct to confirm or refute the original piece of data. This is a moment in time when it truly benefits our profession to have competing measures of similar constructs (and indeed hampers us when we do not). Adding another measure of the same construct can help you determine whether and how much the original one was likely influenced by some external variable, such as environmental distraction. It cannot, of course, help in your decision about whether the original data suffered because of the tele-assessment context (as, presumably, this new measure will also be given this way), but if there are measures that tap similar constructs with different methods, this could help.

Similar to determining if a piece of tele-assessment test data has suffered by using additional comparable tools, if and when you decide that a task has indeed suffered, discard it and try to administer another comparable measure of the construct. For example, suppose when you are administering a Woodcock–Johnson achievement battery, an environmental distraction occurs during the Word Attack test (a task requiring clients to read made-up words phonetically, which assesses phonic and structural analysis skills), and this renders the test an inaccurate representation of the client's abilities. You should discard the Word Attack data and consider administering either another form of that task (the Woodcock–Johnson has alternate forms) or the Wechsler Pseudoword Decoding subtest (a very similar task, assessing the same underlying constructs). You should of course note any likely potential for repeated administration effects, but ultimately you should include an additional task to better represent the clients' ability.

Finally, your training and experience as a psychologist has given you expertise in integrating multiple sources of data and reconciling any inconsistencies or discrepancies in assessment data. Models for being methodical in the combining, integrating, and reconciling of data are presented later in this chapter, but, in general, you will make clinical conclusions and decisions based on *the preponderance of data*. That is, if all signs are pointing toward one conclusion, and one piece of data from one test given in an non-standardized, tele-assessment fashion tells a different story, you will likely make your decisions based on the overwhelming majority of the data, rather than that one outlier.

This is of course a generalization. There are certainly times when a piece of data collected in a particular way actually taps a construct in a way that no other method can, and it can be important to include its result. However, because of the slightly less precise nature of tele-assessment data, you need to consider that some findings may just not quite be accurate. In those cases, look for consistency across measures and methods to inform your clinical decisions.

DON'T FORGET

- Do not use bad data!
- If you are unsure of the quality of any specific data, add in another comparable measure.
- If you cannot use some data but need that information, add in another comparable measure.
- Look for conclusions based on the preponderance of data.

OBVIOUS CONSTRUCT-IRRELEVANT DATA

While every test elicits data that include (hopefully mostly) construct-relevant data (such as reading ability on a reading test, working memory skills on a working memory test, level of narcissism on a narcissism inventory, etc.) *and* construct-irrelevant data (including things like test-taking skills, response bias, etc.), introducing an alternative administration mode like tele-assessment brings with it some extra construct-irrelevant data. Some of these are fairly obvious throughout the process, and our first line of test data contextualization should focus here. That is, when there are obvious, construct-irrelevant factors that are influencing the results of a test, measure, or task, you should interpret those data fully considering those factors. You cannot simply pretend that environmental factors that can clearly influence test results were not present.

The current state of our technology to accomplish tele-assessments means that there is a high likelihood that at some point during the assessment concrete and obvious *technological issues* can present themselves. These can include disruptions in the connectivity that affect the audio and/or video connection between psychologist and client. While some of these may not affect the results significantly (such as video delay during a client taking a self-report inventory), at other points they may impede the accurate administration of certain tasks (such as an auditory working memory task). These are moments when you, as the psychologist, need to make the sometimes tough decision to disqualify or discount a particular test finding, as you have clear evidence that the results do not accurately reflect the client's ability. It is also during these moments when you may need to, if at all possible, supplement your battery with another task to tap the same construct, if you need it for the assessment.

Similar to technological glitches impairing a moment in testing, so too can specific and noticeable *environmental distractions*. Perhaps one of the toughest parts of psychological tele-assessment—and certainly one of the primary criticisms of doing tele-assessment at all—is the significantly restricted ability to maintain a neutral, quiet, comfortable, and private environment for the client. Such an environment is a hallmark of standardized testing because this is how most tests have been developed, standardized, and normed. While you can take measures to move toward a more secure, neutral environment for the client, there is simply no way to guarantee it, even if the client is in a satellite testing office. As such, you need to be extra vigilant to notice environmental distractions.

In tele-assessment with a client in their home, this is a larger issue. Cohabitants (like roommates, spouses, children, etc.) can interfere with the testing session. Electronics in the client's home can turn on and off during the session. Sirens or other noises can present themselves outside the client's window during the session. As with technological issues, it is important to note when distractions occur and how much they are likely to affect the data you are collecting. Again, they may or may not change the way someone responds to a self-report measure, but it is clear that these kinds of distractions can significantly affect performance-based measures like cognitive ability and academic achievement tests.

When working in the tele-assessment context, be aware that your own attention also is necessarily divided throughout the process. While trying to attend to the needs of clients in the moment, administer test materials, check coding guidance in manuals, and monitor the client's environment for distractions or technology glitches, it is simply too easy for you to miss something. Thus, *it is recommended that you record tele-assessment sessions and rewatch them, in their entirety, to focus on such technological or environmental factors that may have influenced test data, when you are no longer juggling the actual administration of tests with the technology and interaction with the client* (Rapid Reference 5.1). Only by rewatching testing sessions can you give undivided attention to the client's experience, including their technology, their environment, and any noticeable reactions on their face that may signify that something weird happened. The psychological tele-assessment context necessarily adds on extra things for you to be aware of and attuned to, much more than is possible to accomplish with 100% accuracy in the moment. As such, rewatching sessions (as boring and tedious as it may be) offers the ability to identify construct-irrelevant data that may have affected the testing.

An important factor to consider that is slightly less obvious than a large environmental distraction or momentary loss of audio is the potential for *technology frustration*. Technology and computer frustration can be the result of even minor goal interruptions due to technology (Bessiere, Ceaparu, Robinson, & Shneiderman, 2004). Having to pause the assessment work because of connectivity issues, having difficulty understanding one another because the technology does not allow both parties to speak at the same time and be heard, and even blaming the technology for shortcomings on a cognitive task that had nothing to do with the technology can all contribute to technology frustration.

The tolerance for technology frustration can be even harder for those who already have computer anxiety, and so cultural and developmental factors can play a role. The result of such frustration can include multiple effects on the testing, including resignation and lack of effort, self-flagellation and self-punitive

≡ Rapid Reference 5.1

It is recommended that you record tele-assessment sessions and rewatch them, in their entirety, to focus on such technological or environmental factors that may have influenced test data, when you are no longer juggling the actual administration of tests with the technology and interaction with the client.

behavior, over-fixation on a specific task, or withdrawal, among other possibilities (Bessiere et al., 2004). All of these results can negatively affect actual testing, and so you need to remain vigilant for behavioral and physical signs that any of these may be occurring. If any of these negative reactions occurs, again, you should be ready to discard the data collected at that moment in time if it seems to have been negatively impacted. As always, you as the psychologist need to determine the likelihood that the test data were negatively affected.

The final obvious variable that can negatively affect the quality of the data elicited from psychological tele-assessment is *fatigue*. While fatigue has always been a factor in psychological assessment, the increased likelihood of eye strain and resulting fatigue is much more serious and deleterious in the tele-assessment context (The Vision Council, 2016). Especially with tasks performed later in sessions with visual stimuli, actual eye strain and fatigue can significantly impact a client's ability to respond. But you should be careful to not assume this only applies to visual-spatial tasks on cognitive tests. The fatigue experienced as a result of staring at a screen for an extended period of time can be global, and thus globally affect client performance. While it is of course best to monitor this throughout testing, going back and noticing when there were signs of obvious fatigue is important for contextualizing the data that emerged during those moments. You, as the psychologist, need to interpret findings accordingly.

> **DON'T FORGET**
> ••
> Make sure to look for and, most importantly, account for in your interpretation of test data some of the obvious factors that can affect tele-assessment test data:
> • Concrete and obvious technological issues
> • Environmental distractions
> • Technology frustration
> • Fatigue

SUBTLE ALTERNATIVE ADMINISTRATION EFFECTS

Unfortunately, not all of the context-irrelevant and potentially harmful variables brought about by the transition to tele-assessment are as obvious as those just listed. Luxton, Pruitt, and Osenbach (2014), for example, discuss thinking thoroughly about client characteristics, including culture, and their interaction with tele-assessment technologies. For example, they highlight that individuals from backgrounds that value and rely on more nonverbal communication may be disadvantaged by the limited view of the whole person with whom they are interacting. They similarly discuss how older adults and those from marginalized and impoverished backgrounds may also be disadvantaged by the tele-assessment medium and perform worse on tasks in this format. Ultimately, you need to account for these client characteristics when interpreting data and consider stating clearly whether results are likely an underestimate of their actual skills and abilities.

DON'T FORGET
....
Consider client characteristics (including culture) and how these may interact with the tele-assessment methodologies.

Additionally, if you are using a parent/guardian/caregiver or some other known person as a proctor or facilitator, you need to consider how this may have affected the way the client performed on different tests. While very little research has included cognitive and academic assessment in the home (see Chapter 1), even less has scrutinized the impact of having a non-neutral third party present during the assessment. It may be unavoidable at times, but it can add an additional set of construct-irrelevant variables. For example, a child may get more nervous with their parent in the room, or they may not be as open and honest during an interview or projective test. Data from measures administered with a non-neutral third party present should be carefully considered, as the potential impact of this person's presence is currently unknown, but could reasonably be expected to have some sort of effect.

In general, regardless of client-specific factors, and even if a non-neutral facilitator is not present, psychologists need to understand what adding a layer of "unknown" to the testing situation is likely to do to the data. Adding the set of possibly negligible (based on some of the early research showing it as such) but not yet fully understood new variables to the testing equation means you need to be more careful, more mindful, and more deliberate about your understanding of what psychological test data are and how to use them to inform decisions.

Holistically, adding the unknowns of tele-assessment makes our measurement less precise, and you should *widen your "confidence intervals"* when interpreting individual test scores (Wright et al., 2020). The words confidence intervals are in quotation marks because there is not a statistical or mathematical calculation that actually accurately reflects just how much less precise tele-assessment measurement is (though if you are more mathematically inclined, you may want to move from 90% to 95% or from 95% to 99% confidence intervals on performance-based tasks). The spirit of this guidance is simply to have slightly less confidence or faith in any one score elicited from tele-assessment procedures, within reason. You should think about which measures, methods, and scores are more likely to be affected by the change in administration method. Self-report measures, for example, may not be significantly affected, so widening the confidence intervals for them may not make as much sense. Performance-based cognitive measures, though, are more likely to suffer from the subtle, unknown variables introduced by the non-standard administration procedures.

It is likely (and hoped!) that the next ten years will bring about much more and increasingly robust research into tele-assessment technologies. Researchers are likely to further study equivalence of traditional measures administered in tele-assessment mode. Test publishers may develop, standardize, and norm formal tele-assessments (no need for equivalency studies!). And finally, psychologists can anticipate research into the psychological processes that are engaged when individuals respond to assessment stimuli via tele-assessment. Researchers should attend, in a methodical way, to the construct-relevant and construct-irrelevant variables captured in the tele-assessment process, so that psychologists can more precisely and accurately use the data. Chapter 4 of this book provides some suggested first steps.

> **DON'T FORGET**
> ....
> When interpreting data from psychological tele-assessments—especially from performance-based measures—recognize the additional potential error of each test score (widen the "confidence intervals"). Be slightly less confident about each score's precise and accurate representation of the underlying psychological construct.

INTEGRATIVE METHODOLOGIES

Although not specific to psychological tele-assessment, it is worth repeating that psychological assessment is more than psychological testing; that is, assessment requires the integration of multiple sources of data, in order to cover the "blind spots" of any one methodology or measure (Meyer et al., 2001). This integrative methodology is even more important in the context of psychological tele-assessment, as we cannot make good clinical decisions based on single scores or data that emerge from non-standardized administration procedures (we should not have been doing so even in traditional assessment, but this becomes even more important with data that we are less confident in). There is some, though not much, guidance on how to integrate data methodically (e.g., Wright, 2020a), as well as making decisions about discrepancies in data. With psychological tele-assessment test data, it is even more important to be methodical and clear about how we are using the data and how we are reconciling test data that seem to contradict other data.

Trusting test data that emerge from tele-assessment administration procedures less means scrutinizing it more. The model presented here for reconciling discrepant data is adapted from Wright (2020a) to include extra steps for doing just that. While the original model includes five steps, this adapted model includes six.

Whenever there are data that seem discrepant, contradictory, or otherwise odd and unexpected, the first step should be to *double-check all coding and scoring*. Errors in coding and scoring of especially performance-based tests are much more common than they should be, even by extremely well-trained and credentialed individuals (e.g., Kaufman, Raiford, & Coalson, 2016; Loe, Kadlubek, & Marks, 2007; Oak, Viezel, Dumont, & Willis, 2018; Rollins & Raiford, 2017a, 2017b; Styck & Walsh, 2016; and many more!). So, the first step should always be to double-check that the data you are looking at is accurately coded and scored. If it is not, you should correct this error. If either the test data are accurately coded and scored or correcting the coding and scoring does not fix the discrepancy, move on to the second step.

DON'T FORGET

Double-check your coding and scoring! Even extremely well-trained psychologists commonly make clerical and other scoring errors when recording, coding, scoring, and converting scores.

The second step, once you are sure all data are accurately coded and scored, is to *identify whether the discrepancy is a true discrepancy or an apparent discrepancy*. The field of *psychology* is rife with constructs that seem like they should be contradictory but are in fact not. For example, when some test data reveal an individual is struggling with low self-esteem, and other test data reveal an over-inflated sense of self-importance, this can seem like a contradiction. However, we know within the field of psychology that this is a mechanism by which defensive narcissism works. The same may be true for adequate attentional ability (as measured in a performance-based and ideal context) and actual, everyday difficulties with attention in school. While these may seem at odds with one another, we in the field of psychology know that there are myriad issues that can cause everyday attentional difficulties, not just a prefrontal cortex attention deficit. Thus, while these things may seem like discrepancies or contradictions in data, they in fact are not.

The third step—and the one added to the model specifically for psychological tele-assessment—is to *scrutinize any discrepant data that emerged from tele-assessment practices that might have affected the data quality*. To do this, you should review the lists in this chapter of variables introduced by the tele-assessment process, rewatch the moments that resulted in the collected data to look specifically for any of these potentially meaningful circumstances, think through what kinds of data they are likely to affect, and consider adopting a broader margin of error for these findings, when appropriate. These steps are not meant to undermine the data that emerge from tele-assessment procedures; conversely, they are meant to rule out the likelihood that the data were in fact significantly affected by the tele-assessment methods so that you can have *more* faith in them. If you can systematically rule out obvious factors like technology problems and environmental distractions, subtle factors like fatigue and cultural effects, and widen the margin of error within which you are interpreting the test finding, and it still emerges as contradictory or discrepant from other collected data, you can maintain the test result and move on to the next step.

The next step is to *think through the potential method and process effects.* While not acknowledged enough in our work, different psychological assessment methodologies engage different psychological processes within clients. Even when constructs are named the same across measures, different underlying abilities, traits, or functioning may be tapped by different methodologies (such as self-report versus performance-based tasks). When we have data that are discrepant, *even when the same name is used for the purported construct they are measuring,* we may have just uncovered some underlying issue using one methodology that simply was not elicited by the other approach. Scales on a collateral-report measure, a self-report inventory, and a performance-based neuropsychological test may all have the same name for some part of executive functioning (like "inhibitory control"), for example, but each may be tapping slightly different underlying constructs. You need to consider if it is *because of* the different methodologies (and processes engaged by them) that different findings emerged (in a logical way). If this does not explain the discrepancies, however, move on to the next step.

The next step, when the previous steps have not effectively explained or reconciled the discrepant data, is to *consider context effects.* That is, look at the moments in time when different pieces of data were collected and think through whether there are notable, significant differences in the client's circumstances between the different moments. This is especially important, as data collected toward the end of long tele-assessment sessions—even without obvious physical or behavioral markers—are likely quite susceptible to eye strain and fatigue. Pay particular attention to this issue when comparing data collected toward the beginning with that collected at the end of sessions. Beyond fatigue, clients can present for different sessions in quite different frames of mind. Rewatching sections of the different sessions to look for behavioral evidence, and even discussing with the client if circumstances were notably different in one session versus the others, may reveal the reasons for the discrepancies in data.

Finally, if none of these strategies explain the discrepant data, consider that because of the imprecision of psychological testing in general (and maybe even more so when conducted via tele-assessment), discrepancies can be due to *test error and outlier-driven*. Now more than ever we need to appreciate the limitations of our measures, especially because (even in traditional, standardized administration) tests can produce data in error. This fact continues to be true, no matter how much we may overly glorify some tests, methods, and data. When we acknowledge the fact that any test can give erroneous data at any random point, it allows us to (methodically and mindfully) discard such data if needed. Sometimes data collected via psychological tests, measures, and inventories are simply inaccurate representations of the client's functioning or abilities. While we cannot discard data mindlessly and haphazardly, if we have gone through each of these steps to try to understand and contextualize the data, to no avail, the data can be discarded as error. Making this decision requires a sophisticated understanding of all the processes and methods that underlie the measures, as well as clear acknowledgment that there is a preponderance of data that supports one conclusion over another. These nuanced decisions are one of the major reasons the assessment process is limited to professionals specifically trained to do it (Rapid Reference 5.2).

CONCLUSION

You, as a psychologist, are a professional specifically trained to understand how to understand and integrate data as part of a comprehensive assessment. The psychological tele-assessment context introduces a host of potentially disruptive variables within the overall, often heavily standardized process. However, early research on the effects of the tele-assessment method (see Chapter 1),

≋ Rapid Reference 5.2

The steps for reconciling discrepant data in a psychological tele-assessment context are as follows:

1. Double-check all coding and scoring
2. Identify whether the discrepancy is a true discrepancy or an apparent discrepancy
3. Scrutinize any discrepant data that emerged from tele-assessment practices that might have affected the data quality
4. Think through the potential method and process effects
5. Consider context effects
6. Acknowledge the possibility of test error and outlier-driven discrepancies

as compared to traditional in-person assessments, has shown promising support for the general disruptiveness being negligible. Nevertheless, psychologists need to be vigilant about the quality of the data that emerge from tele-assessment practices (Wright et al., 2020). Being methodical and deliberate about evaluating data quality (even when it is tedious, such as rewatching entire testing sessions) is a necessary step for ethical and valid psychological tele-assessment.

Six

COGNITIVE AND NEUROPSYCHOLOGICAL TELE-ASSESSMENT

With Katy Genseke

Performance-based cognitive testing (including intelligence, memory, neuropsychological, and language measures) is a cornerstone of psychological assessment, and it is perhaps one of the most difficult types for psychologists to think about managing in a tele-assessment context. The information in this chapter is meant to help psychologists prepare to conduct tele-assessments with performance-based cognitive tests, and much of the detailed footwork and notes you will need for cognitive tele-assessment are provided. This chapter can be used as a training reference as you practice, as well as to refresh and remind yourself of requirements prior to beginning a tele-assessment session.

Before you administer a performance-based test via tele-assessment, you should be aware of the evidence that supports its use in the new mode. This chapter and Chapter 7 reference equivalence evidence by task, much of which was discussed broadly in Chapter 1. The references are drawn from both *direct evidence* (i.e., drawn directly from research on the listed task or measure) and *indirect evidence* (i.e., drawn from research based on other tasks with similar or identical input and output demands) of tele-assessment and face-to-face administration mode equivalence, as discussed in Chapters 1 and 5. Some tasks discussed in this chapter and in Chapter 7 are supported with both direct and indirect evidence, and other tasks are supported with only indirect evidence. We have tried to be extremely clear which tasks are supported by indirect and direct evidence, based on the available research at the time of writing this book.

Direct evidence for a test, measure, or task is based on research studies that have shown equivalence (discussed at length in Chapter 4). However, just because a

Essentials of Psychological Tele-Assessment, First Edition.
A. Jordan Wright and Susan Engi Raiford

task does not have direct evidence—a study that specifically looked at that task—for equivalence across modes does not mean that data that emerge from the task are invalid. *Indirect evidence* focuses on the specific task demands required for the psychologist and the examinee to engage in. The task demands include *input demands*, which are all the necessary stimulus prompts, such as a task requiring the examiner to simply say some stimulus words aloud, the examiner to show the examinee stimulus pictures and prompt verbally, or other such stimulus demands. The task demands also include *output demands*, which are the necessary processes the examinee must engage in to respond to the stimuli of a task. These can include short verbal responses, pointing to a part of a stimulus picture, writing something down, or other such response processes.

As an example, while one test of written math may have been specifically studied and shown to be equivalent in a tele-assessment mode (showing direct evidence of equivalence), another test of written math that has not may have nearly identical input demands (perhaps prompting the examinee to complete math questions that are written in a response booklet given to them) and output demands (the examinee writing math answers on the response booklet). It is reasonable to assume that the direct evidence from the first written math task supports the equivalence—in an indirect way—of the second written math task.

It should be noted that while indirect evidence utilizing input and output demands can be useful for evaluating how likely performance-based tasks are to produce valid data, it should still be used cautiously and judiciously. Evaluating input and output demands provides a basis, but it also does not incorporate the mediating psychological processes involved in tasks. For example, if there is direct evidence of a word reading task (in which the input is a list of written words projected on a screen, and the output is the examinee reading the words aloud verbally for the examiner to hear), the inputs and outputs may be the same for a task that requires different cognitive skills. A task asking an examinee to define words presented visually to them, for example, includes the same input (words printed on the screen) and output (short verbal responses), but the mediating cognitive task is different. While it is hoped that the overwhelming majority of the variance in scores obtained by a task like this would depend on the examinee's capacity to read and define the words, it is possible that the change in mode (from in-person to remote tele-assessment) may somehow interact with the mediating psychological processes as well. It is unlikely, which is why an evaluation of input and output demands can provide strong indirect evidence for task score validity. However, it is not impossible.

It is important to recall from Chapter 4 that *for examinees younger than 5 years there is very little equivalence evidence on tele-assessment and face-to-face administration modes.* Many of the tests reviewed in this chapter and in Chapter 7 include children younger than 5 years within the possible administration age range. Pay close attention to the age ranges examined in the studies that offer administration mode equivalence evidence in the Rapid Reference for each test. Proceed with great caution if testing young children via tele-assessment when interpreting results.

Rapid Reference 1.1 in Chapter 1 provides a broad overview of the existing performance-based cognitive and neuropsychological tele-assessment equivalence studies. We have also developed an online resource, the *Tele-Assessment Equivalence Study Database,* which accompanies this book and provides more in-depth information about each tele-assessment equivalence study and the input and output demands of each researched task. The studies and information in the database are referred to throughout this chapter and Chapter 7.

If you intend to administer a task

DON'T FORGET
....

Some tests, measures, and tasks have direct evidence of equivalence between tele-assessment methods and traditional, in-person methods. This means that they have specifically been studied and shown to be equivalent, to not have a significant method effect that affects the data. Other tasks have indirect evidence of equivalence, such that measures with similar or nearly identical *input demands* (delivery of stimuli to the examinee) and *output demands* (delivery of responses from the examinee) have shown equivalence in research.

CAUTION
....

There is very little evidence on tele-assessment and face-to-face equivalence of performance-based tests with young children. Pay close attention to the age ranges examined for each study in the Rapid Reference that corresponds to a test used with young children. *Proceed with great caution when interpreting results obtained with young children via tele-assessment.*

---

not discussed in this book, the database also can be used to search for evidence of tele-assessment equivalence for tasks with similar input and output demands. It can be filtered by task type or construct for ease of use. The information cataloged in the *Tele-Assessment Equivalence Study Database* are listed in Rapid Reference 6.1.

≡ Rapid Reference 6.1

Detailed Contents of the Tele-Assessment Equivalence Study Database

Tele-Studies and Tasks Tab:
- Rating of each study's rigor and the reasons behind the ratings
- Population studied (e.g., nonclinical, mild cognitive impairment)
- Number and age range of participants
- Tasks or composite scores studied
- Software used
- Analyses performed
- Summary of results

Task Demands Tab:
- Task name
- Task type (e.g., elaborated verbal, visual reasoning, auditory working memory, processing speed)
- Task description (i.e., what the examinee is required to do)
- Task input demands (e.g., brief spoken directions, picture stimuli, spoken stimuli)
- Task output demands (e.g., brief spoken response, multiple choice, pointing, open-ended verbal response, written or fine motor response)

ACCESSING DIGITAL STIMULI

Stimuli for performance-based tests that are available for tele-assessment are provided in various formats. Some digital materials (e.g., interactive PDFs) reside on test publisher platforms and can be used for multiple purposes, including remote administration. Other stimuli reside on digital administration platforms for use in face-to-face environments, and test publishers have given permission to adapt them for remote administration.

Specifically, many test publishers gave permission during the COVID-19 crisis for psychologists to use teleconferencing platforms to display test materials for tele-assessment purposes. *Prior to beginning, it is important to ensure through the publisher's website that this permission is still in*

CAUTION

Several test publishers gave permission during the COVID-19 crisis for psychologists to use teleconferencing platforms to display test materials for tele-assessment purposes. Always verify that this permission is still in place.

place. In a few cases, test publishers created special versions of their tests for remote on-screen administration.

Digital Stimulus Materials

The platforms used for digital stimuli delivery by the major test publishers are described in this section. Each test's section in this chapter and in Chapter 7 lists the platform(s) through which the stimuli (and often manuals) can be accessed.

It is important to utilize the digital stimulus materials created and provided by the test publishers. They have gone to great lengths to ensure that the stimuli are highly comparable to the traditional stimuli. Details like the sound quality of recorded auditory stimuli and the resolution, size, and color quality of visual stimuli are extremely important in simulating standardized administration procedures.

For example, scanning and screen-sharing materials from physical stimulus books or easels may seem feasible, but the scans can produce visual materials that are not faithful in color, quality, or size to the original materials when projected through screen-sharing technology. This can affect the data that emerge from responses related to those stimuli.

When stimulus materials are not available from test publishers, use of a document camera and the original, physical materials may seem to be the best simulation (as discussed in Chapter 3). However, most publishers do not allow this as an acceptable use and consider it to be a violation of the test user agreement.

It is important to remember when administering most tests via tele-assessment that the same physical materials needed for face-to-face administration (e.g., blocks, cards, grids) and paper record forms and

> ### CAUTION
>
> Do not scan stimulus materials. Only use digital stimulus materials provided by the test publishers when they are available.
>
> When they are not available, only use a document camera to project the original, physical stimulus materials if the test publisher has given permission for such use. Many publishers have stated that projecting stimuli on a document camera is a violation of the test user agreement and not permitted.

> ### DON'T FORGET
>
> When administering most tests via tele-assessment, the same physical materials needed for face-to-face administration and paper record forms and response booklets are still necessary. Consumable paper components usually cannot be printed from most test publishers' platforms.

response booklets are still necessary. Consumable paper components usually cannot be printed from most test publishers' platforms.

Multihealth Systems (MHS)

MHS Online Portals has online apps available for some performance-based tests. Psychologists can use the apps as they usually do for face-to face assessment. During the COVID-19 crisis, MHS gave permission for some products to allow the visual and auditory stimuli used through the apps to be displayed to the examinee via screensharing using encrypted videoconferencing software.

Pearson Clinical Assessments

Q-global is Pearson's online administration, scoring, and reporting platform. It can be accessed on any computer or device with a web browser. The digital stimuli, including stimulus books and response booklets, are in the resource library's restricted folders for each product. The response booklets are meant to be used when instructing or prompting the examinee and in some cases are not printable. During the COVID-19 crisis, Pearson gave permission for the digital stimuli to be displayed to the examinee via screensharing using encrypted videoconferencing software.

It should be noted that physical manipulatives (e.g., blocks, puzzles, and cards) and paper record forms and response booklets are still necessary. In general, most paper components cannot be printed from Q-global.

Q-interactive is Pearson's iPad-based digital administration and scoring platform. Assess, the Q-interactive iPad app, is used by connecting two iPads—the examiner's and the examinee's—via Bluetooth. The examinee's iPad, which shows the relevant visual stimuli, can be displayed on the examiner's computer using mirroring software and then shared on the examinee's screen via the teleconferencing platform. During the COVID-19 crisis, Pearson also gave permission for the Q-interactive digital stimuli to be displayed to the examinee via screensharing, as with Q-global. After the examinee's and examiner's iPads are connected, the examiner iPad is used to administer as usual using the subtest instructions in the Assess app. While record forms are not necessary, physical manipulatives (e.g., blocks, puzzles, cards) and response booklets are still needed with Q-interactive.

Pro-Ed

Many Pro-Ed products have virtual components (e.g., manuals, stimulus books) that can be purchased on each product's page on the Pro-Ed website. These are offered in the Other Components and Related Products of each page. After purchasing them, an email code is sent which provides access to the components from their digital delivery partner, *RedShelf.* During the COVID-19 pandemic, Pro-Ed gave permission for the digital stimuli to be displayed to the examinee via screensharing using encrypted videoconferencing software.

Psychological Assessment Resources (PAR)

PARiConnect is the online administration, scoring, and reporting platform for PAR, accessible through all browsers and devices. Some performance-based products are administered directly through PARiConnect, whereas others require accessing the PAR digital library. PAR has given permission to allow some performance-based tests' digital stimuli to be displayed to the examinee via screensharing using encrypted videoconferencing software. In some cases, an integrated experience is provided with all administration and scoring accomplished within the platform. In others, special record forms designed for remote administration are necessary.

Riverside Insights

Riversidescore.com is Riverside Insights' online scoring and reporting platform. The platform contains the visual stimuli and recorded audio stimuli as well. The site can be accessed on any computer or device with a web browser. During the COVID-19 crisis, Riverside Insights gave permission for the digital stimuli to be displayed to the examinee via screensharing using encrypted videoconferencing software.

The examiner's side of the easel test books, where the instructions reside, are not on the Riversidescore.com site as digital files. You must have the physical easel test books available in order to administer the tests. Paper record forms and response books are also necessary.

TELE-ASSESSMENT WITH INTELLIGENCE TESTS

Wechsler Intelligence Scales (WAIS-IV, WISC-V, WISC-V Integrated, WPPSI-IV)

This section reviews the Wechsler Adult Intelligence Scale, Fourth Edition (WAIS-IV; Wechsler, 2008), the Wechsler Intelligence Scale for Children, Fifth Edition (WISC-V; Wechsler, 2014), WISC-V Integrated (Wechsler & Kaplan, 2015), and the Wechsler Preschool and Primary Scale of Intelligence, Fourth Edition (WPPSI-IV; Wechsler, 2012) evidence for equivalence of tele-assessment and face-to-face administration. Special administration considerations are discussed, as are composite score selection related to administration decisions made due to the need for physical materials in the examinee's location.

Wechsler Intelligence Scales Equivalence Evidence

Multiple studies have been conducted to examine equivalence of the Wechsler intelligence scales and tasks in tele-assessment and face-to-face conditions. Notably, in a study conducted on the WISC-V for ages 6–16 (Wright, 2020b), equivalence was supported for all subtests, the primary index scores, and the Full Scale IQ, with the lone exception being Letter–Number Sequencing. There are a variety of other studies that support equivalence of the WAIS-IV tasks (or those with similar input and output demands) in both the child and adult age range that are listed in Rapid Reference 6.2.

Rapid Reference 6.2 provides analysis of each subtest's input and output demands. It also lists both direct and indirect evidence of equivalence for each task, along with the age ranges studied. The Wechsler Abbreviated Scale of Intelligence, Second Edition (WASI-II; Wechsler, 2011) evidence also appears in Rapid Reference 6.2, although the WASI-II itself is discussed in the Brief Intelligence Tests section of this chapter. Because the age range for the Wechsler intelligence scales spans ages 2–90, a review of other tele-assessment equivalence studies with similar tasks and examinees of varied ages is helpful to inform interpretation.

Wechsler Intelligence Scales Administration Considerations

The Wechsler intelligence scales can be administered via tele-assessment in multiple ways. There are two platforms where the digital stimuli are available: Q-global and Q-interactive. Paper response booklets are necessary with both platforms, and a paper record form is necessary with Q-global.

Administering the Wechsler intelligence scales via tele-assessment requires high quality audio and video for nearly all tasks. A headset with a microphone is recommended for both the examinee and examiner.

Special administration considerations are listed by subtest in Rapid Reference 6.3. The WASI-II considerations also appear in this Rapid Reference, although the WASI-II itself is discussed in the Brief Intelligence Tests section later in this chapter.

≣ Rapid Reference 6.2

Wechsler Intelligence Scale Subtest Input and Output Demands and Equivalence Evidence

Subtest(s)	Input	Output	Evidence[a] Citation: Task Abbreviation/Ages
Similarities Vocabulary Information Comprehension	Brief spoken directions, spoken stimuli WPPSI: picture stimuli on early items Vocabulary: picture stimuli WAIS and WASI Vocabulary: Words in Print	Open ended, spoken response WPPSI: multiple choice and pointing or brief spoken response on early items	**Direct evidence:** Hildebrand et al., 2004:VC/60+ Hodge et al., 2019: SI,VC/8–12 Jacobsen et al., 2003:VC/adult Temple et al., 2010:VC/23–63 Wright, 2020b: SI,VC, IN, CO/6–16 **Indirect Evidence:** Dekhtyar et al., 2020: CQ/26–75 Turkstra et al., 2012: MDEP,ABD/21–69 Wright, 2018a: GW,VR/3–19 Wright, 2018b: OV, GI/5–16
Similarities Multiple Choice Vocabulary Multiple Choice Information Multiple Choice Comprehension Multiple Choice	Brief spoken directions, spoken stimuli, words in print	Multiple choice, pointing or brief spoken response	**Indirect Evidence:** Dekhtyar et al., 2020: RCS/26–75 Wright, 2018b: PCO/5–16 Wright, 2020b: SI,VC, IN, CO/6–16

(continued)

Subtest(s)	Input	Output	Evidence[a] Citation: Task Abbreviation/Ages
Picture Naming	Brief spoken directions, picture stimuli	Brief spoken response, open ended	**Indirect Evidence:** Brearly et al., 2017: BNT/adult Cullum et al., 2006: BNT/51–84 Cullum et al., 2014: BNT/46–90 Dekhtyar et al., 2020: PD/26–75 Galusha-Glasscock et al., 2016: PN/58–84 Sutherland et al., 2017: FS, WS/8–12 Vestal et al., 2006: BNT, PD/68–78 Wadsworth et al., 2018: BNT/adult Waite et al., 2010: FS, WS/5–9
Receptive Vocabulary Picture Vocabulary Multiple Choice	Brief spoken directions, picture stimuli	Multiple choice, pointing or brief spoken response	**Indirect Evidence:** Sutherland et al., 2017: WC/8–12 Vestal et al., 2006: ACWP/68–78
Block Design Object Assembly	Brief spoken directions, gestured directions, motor demonstration, physical manipulatives *Block Design:* picture stimuli	Item-level time limit, fine motor response	**Direct Evidence:** Dekhtyar et al., 2020: BD/26–75 Hodge et al., 2019: BD/8–12 Temple et al., 2010: BD/23–63 Wright, 2020b: BD/6–16 Indirect Evidence: Jacobsen et al., 2003: BD, GP/adult Vestal et al., 2006: TKT/68–78

Subtest	Input	Response	Evidence
Visual Puzzles Block Design Multiple Choice Matrix Reasoning Figure Weights Figure Weights Process Approach Picture Concepts Picture Span Picture Memory	Brief spoken directions, gestured directions, picture stimuli *Visual Puzzles, Matrix Reasoning, Figure Weights, Picture Concepts: Color-critical items* *Picture Span and Picture Memory: Timed presentation*	Multiple choice, pointing or brief spoken response *Visual Puzzles, Block Design Multiple Choice, and Figure Weights: Item-level time limit*	**Direct Evidence:** Hildebrand et al., 2004: MR/60+ Hodge et al., 2019: VP, MR, FW, PS/8–12 Wright, 2020b: VP, MR, FW, PC, PS/6–16 Indirect Evidence. Dekhtyar et al., 2020: RPM/26–75 Sutherland et al., 2017: CFD, WC/8–12 Vahia et al., 2015: BVMT/65+ Vestal et al., 2006: ACWP/68–78 Waite et al., 2010: CFD/5–9 Wright, 2018a: NM, OIQ, WM/3–19 Wright, 2018b: CF, VZ/5–16
Picture Completion	Brief spoken directions, gestured directions, picture stimuli	Item-level time limit, open ended, pointing or brief spoken response	**Indirect Evidence:** Dekhtyar et al., 2020: PD/26–75 Vestal et al., 2006: PD/68–78 Wright, 2018a: WM/3–19

(continued)

Subtest(s)	Input	Output	Evidence[a] Citation: Task Abbreviation/Ages
Arithmetic Arithmetic Process Approach	Brief spoken directions, gestured directions, picture stimuli, spoken stimuli	Brief spoken response, item-level time limit, open ended	**Direct Evidence:** Wright, 2020b: AR/6–16 Indirect Evidence: Dekhtyar et al., 2020: SC, SCD/26–75 Sutherland et al., 2017: RS/8–12 Waite et al., 2010: RS/5–9 Wright, 2018b: AP,VA/5–16
Digit Span Letter–Number Sequencing	Brief spoken directions, spoken stimuli	Open ended, spoken response	**Direct Evidence:** Cullum et al., 2006: DS/51–84 Cullum et al., 2014: DS/46–90 Galusha-Glasscock et al., 2016: DS/58–84 Grosch et al., 2015: DS/67–85 Hodge et al., 2019: DS/8–12 Jacobsen et al., 2003: DS/adult Stain et al., 2011: DS/14–27 Vahia et al., 2015: DS/65+ Wadsworth et al., 2018: DS/adult Wright, 2020b: DS, LN/6–16 (LN not equivalent) Indirect Evidence: Wright, 2018b: NR/5–16

Zoo Locations	Brief spoken directions, gestured directions, motor demonstration, physical manipulatives, picture stimuli, timed presentation	Fine motor response	**Indirect Evidence:** Dekhtyar et al., 2020: BD/26–75 Hodge et al., 2019: BD/8–12 Jacobsen et al., 2003: BD, GP/adult Temple et al., 2010: BD/23–63 Vestal et al., 2006: TKT/68–78 Wright, 2018a: NM/3–19 Wright, 2020b: BD/6–16
Coding Symbol Search Cancellation Bug Search Animal Coding	Brief spoken directions, gestured directions, motor demonstration, physical manipulatives, response booklet *Coding and Symbol Search:* Letters digits or symbols in print Cancellation, Bug Search, and Animal Coding: Picture stimuli	Task-level time limit Simple written response Coding: Written response	**Direct Evidence:** Galusha-Glasscock et al., 2016: CD/58–84 Hodge et al., 2019: CD, SS/8–12 Wright, 2020b: CD, SS, CA/6–16 Indirect Evidence: Jacobsen et al., 2003: SDMT/adult Wright, 2018a: SPS/3–19 Wright, 2018b: LPM, MFF/5–16

(continued)

Subtest(s)	Input	Output	Evidence[a] Citation: Task Abbreviation/Ages
Naming Speed subtests	Brief spoken directions, gestured directions, picture stimuli	Open ended, spoken response, task-level time limit	**Indirect Evidence:** Wright, 2018a: SNT/7–19
Symbol Translation subtests	Brief spoken directions, gestured directions, picture stimuli, timed presentation	Pointing or brief spoken response *Recognition items:* multiple choice, brief spoken response	**Indirect Evidence:** Wright, 2018b: NM/3–19

Note. In-person digital/paper format equivalence evidence for the Wechsler intelligence scale tasks spans ages 2–90: Daniel (2012a, 2012b); Daniel et al. (2014); Drozdick, Getz, Raiford, and Zhang (2016); Raiford, Holdnack, et al. (2014, 2015, 2016).

[a]**Evidence column task abbreviations:** ABD = AphasiaBank discourse tasks; ACWP = Aural Comprehension of Words and Phrases; AP = Applied Problems; AR = Arithmetic; BD = Block Design; BNT = Boston Naming Test; BVMT = BriefVisuospatial Memory Test; CA = Cancellation; CD = Coding; CF Concept Formation; CFD = Concepts and Following Directions; CO = Comprehension; CQ = Conversational Questions; DS = Digit Span; FW = Figure Weights; FS = Formulated Sentences; GI = General v. GP = Grooved Pegboard; GW = Guess What; IN = Information; LN = Letter–Number Sequencing; LPM = Letter–Pattern Matching; MDEP = Mediated Discourse Elicitation Protocol; MFF = Math Facts Fluency; MR = Matrix Reasoning; NM = Nonverbal Memory; NR = Numbers Reversed; OIO = Odd-Item Out; OV = Oral Vocabulary; PC = Picture Concepts; PD = Picture Description; PN = Picture Naming; PS = Picture Span; RPM = Raven's Progressive Matrices; RS = Recalling Sentences; SC = Sentence Completion; SCD = Sequential Commands; SDMT = Symbol Digit Modalities Test; SI = Similarities; SNT = Speeded Naming Task; SS = Symbol Search; TKT = Token Test; VA = Verbal Attention; VC = Vocabulary; VP = Visual Puzzles; VR = Verbal Reasoning; VZ = Visualization; WC = Word Classes; WM = What's Missing; WS = Word Structure.

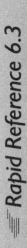

Rapid Reference 6.3

Wechsler Intelligence Scales Administration Considerations

Subtests	Administration Considerations
Similarities Vocabulary Information Comprehension WPPSI-IV only: Picture Naming	• For picture items, examiner uses mouse/cursor to point to stimuli on screen • Some items may elicit pointing or gestured responses if examinee is in home environment; ask examinee to say answer using words **WAIS-IV** • *Vocabulary:* Items 4 and 5 may elicit pointing responses; examiner uses mouse/cursor to point to stimuli on screen • *Information:* Item 2 may elicit gestured response **WISC-V** • *Vocabulary:* Some items (e.g., 5, 6, 7, 8) may elicit pointing responses • *Information:* Items 1–2 require a pointing response, and Items 4, 5, 8, 11, 12, and 13 may precipitate pointing or gestured responses **WPPSI-IV** • *Similarities, Information, Comprehension picture items:* examinee may say number of choice, or peripheral camera/device can be placed in a stable position that shows examinee's screen and provides a view of choices made nonverbally (e.g, pointing) • Picture item instructions may be altered to ask examinee to say number of response. For example (not a real item), change "Show me what you can drink" to "Which one can you drink? Is it (point with mouse) 1, 2, 3, or 4?" • *Information:* Items 1, 2, 3, 4, 9, and 12 may elicit pointing or gestured responses • *Vocabulary:* Items 4, 5, 7, and 11 may elicit pointing or gestured responses

(continued)

Subtests	Administration Considerations
	WASI-II
	• *Vocabulary items, Similarities Items 1–3:* examiner uses mouse/cursor to point to stimuli on screen
	• Some items may elicit pointing or gestured responses, especially if examinee is in home environment; ask examinee to answer using words
	– *Vocabulary:* 4–12
	– *Similarities:* 1–3
	• Optional: *Similarities* Items 1–3: Examinee can use mouse to point at choices
Block Design	• Onsite professional, if available, should assist with administration of these subtests
WPPSI-IV only:	• Train new onsite professionals until presentation of manipulatives during instructions and items is
Object Assembly	performed according to directions
Zoo Locations	• Do not allow non-professionals to present manipulative stimuli nor attempt to have examinee
	scramble blocks or present their own stimuli
WISC-V Integrated only:	• Onsite professional presents stimuli while *examiner* provides all verbal instructions
Spatial Span	• Examiner uses stopwatch and stops examinee at item time limit
	• Peripheral camera/device should be placed in a stable position to show examinee's responses (i.e.,
	constructions, card placements; touching blocks)
	• *Spatial Span:* situate camera/device to allow examiner to view board looking slightly downward on
	letter side as examinee responds; onsite professional should also record examinee's responses
	• *Block Design:*
	– Onsite professional should show sides of blocks during instruction, present blocks for each item,
	and build model for items that require it, while *examiner* provides verbal instructions
	– Requires a print stimulus book in examinee's location or digital stimulus book on a tablet
	– Stimuli should lay flat on table, not presented on vertical screen (impact of vertical presentation
	is unknown)

- Train onsite professional to present stimuli facing correct direction, as items easily become rotated 180°
- Do not allow examinee to rotate stimuli
- Examiner uses mouse/cursor to point to design stimuli on screen

- Examiner uses mouse/cursor to point to stimuli on screen
- Examinee can use mouse/cursor to point at choices
- *Visual Puzzles, Picture Concepts, Picture Span, Picture Memory:* It is not recommended to allow examinee to use mouse/cursor to point at choices as intended responses cannot always be clearly determined
- Multiple choice item instructions may be altered to ask examinee to say number(s) or letter(s) of response to clarify if necessary
- Optional: Peripheral camera/device can be placed in stable position that shows examinee's screen and provides a view of choices made nonverbally (e.g., pointing)
- *Block Design Multiple Choice, Visual Puzzles, Figure Weights, Figure Weights Process Approach, Picture Completion, Picture Memory, Picture Span:* Examiner uses stopwatch when necessary
- *Picture Completion:* Some verbal responses must be clarified with a correct pointing response

Visual Puzzles
Matrix Reasoning
Figure Weights
Picture Concepts

WAIS-IV only:
Picture Completion

WISC-V only:
Picture Span

WISC-V Integrated only:
Picture Vocabulary Multiple Choice
Block Design Multiple Choice
Figure Weights Process Approach

WPPSI-IV only:
Receptive Vocabulary
Picture Memory

(continued)

Subtests	Administration Considerations
Arithmetic *WISC-V Integrated only:* Arithmetic Process Approach	• Optional: Peripheral camera/device can be placed in stable position that shows examinee's screen and provides a view of choices made nonverbally (e.g., pointing) • Picture items: examiner points to stimuli on screen • Examinee must point to stimuli on screen for Items 1–2 and may provide other responses by holding up fingers • Examiner uses stopwatch • Do not repeat any item except as allowed in manual unless it was not heard due to technical problems
Digit Span Letter–Number Sequencing *WISC-V Integrated only:* Sentence Recall	• Do not repeat stimuli unless it was not heard due to technical problems
Coding Symbol Search Cancellation *WISC-V Integrated only:* Cancellation Abstract Written Arithmetic *WPPSI-IV only:* Bug Search Animal Coding	• Peripheral camera/device should be placed in a stable position that shows examinee's response booklet and provides examiner a view of examinee's written responses • Examiner can complete demonstration items in examinee's response booklets prior to sending and can also demonstrate on screen during testing session • Examiner points to stimuli on screen and may fill in demonstration items on digital copy of response booklet displayed on screen with writing utensil tool (if a good one exists in teleconference platform) • Coding: Remove response booklet from screensharing display for sample and test items as examinees tend to look up at digital response booklet key instead of their own copy • Examiner uses stopwatch and must ensure examinee stops at task time limit

- It may be helpful to have a printed copy of response booklets in examiner's location also in order to show briefly on camera additional response booklet pages if applicable or how to turn to correct item for *Cancellation* when giving test item directions
- Ensure response booklet is opened only to correct page when directed
- Ensure response booklet is placed correctly to show demonstration and sample items, and to show test items correctly

WPPSI-IV:
- Any ink dauber in examinee's location that comfortably fits examinee's hand size can be used; subtests were standardized with multiple types of ink daubers
- Ensure response booklets are set aside to dry before placing in sealed envelopes

WISC-V only:
Naming Speed subtests
- Examiner points to stimuli on screen
- Younger examinees use finger tracking; peripheral camera/device should be placed in a stable position that shows examinee's screen and provides examiner a view of examinee's finger tracking
- Examiner uses stopwatch

WISC-V only:
Symbol Translation subtests
- Peripheral camera/device should be placed in a stable position that shows examinee's screen and provides examiner a view of examinee pointing at symbols
- Examiner points to stimuli on screen
- *Immediate and Delayed:* Examinee may often point to stimuli on screen and may skip some symbols

(continued)

Subtests	Administration Considerations
WISC-V Integrated only: Similarities Multiple Choice Vocabulary Multiple Choice Information Multiple Choice Comprehension Multiple Choice	• Examiner uses mouse/cursor to point to stimuli on screen • Examiner reads stimuli • Examinee can use mouse/cursor to point at choices • Multiple choice item instructions may be altered to ask examinee to say letter of response to clarify if necessary • Optional: Peripheral camera/device can be placed in stable position that shows examinee's screen and provides a view of choices made nonverbally (e.g., pointing)

Wechsler Intelligence Scales Composite Score Considerations

The data validating tele-assessment have generally involved onsite professionals (i.e., non-interested third parties, though often not specifically psychologists or other mental health or educational professionals) working with the psychologist. If available and trained, the onsite professional can present Wechsler intelligence scale manipulatives (e.g., blocks, puzzles, cards) and response booklets. Psychologists using this approach can obtain the typical composite scores that are available in face-to-face administrations.

If an onsite professional is not available, some subtests are not feasible for tele-assessment. This impacts the session workflow, subtest selection, and the approach to deriving composite scores. The impact varies depending on which Wechsler intelligence scale is being administered.

WAIS-IV

Without Block Design: For the WAIS-IV, assuming all necessary subtests apart from Block Design are administered, Figure Weights or Picture Completion can be substituted for Block Design when calculating the Perceptual Reasoning Index (PRI), the Full Scale IQ, and/or the General Ability Index (GAI). Alternately, the PRI and the Full Scale IQ can be prorated. This approach allows all WAIS-IV composite scores to be derived.

> **DON'T FORGET**
>
> If an onsite professional is not available, some subtests are not feasible for tele-assessment. This impacts the session workflow and composite score selection. The impact varies depending on which Wechsler intelligence scale is being administered.

Without Block Design or Response Booklets: If Block Design is omitted *and* response booklets are not used, subtest selection and the composite score approach is different. Assuming all other necessary subtests apart from Block Design, Symbol Search, Coding, and Cancellation are administered, the following composites can be obtained: Verbal Comprehension Index (VCI), PRI (by substitution or proration), Working Memory Index (WMI), and GAI (by substitution). In this situation, no Full Scale IQ can be obtained, because three of the ten core subtests are missing and all Processing Speed subtests are missing (refer to the administration and scoring manual for limits on substitution and proration).

Rapid Reference 6.4 presents the composite score selection, which varies depending on if Block Design and response booklets are used.

≡ Rapid Reference 6.4

WAIS-IV Composite Score Selection According to Block Design and Response Booklet Use

	Full Administration	No Block Design	No Block Design or Response Booklets
Composite Score	Composite Score Available?		
VCI	✓	✓	✓
PRI	✓	*Substitute Figure Weights or Picture Completion for Block Design; or prorate	*Substitute Figure Weights or Picture Completion for Block Design; or prorate
WMI	✓	✓	✓
PSI	✓	✓	No
Full Scale IQ	✓	*Substitute Figure Weights or Picture Completion for Block Design; or prorate	No
GAI	✓	*Substitute Figure Weights or Picture Completion for Block Design	*Substitute Figure Weights or Picture Completion for Block Design

*See page 29 in the WAIS-IV Administration and Scoring Manual.

WISC-V and WISC-V Integrated

Without Block Design: Assuming all necessary subtests apart from Block Design are administered, Visual Puzzles can be substituted or the Full Scale IQ can be prorated. This method makes available all WISC-V composite scores except for the Visual Spatial Index (VSI), the Nonverbal Index (NVI), and the GAI.

Without Block Design or Response Booklets: If Block Design is omitted *and* response booklets are not used, and if other WISC-V subtests are administered, all WISC-V composite scores except for the VSI, Processing Speed Index (PSI),

Full Scale IQ, NVI, and GAI are available. Rather than the PSI, the Naming Speed Index (NSI) can be used to provide a measure of cognitive speed.

Additionally, the missing composite scores can be replaced with highly similar composite scores using a combination of the WISC-V and WISC-V Integrated (Wechsler & Kaplan, 2015) subtests and portions of *Essentials of WISC-V Integrated Assessment* (Raiford, 2017). The book excerpts are available to customers within the Q-global Resource Library courtesy of John Wiley & Sons. These are referred to as *Essentials nonmotor composites*. These scores make use of Block Design Multiple Choice in place of Block Design and Naming Speed Quantity in place of Coding. The following nonmotor composites are available in place of the missing WISC-V composites: Nonmotor Full Scale Score, Nonmotor VSI, Nonmotor GAI, and Nonmotor NVI. Reliability, validity, clinical utility, interpretive information, and norms are provided in the *Essentials of WISC-V Integrated Assessment* book excerpt.

Rapid Reference 6.5 presents the WISC-V composite score selection, which varies depending on Block Design and response booklet use.

≡ Rapid Reference 6.5

WISC-V and WISC-V Integrated Composite Score Selection According to Block Design and Response Booklet Use

	Full Administration	No Block Design	No Manipulatives or Response Booklets
Composite Score	*Composite Score Available?*		
VCI	✓	✓	✓
VSI	✓	Replace with Nonmotor VSI**, using Block Design Multiple Choice instead of Block Design	Replace with Nonmotor VSI**, using Block Design Multiple Choice instead of Block Design
FRI	✓	✓	✓
WMI	✓	✓	✓

(continued)

	Full Administration	No Block Design	No Manipulatives or Response Booklets
PSI	✓	✓	Replace with NSI**
Full Scale IQ	✓	Substitute Visual Puzzles for Block Design	Replace with Nonmotor Full Scale Score**, using Block Design Multiple Choice and Naming Speed Quantity instead of Block Design and Processing Speed tasks, respectively
Verbal Expanded Crystallized Index	✓	✓	✓
*Multiple Choice VCI	✓	✓	✓
Expanded Fluid Index	✓	✓	✓
Quantitative Reasoning Index	✓	✓	✓
Auditory WMI	✓	✓	✓
NVI	✓	Replace with Nonmotor NVI**, using Block Design Multiple Choice instead of Block Design	Replace with Nonmotor NVI**, using Block Design Multiple Choice instead of Block Design
GAI	✓	Replace with Nonmotor GAI**, using Block Design Multiple Choice instead of Block Design	Replace with Nonmotor GAI**, using Block Design Multiple Choice instead of Block Design
CPI	✓	✓	No

	Full Administration	No Block Design	No Manipulatives or Response Booklets
NSI	✓	✓	✓
Symbol Translation Index	✓	✓	✓
Storage and Retrieval Index	✓	✓	✓

*WISC-V Integrated composite score
**Essentials of WISC-V Integrated nonmotor composite

WPPSI-IV

The WPPSI-IV contains many subtests with manipulatives and response booklets. When they are not administered, composite scores are limited. However, several additional composites were developed using the publisher's norming method and appear in *Essentials of WPPSI-IV Assessment* (Raiford & Coalson, 2014). These can help to round out the information obtained when the WPPSI-IV manipulatives and/or response booklets are not used, because none require response booklets. Remember, though, that very little evidence exists for validity of data obtained via tele-assessment for children under 5.

The additional composite scores include the *Comprehensive Verbal Index (CVI)*, which is derived using Information, Similarities, Vocabulary, and Comprehension. The CVI was created to provide a comprehensive

DON'T FORGET

If you are using the WISC-V and not using blocks or response booklets, if you wish to obtain the Nonmotor Full Scale Score and other nonmotor composites, administer Naming Speed Quantity and WISC-V Integrated Block Design Multiple Choice, along with WISC-V Similarities, Vocabulary, Matrix Reasoning, Figure Weights, and Digit Span.

Many other composite scores that use Block Design and response booklets can be replaced with highly similar composite scores using a combination of the WISC-V and WISC-V Integrated subtests and portions of *Essentials of WISC-V Integrated Assessment*. **Portions of that book are available within the Q-global Resource Library, along with an Excel-based tool used to calculate the Essentials nonmotor composites** (*WISC-V Integrated Interpretive Assistant 1.2*), courtesy of John Wiley & Sons.

measure of a wide variety of abilities primarily requiring verbal expression, including crystallized knowledge, concept formation and conceptualization, abstract reasoning, categorical and associative thinking, word/lexical knowledge, vocabulary development, learning, and practical judgment. It was discussed as useful for children with motor difficulties because the other broad composite scores involve manipulatives, so it has obvious applications for WPPSI-IV tele-assessment.

There are several other additional composites in Raiford and Coalson (2014) that can be used in a tele-assessment context and do not require manipulatives or response booklets. These include composites for general information, lexical knowledge, inductive reasoning with verbal stimuli, word knowledge, concept recognition and generation, and complex expressive ability.

Without Manipulatives: For the younger battery, assuming all necessary subtests apart from Block Design, Object Assembly, and Zoo Locations are administered, two composite scores can be obtained: The VCI and the Vocabulary Acquisition Index (VAI). However, the VSI, WMI, Full Scale IQ, NVI, and GAI cannot.

For the older battery, if all necessary subtests apart from Block Design, Object Assembly, and Zoo Locations are administered, more composite scores relative to the younger battery can be obtained. The VCI, Fluid Reasoning Index (FRI), PSI, and VAI can be derived as usual, and the Full Scale IQ can be obtained by proration (due to the missing Block Design score). The additional composite scores that appear in *Essentials of WPPSI-IV Assessment* (Raiford & Coalson, 2014) can also be obtained. However, the VSI, WMI, NVI, GAI, and Cognitive Proficiency Index (CPI) cannot be calculated.

Without Manipulatives or Response Booklets: The younger battery is unaffected by use of response booklets. The composite scores that can be obtained are the same as if the subtests that use manipulatives are omitted.

For the older battery, if all necessary subtests apart from Block Design, Object Assembly, Zoo Locations, and the Processing Speed subtests are administered, some composite scores can be obtained. The VCI, FRI, PSI, and VAI can be derived as usual. The additional composite scores (Raiford & Coalson, 2014) can also be obtained. However, the Full Scale IQ, VSI, WMI, NVI, GAI, and CPI cannot be derived.

Rapid Reference 6.6 presents the WPPSI-IV composite score selection, which varies depending on manipulative and response booklet use and examinee age.

DON'T FORGET

....

If you are using the WPPSI-IV, many other composite scores that do not involve subtests with manipulatives or response booklets are available in the book *Essentials of WPPSI-IV Assessment*.

≋ Rapid Reference 6.6

WPPSI-IV Composite Score Selection According to Manipulatives and Response Booklet Use, by Battery

	Full Administration		No Manipulatives		No Manipulatives or Response Booklets
Composite Score	Composite Score Available?				
	Younger Battery	Older Battery	Younger Battery	Older Battery	Older Battery
VCI	✓	✓	✓	✓	✓
VSI	✓	✓	No	No	No
FRI		✓		✓	✓
WMI	✓	✓	No	No	No
PSI		✓		✓	No
Full Scale IQ	✓	✓	No	**Prorate for Block Design	No
VAI	✓	✓	✓	✓	✓
NVI	✓	✓	No	No	No
GAI	✓	✓	No	No	No
CPI		✓		No	No
*CVI		✓		✓	✓
*Gc-K0		✓		✓	✓
*Gc-VL		✓		✓	✓
*Gf-Verbal		✓		✓	✓
*Word Knowledge Index		✓		✓	✓
*Concept Recognition and Generation Index		✓		✓	✓
*Complex Expressive Index		✓		✓	✓

* = Additional composite score available in *Essentials of WPPSI-IV Assessment* (Raiford & Coalson, 2014)
**See page 29–30 in the WPPSI-IV Administration and Scoring Manual.

Composite score abbreviations: *Gc-K0* = Gc narrow ability of general information. *Gc-VL*: Gc narrow ability of lexical knowledge. *Gf*-Verbal = inductive reasoning with verbal stimuli.

Woodcock Johnson IV Cognitive Tests (WJ-IV-Cog and WJ-IV-ECAD)

This section reviews the WJ-IV Cognitive Battery (WJ-IV-Cog; Schrank, McGrew, & Mather, 2014b) and the WJ-IV Early Cognitive and Academic Development (ECAD; Schrank, McGrew, & Mather, 2015) evidence for equivalence of tele-assessment and face-to-face administration. Special administration considerations are discussed, as is composite score selection related to the need for response booklets in the examinee's location.

WJ Cog and ECAD Equivalence Evidence

A study was conducted to examine equivalence of the first ten subtests of the WJ-IV-Cog in tele-assessment and face-to-face conditions for ages 5–16 (Wright, 2018b). Equivalence was supported for all subtest and composite scores that were studied.

Because the WJ-IV-Cog can be used with examinees ages 2–90+ and the age range for Wright's (2018b) equivalence study was only 5–16, a review of other tele-assessment equivalence studies with examinees of varied ages is helpful to inform interpretation. Rapid Reference 6.7 provides analysis of each test's input and output demands. It lists both direct and indirect evidence of equivalence for each task, along with the age ranges studied.

WJ-IV-Cog and ECAD Administration Considerations

The WJ-IV-Cog and ECAD can be administered via tele-assessment using the stimuli on the Riversidescore.com platform. The WJ-IV-Cog and ECAD require high quality audio and video and a headset with a microphone for both the examinee and examiner for nearly all tasks. The examiner and examinee should almost always be positioned to see one another's mouths. The examiner must have access to test directions through the physical test book easels. Special administration considerations are listed by test in Rapid References 6.8 and 6.9.

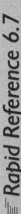

≋ Rapid Reference 6.7

WJ-IV-Cog and ECAD Input and Output Demands and Equivalence Evidence

Test(s)	Input	Output	Evidence[a] Citation: Task Abbreviation/Ages
Oral Vocabulary General Information Verbal Analogies (ECAD)	Brief spoken directions *Oral Vocabulary:* Gestured directions *General Information and Verbal Analogies:* Spoken stimuli	Open ended, spoken response	**Direct Evidence:** Wright, 2018b: OV, GI/5–16 **Indirect Evidence:** Dekhtyar et al., 2020: CQ/26–75 Hildebrand et al., 2004: VC/60+ Hodge et al., 2019: SI, VC/8–12 Jacobsen et al., 2003: VC/adult Temple et al., 2010: VC/23–63 Turkstra et al., 2012: MDEP, ABD/21–69 Wright, 2018a: GW, VR/3–19 Wright, 2020b: SI, VC, IN, CO/6–16
Number Series	Brief spoken directions, numbers in print, gestured directions, spoken stimuli	Brief spoken response, item-level time limit	**Direct Evidence:** Wright, 2018b: LWI, NS, WA/5–16 Indirect Evidence: Dekhtyar et al., 2020: CL/26–75

(continued)

Test(s)	Input	Output	Evidence[a] Citation:Task Abbreviation/Ages
Verbal Attention	Brief spoken directions, spoken stimuli	Brief spoken response	**Direct Evidence:** Wright, 2018b: APVA/5–16 **Indirect Evidence:** Dekhtyar et al., 2020: SC, SCD/26–75 Sutherland et al., 2017: RS/8–12 Waite et al., 2010: RS/5–9 Wright, 2020b: AR/6–16
Letter–Pattern Matching Number—Pattern Matching Pair Cancellation	Brief spoken directions, gestured directions, picture stimuli, spoken stimuli *Letter–Pattern and Number–Pattern:* Letters digits or symbols in print	Simple written response, task-level time limit	**Direct Evidence:** Wright, 2018b: LPM, MFF/5–16 **Indirect Evidence:** Galusha-Glasscock et al., 2016: CD/58–84 Hodge et al., 2019: CD, SS/8–12 Jacobsen et al., 2003: SDMT/adult Wright, 2018a: SPS/3–19 Wright, 2020b: CD, SS, CA/6–16

Phonological Processing (Word Access, Word Fluency, & Substitution)	Brief spoken directions, picture stimuli, spoken stimuli: (Pre-K-K) Spoken stimuli: (Grade 1–Adult)	Pointing response (Pre-K-K) Spoken response (Grade 1–Adult)	**Direct Evidence:** Wright, 2018b: PP/5–16 **Indirect Evidence:** Brearly et al., 2017: SF/adult
Sound Blending (ECAD)	Sound Blending: audio recorded stimuli, brief spoken directions	Brief spoken response	Dekhtyar et al., 2020: WF/26–75 Galusha-Glasscock et al., 2016: SF/58–84 Hildebrand et al., 2004: CWAT/60+ Stain et al., 2011: CWAT/14–27
Story Recall	Brief spoken directions, spoken stimuli	Open ended, spoken response	**Direct Evidence:** Wright, 2018b: SR/5–16 **Indirect Evidence:** Jacobsen et al., 2003: LM/adult (not equivalent) Stain et al., 2011: LM/14–27 Wright, 2018a: VM/3–19

(continued)

Test(s)	Input	Output	Evidence[a] Citation: Task Abbreviation/Ages
Visualization Concept Formation Picture Recognition Visual Closure (ECAD)	Brief spoken directions, color-critical items, gestured directions, picture stimuli	Multiple choice, pointing or brief spoken response	**Direct Evidence:** Wright, 2018b: CF, VZ/5–16 **Indirect Evidence:** Dekhtyar et al., 2020: RPM/26–75 Hildebrand et al., 2004: MR/60+ Hodge et al., 2019: VP, MR, FW, PS/8–12 Sutherland et al., 2017: CFD, WC/8–12 Vahia et al., 2015: BVMT/65+ Vestal et al., 2006: ACWP/68–78 Waite et al., 2010: CFD/5–9 Wright, 2018a: NM, OIO, WM/3–19 Wright, 2020b: FW, MR, PC, PS, VP/6–16

Numbers Reversed Nonword Repetition Object–Number Sequencing Memory for Words Sentence Repetition	Brief spoken directions *Numbers Reversed, Nonword Repetition, and Memory for Words:* Spoken stimuli *Object–Number Sequencing and Sentence Repetition:* Audio recorded stimuli	Open ended, spoken response	**Direct Evidence:** Wright, 2018b: NR/5-16 **Indirect Evidence:** Cullum et al., 2006: DS/51–84 Cullum et al., 2014: DS/46–90 Galusha-Glasscock et al., 2016: DS/58–84 Grosch et al., 2015: DS/67–85 Hodge et al., 2019: DS/8–12 Jacobsen et al., 2003: DS/adult Stain et al., 2011: DS/14–27 Vahia et al., 2015: DS/65+ Wadsworth et al., 2018: DS/adult Wright, 2020b/6–16 DS, LN (LN not equivalent)
Visual–Auditory Learning	Brief spoken directions, gestured directions, picture stimuli; timed presentation	Multiple choice, pointing or brief spoken response	**Indirect Evidence:** Wright, 2018b: NM/3–19
Analysis-Synthesis Memory for Names (ECAD)	Brief spoken directions, gestured directions, picture stimuli; spoken stimuli *Memory for Names:* Color-critical items	Open ended, spoken response	**Indirect Evidence:** Jacobsen et al., 2003: SL/adult Sutherland et al., 2017: FS, WC/8–12 Waite et al., 2010: FS, WS/5–9

(continued)

Test(s)	Input	Output	Evidence[a] Citation: Task Abbreviation/Ages
Picture Vocabulary (ECAD)	Brief spoken directions, picture stimuli	Brief spoken response, open ended	**Indirect Evidence:** Brearly et al., 2017: BNT/adult Cullum et al., 2006: BNT/51–84 Cullum et al., 2014: BNT/46–90 Dekhtyar et al., 2020: PD/26–75 Galusha-Glasscock et al., 2016: PNJ/58–84 Vestal et al., 2006: BNT, PD/68–78 Wadsworth et al., 2018: BNT/adult Waite et al., 2010: FS, WS/5–9
Rapid Picture Naming (ECAD)	Brief spoken directions, gestured directions, picture stimuli	Open ended, spoken response, task-level time limit	Wright, 2018a: SNT/7–19
Letter—Word Identification (ECAD)	Brief spoken directions, gestured directions, letters digits or symbols in print, words in print	Brief spoken response, item-level time limit	**Direct Evidence:** Wright, 2018b: NS, LWI, WA/5–16 Indirect Evidence: Dekhtyar et al., 2020: CL/26–75

			Indirect Evidence:
Number Sense (ECAD)	Brief spoken directions, gestured directions, picture stimuli	Open ended, pointing or brief spoken response	Brearly et al., 2017: BNT/adult Cullum et al., 2006: BNT/51–84 Cullum et al., 2014: BNT/46–90 Dekhtyar et al., 2020: PD/26–75 Galusha-Glasscock et al., 2016: PN/58–84 Sutherland et al., 2017: FS, WS/8–12 Vestal et al., 2006: BNT, PD/68–78 Wadsworth et al., 2018: BNT/adult Waite et al., 2010: FS, WS/5–9
Writing (ECAD)	Brief spoken directions, response booklet, spoken stimuli	Written response	**Direct Evidence:** Wright, 2018b: SP/5–16 **Indirect Evidence:** Dekhtyar et al., 2020: WID, WND/26–75

Evidence column task abbreviations: ABD = AphasiaBank discourse tasks, ACWP = Aural Comprehension of Words and Phrases, AP = Applied Problems, AR = Arithmetic, BNT = Boston Naming Test, BVMT = BriefVisuospatial Memory Test, CA = Cancellation, CD = Coding, CF = Concept Formation, CFD = Concepts and Following Directions, CL = Calculation, CO = Comprehension, CQ = Conversational Questions, CWAT = Controlled Word Association Test, DS = Digit Span, FW = Figure Weights, FS = Formulated Sentences, GI = General Information, GW = Guess What, IN = Information, LM = Logical Memory, LN = Letter–Number Sequencing, LPM = Letter–Pattern Matching, LWI = Letter–Word Identification, MDEP = Mediated Discourse Elicitation Protocol, MFF = Math Facts Fluency, MR = Matrix Reasoning, NM = Nonverbal Memory, NR = Numbers Reversed, NS = Number Series, OIO = Odd-Item Out, OV = Oral Vocabulary, PC = Picture Concepts, PD = Picture Description, PN = Picture Naming, PP = Phonological Processing, PS = Picture Span, RPM = Raven's Progressive Matrices, RS = Recalling Sentences, SC = Sentence Completion; SCD = Sequential Commands, SDMT = Symbol Digit Modalities Test, SF = Semantic Fluency, SI = Similarities, SL = Silhouettes, SNT = Speeded Naming Task, SPS = Speeded Picture Search, SR = Story Recall, SS = Symbol Search, VA = Verbal Attention, VC = Vocabulary, VM = Verbal Memory, VP = Visual Puzzles, VR = Verbal Reasoning, VZ = Visualization, WA = Word Attack, WC = Word Classes, WF = Word Fluency, WID = Writing Irregular Words to Dictation, WM = What's Missing, WND = Writing Nonwords to Dictation, WS = Word Structure.

≡ Rapid Reference 6.8

WJ-IV-Cog Administration Considerations

Test(s)	Administration Considerations
COG 1: Oral Vocabulary (Synonyms & Antonyms)	• Examiner uses mouse/cursor to point to stimuli on screen • Examiner must monitor response time using stopwatch or timer
COG 2: Number Series	• Examiner uses mouse/cursor to point to stimuli on screen • Examiner must monitor response time using stopwatch or timer • Requires response book or blank sheet of paper • Requires examinee to have pencil
COG 3: Verbal Attention	• Examiner streams and shares audio from online platform • If streaming audio from platform does not produce best quality audio, follow guidance in Examiner's Manual for presenting items orally
COG 4: Letter–Pattern Matching	• Requires use of response book and pencil • Examiner displays response book while walking through sample items • Requires facilitator or examinee to position web camera or peripheral camera on examinee's response book when completing sample items and test items • Examiner must monitor response time using stopwatch or timer
COG 5: Phonological Processing (Word Access, Word Fluency, & Substitution)	*Word Access* • Examiner streams and shares audio from online platform • Sample Items and Test Items 1–3 require examiner to display and point to stimuli projected on examinee's monitor; examinee must point to response (dual controls can be given to mouse or peripheral camera can be utilized) • Requires examiner to stream audio from online platform starting at Item 4 • If streaming audio from platform does not produce best quality audio, follow guidance in Examiner's Manual for presenting items orally *Word Fluency* additionally requires stopwatch or timer *Substitution* • Sample Items A & B and Test Items 1–2 are administered orally by examiner

Test(s)	Administration Considerations
	• Requires examiner to stream audio from online platform for Sample Items C & D, and Test Items 3–15 • If streaming audio from platform does not produce best quality audio, follow guidance in Examiner's Manual for presenting items orally
COG 6: Story Recall	• Requires examiner to stream audio from online platform • If streaming audio from platform does not produce best quality audio, follow guidance in Examiner's Manual for presenting items orally
COG 7: Visualization (Spatial Relations & Block Rotation)	• Examiner uses mouse/cursor to point to stimuli on screen • *Block Rotation*: examiner must monitor response time using stopwatch or timer
COG 8: General Information (What & Where)	• Requires high quality video for examiner and examinee (positioned to see mouths)
COG 9: Concept Formation	• Examiner uses mouse/cursor to point to responses on screen on Items 1–5 • Requires examiner to monitor examinee's response time using stopwatch or watch
COG 10: Numbers Reversed	• Sample Item A, Items 1–5; Sample Item B, Items 6–10, and Sample C, are orally presented by examiner • Requires examiner to stream audio from online platform for Sample item D, and Test Items 11–34 • If streaming audio from platform does not produce best quality audio, follow guidance in Examiner's Manual for presenting items orally
COG 11: Number–Pattern Matching COG 17: Pair Cancellation	• Requires use of response book • Requires examiner to be able to display response book while walking through sample items • Requires facilitator or examinee to position web camera or peripheral camera on examinee's response book when completing sample items and test items • Requires stopwatch or timer for 3-minute time limit
COG 12: Nonword Repetition	• Sample Items A & B and Items 1–7 are presented orally • Items 8–46: Examiner streams and shares audio from online platform • If streaming audio from platform does not produce best quality audio, follow guidance in Examiner's Manual for presenting items orally

(continued)

Test(s)	Administration Considerations
COG 13: Visual–Auditory Learning	• Examiner uses mouse/cursor to point to stimuli on screen
COG 14: Picture Recognition COG 15: Analysis-Synthesis	• Examinee can use mouse/cursor to point at items on screen • *Optional*: peripheral camera/device can be positioned in stable position to show examinee's screen and provide view of responses given nonverbally through pointing • *Analysis-Synthesis*: requires stopwatch or timer
COG 16: Object–Number Sequencing	• Sample A presented orally • Sample B & C & Items 1–31: Examiner streams and shares audio from online platform • If streaming audio from platform does not produce best quality audio, follow guidance in Examiner's Manual for presenting items orally
COG 18: Memory for Words	• Sample A presented orally • Sample B & Items 1–26: Examiner streams and shares audio from online platform • If streaming audio from platform does not produce best quality audio, follow guidance in Examiner's Manual for presenting items orally

≡ Rapid Reference 6.9

. . . .

WJ IV ECAD Administration Considerations

Test	Administration Considerations
Memory for Names	• Examiner uses mouse/cursor to point to stimuli on screen • Examinee can use mouse/cursor to point at choices for earlier items • *Optional*: solutions that require pointing responses: peripheral camera/device should be positioned in stable position to show examinee's screen and provide view of responses given nonverbally through pointing

Test	Administration Considerations
Sound Blending	• Requires examiner to stream audio from online platform • If streaming audio from platform does not produce best quality audio, follow guidance in Examiner's Manual for presenting items orally • Examiner presents Sample Items A orally • Examiner presents Sample Items B and all test items require audio streaming
Picture Vocabulary	• Examiner uses mouse/cursor to point to stimuli on screen • Examinee can use mouse/cursor to point at choices for earlier items • Examinee points to Sample Item A, Items 3, 5, 6, 7, 8, and 9 • *Optional*: peripheral camera/device can be positioned in stable position to show examinee's screen and provide view of responses given nonverbally through pointing
Verbal Analogies	• No requirements other than examiner having access to test directions through test book easel
Visual Closure	• Examiner uses mouse/cursor to point to stimuli on screen • *Optional*: peripheral camera/device can be positioned in stable position to show examinee's screen and provide view of responses given nonverbally through pointing
Sentence Repetition	• Examiner presents Sample Item A and Items 1–15 orally • Examiner presents Sample Item B and remaining test items from audio recording (if streaming audio from platform does not produce best quality audio, follow guidance in Examiner's Manual for presenting items orally)
Rapid Picture Naming	• Examiner uses mouse/cursor to point to stimuli on screen • Requires examiner to monitor examinee's responses and testing time (2 minutes) using stopwatch or watch • *Important*: Examiner needs to be ready to scroll to next page as soon as examinee names Item 30
Letter–Word Identification	• Examiner uses mouse/cursor to point to stimuli on screen • Examinee points to Items 1–10; 19–23 • *Optional*: peripheral camera/device can be positioned in stable position to show examinee's screen and provide view of responses given nonverbally through pointing

(continued)

Test	Administration Considerations
Number Sense	• Examiner uses mouse/cursor to point to stimuli on screen • Examinee can use mouse/cursor to point at choices for Items 5, 8, 9, 11, and 20 • *Optional:* peripheral camera/device can be positioned in stable position to show examinee's screen and provide view of responses given nonverbally through pointing
Writing	• Requires examiner to demonstrate Items 1–6 (*Optional:* use of peripheral camera/device for examiner) • Response book required for examinee to write responses • Position computer camera to show examinee's handwriting or use peripheral camera/device positioned in stable place to show examinee's response book and written responses

WJ-IV-Cog and ECAD Composite Score Considerations

If available, an onsite professional can present response books. Psychologists using this approach can administer all subtests and obtain all typical composite scores that are available in face-to face administrations.

It is recommended if possible that psychologists use response books when administering the WJ-IV-Cog and ECAD. If response books are not used, refer to the Selective Testing Tables in the Test Books and Examiner Manual to determine which composite scores can and cannot be obtained.

For the WJ-IV-Cog, the Brief Intellectual Ability (BIA) and *Gf-Gc* composites do not require use of a response book. Although there is space in the response book to use during the Number Series test, a sheet of blank paper can be used in its place. Many other composite scores can be obtained without using response books, including those representing several of the broad CHC factors, narrow abilities, and clinical clusters.

For the WJ-IV ECAD, the response book is only used for the Writing test. If Writing is not administered, all clusters still can be obtained except for Early Academic Skills.

Rapid References 6.10 and 6.11 describe the WJ IV Cog and ECAD composite score selections, which vary if response booklets are not used.

Stanford–Binet Intelligence Scales, Fifth Edition (SB5)

The Stanford-Binet Intelligence Scales, Fifth Edition (SB5; Roid, 2003) can be administered using virtual manuals and virtual item books that can be

≡Rapid Reference 6.10

WJ-IV-Cog Composite Score Selection According to Response Booklet Use

Composite Score	Full Administration	No Response Booklets
	Composite Score Available?	
General Intellectual Ability	✓	No
BIA	✓	✓
Gf-Gc Composite	✓	✓
Comprehension-Knowledge (Gc)	✓	✓
Fluid Reasoning (Gf)	✓	✓
Short-Term Working Memory (Gwm)	✓	✓
Cognitive Processing Speed (Gs)	✓	No
Auditory Processing (Ga)	✓	✓
Long-term Retrieval (Glr)	✓	✓
Visual Processing (Gv)	✓	✓
Quantitative Reasoning (RQ)	✓	✓
Auditory Memory Span (MS)	✓	✓
Number Facility (N)	✓	No
Perceptual Speed (P)	✓	No
Vocabulary (VL/LD)	✓	✓
Cognitive Efficiency	✓	No

purchased on the product's page on the Pro-Ed website and are delivered via RedShelf. The virtual stimuli can be displayed to the examinee by the onsite professional via a digital device, such as a tablet. The virtual item books are useful during the COVID-19 pandemic, during which paper materials are problematic.

We do not recommend attempting to administer the SB5 without a trained, onsite professional at the examinee's location. It is not always possible to predict

⇐ Rapid Reference 6.11

WJ-IV ECAD Composite Score Selection According to Response Booklet Use

Composite Score	Full Administration	No Response Booklets
	Composite Score Available?	
General Intellectual Ability–Early Development	✓	✓
Early Academic Skills	✓	No
Expressive Language	✓	✓

CAUTION

Do not administer the SB5 remotely without an onsite professional, as manipulatives may be required heavily throughout.

if and when the testlets involving manipulatives will be required. If an onsite professional is not available, several testlets (small sets of items) within the subtests are not feasible. These testlets can impact almost all subtests and composite scores. Further, because the SB5 uses manipulatives so extensively (e.g., blocks, toys, chips, rods, cards), it is recommended that the onsite professional be very well trained as a technician.

TELE-ASSESSMENT WITH BRIEFER INTELLIGENCE TESTS

Kaufman Brief Intelligence Test, Second Edition (KBIT-2)

This section reviews the Kaufman Brief Intelligence Test, Second Edition (KBIT-2; Kaufman & Kaufman, 2004) evidence for equivalence of tele-assessment and face-to-face administration. Special administration considerations are discussed.

KBIT-2 Equivalence Evidence

There have been no direct studies on the KBIT-2 and tele-assessment; however, the basic input and output demands of the tasks have support. Rapid Reference 6.12 provides analysis of the input and output demands and lists relevant indirect evidence by age range.

Rapid Reference 6.12

KBIT-2 Subtest Input and Output Demands and Equivalence Evidence

Subtest	Input	Output	Evidence[a] Citation: Task Abbreviation/Ages
Verbal Knowledge	Brief spoken directions, gestured directions, picture stimuli	Multiple choice, pointing or brief spoken response	**Indirect Evidence:** Dekhtyar et al., 2020: CQ/26–75 Hildebrand et al., 2004: VC/60+ Hodge et al., 2019: SI, VC/8–12 Jacobsen et al., 2003: VC/adult Temple et al., 2010: VC/23–63 Turkstra et al., 2012: MDEP, ABD/21–69 Wright, 2018a: GW, VR/3–19 Wright, 2018b: OV, GI/5–16 Wright, 2020b: SI, VC, IN, CO/6–16
Matrices	Brief spoken directions, color-critical items, gestured directions, picture stimuli	Multiple choice, pointing or brief spoken response	**Indirect Evidence:** Dekhtyar et al., 2020: RPM/26–75 Hildebrand et al., 2004: MR/60+ Hodge et al., 2019: VP, MR, FW, PS/8–12 Sutherland et al., 2017: CFD, WC/8–12

(continued)

Subtest	Input	Output	Evidence[a] Citation: Task Abbreviation/Ages
			Vestal et al., 2006: ACWP/68–78
			Waite et al., 2010: CFD/5–9
			Wright, 2018a: NM, OIO,WM/3–19
			Wright, 2018b: CF,VZ/5–16
			Wright, 2020b:VP, MR, FW, PC, PS/6–16
Riddles	Brief spoken directions, gestured directions, picture stimuli, spoken stimuli	Open ended, pointing or brief spoken response	**Indirect Evidence:**
			Dekhtyar et al., 2020: CQ/26–75
			Hildebrand et al., 2004:VC/60+
			Hodge et al., 2019: SI,VC/8–12
			Jacobsen et al., 2003:VC/adult
			Temple et al., 2010:VC/23–63
			Turkstra et al., 2012: MDEP, ABD/21–69
			Wright, 2018a: GW,VR/3–19
			Wright, 2018b: GI, OV/5–16
			Wright, 2020b: SI,VC, IN, CO/6–16

[a]**Evidence column task abbreviations:** ABD = AphasiaBank discourse tasks, ACWP = Aural Comprehension of Words and Phrases, CF = Concept Formation, CFD = Concepts and Following Directions, CO = Comprehension, CQ = Conversational Questions, FW = Figure Weights, GI = General Information, GW = Guess What, IN = Information, MDEP = Mediated Discourse Elicitation Protocol, MR = Matrix Reasoning, NM = Nonverbal Memory, OIO = Odd-Item Out, OV = Oral Vocabulary, PC = Picture Concepts, PS = Picture Span, RPM = Raven's Progressive Matrices, SI = Similarities, VC = Vocabulary,VP = Visual Puzzles,VR = Verbal Reasoning,VZ = Visualization,WA = Word Attack,WC = Word Classes, WM = What's Missing.

KBIT-2 Administration Considerations

The KBIT-2 can be administered via tele-assessment using the manual and digital stimuli available on Q-global. The KBIT-2 is brief and easy to administer via tele-assessment. A paper record form is needed. There are no physical manipulatives or response booklets, so materials in the examinee's location are not needed. All subtest and composite scores can be obtained.

Administering the KBIT-2 via tele-assessment requires high quality audio and video. A headset with a microphone is recommended for both the examinee and examiner. Special administration considerations are listed by subtest in Rapid Reference 6.13.

≡ Rapid Reference 6.13

KBIT-2 Administration Considerations

Subtest(s)	Administration Considerations
Verbal Knowledge Matrices	• Examiner uses mouse/cursor to point to stimuli on screen • Examinee can use mouse/cursor to point at choices • Optional: Peripheral camera/device can be placed in a stable position that shows examinee's screen and provides view of choices made nonverbally (e.g., pointing)
Riddles	Examiner presents most items verbally, and examinee responds verbally For Items 1–8: • Examiner uses mouse/cursor to point to stimuli on screen • Examinee can use mouse/cursor to point at choices • Optional: Peripheral camera/device can be placed in a stable position that shows examinee's screen and provides view of choices made nonverbally (e.g., pointing)

Reynolds Adaptable Intelligence Test (RAIT)

This section reviews the Reynolds Adaptable Intelligence Test (RAIT; Reynolds, 2014) evidence for equivalence of tele-assessment and face-to-face administration. Special administration considerations are discussed.

RAIT Equivalence Evidence

The RAIT manual indicates the normative sample consisted of 484 examinees who completed the booklet version and 1640 examinees who completed the computer version. The manual does not state this explicitly, but additional information obtained from PAR indicated that all examinees who completed the computer version were tested with the examinee in a remote location relative to the examiner.

Equivalence across the two formats/modes was examined in a manner different than the typical equivalence study approaches described in Chapter 4, which were all performed after a test was already in use with its norms derived for face-to-face administration. The RAIT was clearly designed and planned from the beginning to be self-administered and to have the flexibility of paper/face-to-face or digital/remote administration. For that reason, a different approach was taken because combined norms across modes were the most likely possibility (or perhaps only minor adjustments would have been required).

A multivariate analysis of covariance (MANCOVA) was performed to examine differences across format after gender, ethnicity, education level, and region were controlled. Results suggested that format/mode accounted for less than 3% of the variance in mean score levels. Hence, the two formats/modes were deemed equivalent and the two samples were pooled to form the overall normative sample. That is, adjustment or equating techniques (like those described in Chapter 4) were *not* performed; the same raw score for each format/mode results in the identical derived score. The subtest and composite score means from the two formats/modes (i.e., paper/face-to-face and digital/remote) have not been published, so they cannot be directly examined for equivalence beyond the information provided here (which is everything that the manual provides).

While the information about equivalence of the two formats/modes is helpful for evaluating the RAIT, psychologists are cautioned that this evidence may not generalize well to the performance-based cognitive and neuropsychological tests typically used by psychologists (and described in this chapter) that involve an examiner playing an active role. The RAIT examiner is not an active participant in either the face-to-face or a remote session; rather, the examiner serves as a proctor. The test is largely self-administered, with the examinee reading their own instructions and working independently by selecting responses on a computer (or filling in bubbles on an answer sheet to indicate responses). Thus, it involves almost no examiner–examinee interaction, like a fully computer-administered test. In fact, for the computer-administered version of the test, the examiner does not even have to track time limits for the subtests as they must for a paper administration; the computer manages the time limits for each task.

Even without the combined norms, indirect evidence also supports that these tasks would likely be deemed equivalent. Rapid Reference 6.14 lists the direct and indirect evidence of equivalence for each task, along with the age ranges studied.

≡ Rapid Reference 6.14

. . . .

RAIT Input and Output Demands and Equivalence Evidence

Subtests	Input	Output	Evidence[a] Citation: Task Abbreviation/Ages
General Knowledge Odd Word Out Word Opposites Quantitative Knowledge Quantitative Reasoning	Written Directions, words in print	Multiple choice, pointing response, task-level time limit	**Direct Evidence:** Reynolds, 2014: all tasks/10–75 **Indirect Evidence:** Brearly et al., 2017: SF/adult Dekhtyar et al., 2020: WF/26–75 Galusha-Glasscock et al., 2016: SF/58–84 Hildebrand et al., 2004: CWAT/60+ Stain et al., 2011: CWAT/14–27 Wright, 2018b: PP/5–16
Nonverbal Analogies Sequences	Color-critical items, picture stimuli, written directions	Multiple choice, pointing response, task-level time limit	**Direct Evidence:** Reynolds, 2014: all tasks/10–75 **Indirect Evidence:** Dekhtyar et al., 2020: RPM/26–75 Hildebrand et al., 2004: MR/60+ Hodge et al., 2019: VP, MR, FW, PS/8–12 Sutherland et al., 2017: CFD, WC/8–12 Vahia et al., 2015: BVMT/65+ Vestal et al., 2006: ACWP/68–78 Waite et al., 2010: CFD/5–9 Wright, 2018a: NM, OIO, WM/3–19 Wright, 2018b: CF, VZ/5–16 Wright, 2020b: VP, MR, FW, PC, PS/6–16

[a]**Evidence column task abbreviations:** ACWP = Aural Comprehension of Words and Phrases, BVMT = Brief Visuospatial Memory Test, CF = Concept Formation, CFD = Concepts and Following Directions, CWAT = Controlled Word Association Test, FW = Figure Weights, MR = Matrix Reasoning, NM = Nonverbal Memory, OIO = Odd-Item Out, PC = Picture Concepts, PP = Phonological Processing, PS = Picture Span, RPM = Raven's Progressive Matrices, SF = Semantic Fluency, VP = Visual Puzzles, VZ = Visualization, WC = Word Classes, WF = Word Fluency.

RAIT Administration Considerations

The RAIT can be administered digitally via PARiConnect. During the COVID-19 pandemic, the test publisher indicated that the RAIT could be administered remotely using screensharing and giving the examinee remote control of the mouse. The test is largely self-administered and formatted as multiple-choice items. The psychologist should proctor the examinee throughout the tele-assessment through videoconferencing. PAR instructs that the digital stimuli should be displayed to the examinee via screensharing using encrypted videoconferencing software. There are no physical manipulatives or response booklets.

Administering the RAIT via tele-assessment requires high quality video and an audio connection. Special administration considerations are listed by subtest in Rapid Reference 6.15. There are few to no demands on the examiner except to observe the examinee during testing.

≋Rapid Reference 6.15

RAIT Administration Considerations

Subtests	Administration Considerations
General Knowledge Odd Word Out Word Opposites Quantitative Knowledge Quantitative Reasoning	• Examinee reads stimuli on screen • Examinee should use mouse/cursor to select choices • Computer times subtest and stops examinee at subtest time limit
Nonverbal Analogies Sequences	• Examinee views picture stimuli on screen • Examinee can use mouse/cursor to select choices • Computer times subtest and stops examinee at subtest time limit

Reynolds Intellectual Assessment Scales, Second Edition, Remote (RIAS-2 Remote)

The evidence (direct and indirect) for equivalence of tele-assessment and face-to-face administration relevant to the Reynolds Intellectual Assessment Scales, Second Edition (RIAS-2; Reynolds, 2014) is reviewed in this section. Special administration considerations are discussed.

RIAS-2 Equivalence Evidence

A study was conducted to examine equivalence of the RIAS-2 in tele-assessment and face-to-face conditions for ages 3–19 (Wright, 2018a). Equivalence was supported for all subtests except for the Speeded Naming Test for ages 3–6, as well as for all composite scores except the Speeded Processing Index. Because equivalence of the Speeded Naming Test and the Speeded Processing Index were not supported, the speeded tasks are not included in the RIAS-2 Remote.

Because the RIAS-2 Remote and a two-subtest shorter form of the RIAS-2 (the Reynolds Intellectual Screening Test, Second Edition; RIST-2) can be used with examinees ages 3–94, and Wright's equivalence study only ranged from ages 3–19, a review of other tele-assessment equivalence studies with examinees of varied ages is helpful to inform interpretation. Rapid Reference 6.16 provides analysis of each subtest's input and output demands. It lists both direct and indirect evidence of equivalence for each task, along with the age ranges studied.

≡ Rapid Reference 6.16

RIAS-2 and RIST-2 Input and Output Demands and Equivalence Evidence

Subtest	Input	Output	Evidence[a] Citation: Task Abbreviation/ Ages
Guess What (also RIST-2) Verbal Reasoning	Brief spoken directions	Open ended, spoken response	**Direct evidence:** Wright, 2018a: GW, VR/3–19 **Indirect evidence:** Dekhtyar et al., 2020: CQ/26–75 Hildebrand et al., 2004: VC/60+ Hodge et al., 2019: SI, VC/8–12 Jacobsen et al., 2003: VC/adult Temple et al., 2010: VC/23–63 Turkstra et al., 2012: ABD, MDEP/21–69 Wright, 2018b: GI, OV/5–16 Wright, 2020b: SI, VC, IN, CO/6–16

(continued)

Subtest	Input	Output	Evidence[a] Citation: Task Abbreviation/ Ages
Odd-Item Out (also RIST-2) Nonverbal Memory	Brief spoken directions, color-critical, picture stimuli	Item-level time limit, multiple choice, pointing response with drawing tool	**Direct evidence:** Wright, 2018a: NM, OIO, WM/3–19 **Indirect evidence:** Dekhtyar et al., 2020: RPM/26–75 Hildebrand et al., 2004: MR/60+ Hodge et al., 2019: VP, MR, FW, PS/8–12 Sutherland et al., 2017: CFD, WC/8–12 Vahia et al., 2015: BVMT/65+ Vestal et al., 2006: ACWP/68–78 Waite et al., 2010: CFD/5–9 Wright, 2018b: CF, VZ/5–16 Wright, 2020b: FW, MR, PC, PS, VP/6–16
What's Missing	Brief spoken directions, gestured directions, picture stimuli	Item-level time limit, open ended, pointing response with drawing tool	**Direct evidence:** Wright, 2018a: WM/3–19 **Indirect evidence:** Dekhtyar et al., 2020: PD/26–75 Vestal et al., 2006: PD/68–78
Verbal Memory	Brief spoken directions	Spoken response	**Direct evidence:** Wright, 2018a: VM/3–19 **Indirect evidence:** Jacobsen et al., 2003: LM/adult (not equivalent) Stain et al., 2011: LM/14–27 Wright, 2018b: SR/5–16

[a]**Evidence column task abbreviations:** ABD = AphasiaBank discourse tasks, CF = Concept Formation, CFD = Concepts and Following Directions, CO = Comprehension, CQ = Conversational Questions, FW = Figure Weights, GI = General Information, GW = Guess What, IN = Information, LM = Logical Memory, MDEP = Mediated Discourse Elicitation Protocol, MR = Matrix Reasoning, NM = Nonverbal Memory, OIO = Odd-Item Out, OV = Oral Vocabulary, PC = Picture Concepts, PD = Picture Description, PS = Picture Span, RPM = Raven's Progressive Matrices, SI = Similarities, SR = Story Recall, VC = Vocabulary, VM = Verbal Memory, VP = Visual Puzzles, VR = Verbal Reasoning, VZ = Visualization, WM = What's Missing.

RIAS-2 Administration Considerations

Six subtests drawn from the RIAS-2 make up the RIAS-2 Remote. The RIST-2 also has a remote form, the RIST-2 Remote, that can be administered via tele-assessment.

The RIAS-2 downloadable e-stimulus book is provided in digital format. A downloadable e-stimulus book is available separately for the RIST-2. The RIAS-2 Remote record form is a paper-and-pencil form formatted to be used with the RIAS-2 Remote. A RIST-2 Remote record form is separately available. The RIAS-2/RIST-2 professional manual is the same manual included in the physical kit. PAR instructs that the digital stimuli should be displayed to the examinee via screensharing using encrypted videoconferencing software.

There are no physical manipulatives or response booklets for either version of the test. Therefore, there are no demands to manage materials. All RIAS-2 subtest and composite scores can be obtained except for the speeded subtests and the SPI.

Administering the RIAS-2 via tele-assessment requires high quality audio and video for most tasks. A headset with a microphone is recommended for both the examinee and examiner. Special administration considerations are listed by subtest in Rapid Reference 6.17.

≡Rapid Reference 6.17

RIAS-2 Remote Administration Considerations

Subtest	Administration Considerations
Guess Whata	Examiner presents items verbally
	Examinee responds verbally
Odd-Item Outa	Examiner uses stopwatch; examiner must ensure examinee stops at item time limit
	Items require pointing responses (via drawing tool) in remote e-stimulus book
	Examinee either responds verbally or points with drawing tool to stimuli on screen in remote e-stimulus book
Verbal Reasoning	Examiner presents items verbally
	Examinee responds verbally

(continued)

Subtest	Administration Considerations
What's Missing	Examiner uses stopwatch; examiner must ensure examinee stops at item time limit
	Examinee either responds verbally or points with drawing tool to stimuli on screen in remote e-stimulus book
Verbal Memory	Examiner presents items verbally
	Examinee responds verbally
Nonverbal Memory	Examiner uses stopwatch; examiner must ensure examinee stops at item time limit
	Items require pointing responses (via drawing tool) in remote e-stimulus book
	Examinee points with drawing tool to stimuli on screen

ªAlso a RIST-2 Remote subtest

Wechsler Abbreviated Scale of Intelligence, Second Edition (WASI-II)

The WASI-II equivalence evidence and subtest administration considerations are discussed in the Wechsler Intelligence Scales portion of this chapter. This section discusses the location of WASI-II digital stimuli, and composite score selection related to the need for physical materials in the examinee's location. Equivalence evidence, based on input and output demands, was presented earlier in this chapter alongside the other Wechsler scales.

WASI-II Administration Considerations
The WASI-II can be administered via Q-global. Blocks and a paper record form are still necessary, and paper components cannot be printed from Q-global. The WASI-II was not available on Q-interactive as of the time this book was written.

WASI-II Composite Score Selection Considerations
If available, the onsite professional can present the blocks for Block Design. Psychologists using this approach can obtain the typical composite scores that are available in face-to-face administrations. If an onsite professional is not used, Block Design is not feasible for tele-assessment. Omitting Block Design impacts the WASI-II composite scores that can be obtained.

If Vocabulary, Matrix Reasoning, and Similarities are administered, the VCI and the Full Scale IQ-2 subtest (which uses only Vocabulary and Matrix Reasoning) can be obtained. The PRI and the Full Scale IQ-4 subtest (which uses all four subtests) cannot be calculated. However, the information obtained from the WASI-II subtests can be supplemented with information from the WISC-V or the WAIS-IV to provide a composite measure of reasoning with tasks not requiring verbal output to expand the options, as follows.

For examinees aged 6–16, WISC-V Figure Weights may be administered, and the WASI-II (not the WISC-V) Matrix Reasoning score can be used with the WISC-V Figure Weights score to calculate the WISC-V FRI (Raiford, Zhou, & Drozdick, 2016). For examinees aged 16–90, the WASI-II (not the WAIS-IV) Matrix Reasoning score can be used with the WAIS-IV Visual Puzzles and either the WAIS-IV Figure Weights or Picture Completion score to calculate the WAIS-IV PRI (Zhou & Raiford, 2011). In both cases, you can obtain a VCI, a nonverbal measure of reasoning (i.e., either the FRI or the Perceptual Reasoning Index, depending on age), and a Full Scale IQ-2 Subtest (using just Vocabulary and Matrix Reasoning).

Rapid Reference 6.18 presents the composite score selection, which varies according to Block Design use and the age of the examinee.

≡Rapid Reference 6.18

WASI-II Composite Score Selection According to Block Design Use, by Age

	Full Administration	Without Block Design	
	Examinee Age		
	6–90	6–16	16–90
Composite Score		Composite Score Available?	
VCI	✓	✓	✓

(continued)

	Full Administration	Without Block Design	
Perceptual Reasoning Index	✓	• Convert WASI-II Matrix Reasoning to scaled score using WASI-II Table A.2 • Administer WISC-V Figure Weights • Sum the WASI-II Matrix Reasoning and WISC-V Figure Weights scaled scores • Convert the sum of scaled scores to the WISC-V FRI using WISC-V Table A.4	• Convert WASI-II Matrix Reasoning to scaled score using WASI-II Table A.2 • Administer WAIS-IV Visual Puzzles and either Picture Completion or Figure Weights • Sum the WASI-II Matrix Reasoning, WAIS-IV Visual Puzzles, and WAIS-IV (either Picture Completion or Figure Weights) scaled scores • Convert that sum of scaled scores to the WAIS-IV PRI using WAIS-IV Table A.4
Full Scale IQ-2 Subtest	✓	Yes	Yes
Full Scale IQ-4 Subtest	✓	No	No

TELE-ASSESSMENT WITH NONVERBAL INTELLIGENCE TESTS

CTONI-2, TONI-4, and PTONI

The evidence for equivalence of tele-assessment and face-to-face administration relevant to the Comprehensive Test of Nonverbal Intelligence, Second Edition (CTONI-2; Hammill, Pearson, & Wiederholt, 2009), the Test of Nonverbal Intelligence, Fourth Edition (TONI-4; Brown, Sherbenou, & Johnsen, 2010), and the Primary Test of Nonverbal Intelligence (PTONI; Ehrler & McGhee, 2008) are reviewed in this section. These three tests are not a suite of tests by the same author, but they have very similar input and output demands and hail from the same publisher, so they are grouped to avoid repetitiveness. Special administration considerations are discussed.

CTONI-2, TONI-4, and PTONI Equivalence Evidence

There have been no direct studies on these tests and tele-assessment; however, the basic input and output demands of the tasks have support. Rapid Reference 6.19 provides analysis of the input and output demands and lists relevant indirect evidence by age range.

≋ Rapid Reference 6.19

CTONI-2, TONI-4, and PTONI Input and Output Demands and Equivalence Evidence

Tests	Input	Output	Evidence[a] Citation: Task Abbreviation/Ages
TONI-4 PTONI CTONI-2	Brief spoken directions, color-critical items, gestured directions, picture stimuli	Multiple choice, pointing response	**Indirect evidence:** Dekhtyar et al., 2020: RPM/26–75 Hildebrand et al., 2004: MR/60+ Hodge et al., 2019: VP, MR, FW, PS/8–12 Sutherland et al., 2017: CFD, WC/8–12 Vahia et al., 2015: BVMT/65+ Vestal et al., 2006: ACWP/68–78 Waite et al., 2010: CFD/5–9 Wright, 2018a: NM, OIO, WM/3–19 Wright, 2018b: CF, PCO, VZ/5–16 Wright, 2020b: VP, MR, FW, PC, PS/6–16

[a]**Evidence column task abbreviations:** BVMT = Brief Visuospatial Memory Test, CF = Concept Formation, CFD = Concepts and Following Directions, FW = Figure Weights, MR = Matrix Reasoning, NM = Nonverbal Memory, OIO = Odd-Item Out, PC = Picture Concepts, PS = Picture Span, RPM = Raven's Progressive Matrices, VP = Visual Puzzles, VZ = Visualization, WC = Word Classes, WM = What's Missing.

C-TONI-2, TONI-4, and PTONI Administration Considerations

These tests can be administered via tele-assessment using virtual components of the test which are available from the test's publisher, Pro-Ed, and delivered by RedShelf. Pro-Ed instructs that the digital stimuli should be displayed to the examinee via screensharing using encrypted videoconferencing software.

There are no physical manipulatives or response booklets for any of these tests. Therefore, there are no demands for materials in the examinee's location.

Administering the CTONI-2, TONI-4, or the PTONI via tele-assessment requires high quality audio and video. A headset with a microphone is recommended for both the examinee and examiner. Special administration considerations are listed in Rapid Reference 6.20.

≡ Rapid Reference 6.20

CTONI-2, TONI-4, and PTONI Administration Considerations

Administration Considerations

- Examiner uses mouse/cursor to point to stimuli on screen
- Examinee can use mouse/cursor to point at choices
- *Optional* (preferred for very young children): Peripheral camera/device can be placed in stable position that shows examinee's screen and provides a view of choices made nonverbally (e.g., pointing)

Universal Nonverbal Intelligence Test, Second Edition (UNIT2)

The evidence and administration considerations for the Universal Nonverbal Intelligence Test, Second Edition (UNIT2; Bracken & McCallum, 2016) are discussed in this section. Subtest selection and composite score adaptations related to the need for physical materials in the examinee's location are also discussed.

UNIT2 Equivalence Evidence

There have been no direct studies on the UNIT2 and tele-assessment; however, the basic input and output demands of the tasks have support. Rapid Reference 6.21 provides analysis of the input and output demands and lists relevant indirect evidence by age range.

UNIT2 Administration Considerations

The UNIT2 can be administered via tele-assessment using virtual components of the test, which are available from the test's publisher, Pro-Ed, delivered by RedShelf. Pro-Ed instructs that the digital stimuli should be displayed to the examinee via screensharing using encrypted videoconferencing software.

≡Rapid Reference 6.21

••

UNIT2 Input and Output Demands and Equivalence Evidence

Subtests	Input	Output	Evidence[a] Citation: Task Abbreviation/Ages
Analogic Reasoning Nonsymbolic Quantity Numerical Series Younger Items for: • Cube Design • Spatial Memory • Symbolic Memory	Gestured directions *All subtests except Numerical Series:* Picture stimuli *Numerical Series:* Letters digits or symbols in print *Memory tasks:* Timed presentation	Multiple choice, pointing response	**Indirect evidence:** Dekhtyar et al., 2020: RPM/26–75 Hildebrand et al., 2004: MR/60+ Hodge et al., 2019: VP, MR, FW, PS/8–12 Vahia et al., 2015: BVMT/65+ Waite et al., 2010: CFD/5–9 Wright, 2018a: NM, OIO, WM/3–19 Wright, 2018b: CF, NS, VZ/5–16 Wright, 2020b: VP, MR, FW, PC, PS/6–16
Older Items for: • Cube Design • Spatial Memory • Symbolic Memory	Gestured directions, motor demonstration, physical manipulatives, picture stimuli *Memory Tasks:* Timed presentation	Fine motor response Cube Design: Item-level time limit	**Indirect evidence:** Dekhtyar et al., 2020: BD/26–75 Hodge et al., 2019: BD/8–12 Jacobsen et al., 2003: BD, GP/ adult Temple et al., 2010: BD/23–63 Vestal et al., 2006: TKT/68–78 Wright, 2020b: BD/6–16

[a]Evidence column task abbreviations: BD = Block Design, BVMT = Brief Visuospatial Memory Test, CF = Concept Formation, CFD = Concepts and Following Directions, FW = Figure Weights, GP = Grooved Pegboard, MR = Matrix Reasoning, NM = Nonverbal Memory, NS = Number Series, OIO = Odd-Item Out, PC = Picture Concepts, PS = Picture Span, RPM = Raven's Progressive Matrices, TKT = Token Test, VP = Visual Puzzles, VZ = Visualization, WM = What's Missing.

Administering the UNIT2 via tele-assessment requires high quality audio and video. A headset with a microphone is recommended for both the examinee and examiner. Special administration considerations are listed in Rapid Reference 6.22.

≡ Rapid Reference 6.22

UNIT2 Administration Considerations

Subtests	Administration Considerations
Analogic Reasoning Nonsymbolic Quantity Numerical Series Earlier Items for: • Cube Design • Spatial Memory • Symbolic Memory	• Examiner uses mouse/cursor to point to stimuli on screen • Examinee can use mouse/cursor to point at choices • Optional: Peripheral camera/device can be placed in stable position that shows examinee's screen and provides a view of choices made nonverbally (e.g., pointing)
Later Items for: • Cube Design • Spatial Memory • Symbolic Memory	• Onsite professional should assist with administration of these subtests • Train new onsite professionals until presentation of manipulatives during instructions and items is performed according to administration directions • Do not allow non-professionals to present manipulative stimuli or attempt to have examinee present their own stimuli • Examiner uses stopwatch to time stimuli presentation or to stop examinee at item time limit • Examiner uses mouse/cursor to gesture or point to stimuli on screen • Onsite professional should manipulate cubes, chips, and cards and be trained to provide gestured instructions as eye contact while moving or gesturing to physical stimuli is required • Peripheral camera/device should be placed in a stable position to show examinee's responses (i.e., constructions, card placements)

UNIT2 Composite Score Selection Considerations

If available, an onsite professional can present the manipulatives (blocks and response mat for Cube Design, chips and grid for Spatial Memory, and cards for Symbolic Memory). Psychologists using this approach can obtain the typical composite scores that are available in face-to-face administrations.

If an onsite professional is not used, Cube Design, Spatial Memory, and Symbolic Memory are not feasible for tele-assessment. If these three subtests are omitted, only the Abbreviated Battery IQ and the Quantitative composite can be obtained.

Rapid Reference 6.23 presents the composite score selection, which varies according to manipulative use.

≡Rapid Reference 6.23

UNIT2 Composite Score Selection According to Manipulative Use

	Full Administration	Without Manipulatives
Composite Score	Composite Score Available?	
Memory	✓	No
Reasoning	✓	No
Quantitative	✓	✓
Abbreviated Battery IQ	✓	✓
Standard Battery IQ with Memory	✓	No
Standard Battery IQ	✓	No
Full Scale Battery IQ	✓	No

TELE-ASSESSMENT WITH MEMORY TESTS

California Verbal Learning Test, Third Edition (CVLT-3) and CVLT Children's Version (CVLT-C)

The evidence and administration considerations for the California Verbal Learning Test, Third Edition (CVLT-3; Delis, Kramer, Kaplan, & Ober, 2017) and CVLT Children's Version (CVLT-C; Delis, Kramer, Kaplan, & Ober, 1994) are discussed in this section.

CVLT-3 and CVLT-C Equivalence Evidence

Rapid Reference 6.24 provides analysis of the input and output demands. It also lists both direct and indirect evidence of equivalence, along with the age ranges studied. Because the tests can be administered to a broad age range and the direct evidence only covers ages 18–69 from a specific clinical population, a review of other tele-assessment equivalence studies with examinees of varied ages is helpful to inform interpretation.

≋ Rapid Reference 6.24

CVLT-3 and CVLT-C Input and Output Demands and Equivalence Evidence

Input	Output	Evidence[a] Citation: Task Abbreviation/Ages
Brief spoken directions, spoken stimuli	Open ended, spoken response	**Direct evidence:** Barcellos et al., 2017: CVLT/18–69 **Indirect evidence:** Brearly et al., 2017: LL/Adult Cullum et al., 2006: HVLT/51–84 (not equivalent) Cullum et al., 2014: HVLT/46–90 (not equivalent) Galusha-Glasscock et al., 2016: LL, LR, LRg Hildebrand et al., 2004: RAVLT/60+ Vahia et al., 2015: HVLT/65+

Note. Digital/paper format equivalence evidence is also available for the CVLT–II (Daniel, 2012c).

[a]**Evidence column task abbreviations:** CVLT = California Verbal Learning Test, HVLT = Hopkins Verbal Learning Test, LL = List Learning, LR = List Recall, LRg = List Recognition, RAVLT = Rey Auditory Verbal Learning Test.

CVLT-3 and CVLT-C Administration Considerations

These tests can be administered via tele-assessment using paper materials, Q-global, and Q-interactive. If an examiner has a paper manual and paper record form, these tasks can be administered via videoconferencing. There is no need to access digital stimuli in this case.

Administering these tests via tele-assessment requires high quality audio. A headset with a microphone is recommended for both the examinee and examiner. The only special tele-assessment consideration concerns repetition of items. Do not repeat any stimuli unless they were not heard due to technical problems; however, some item types (e.g., recognition or cued) allow repetition according to the manuals.

Test of Memory Malingering (TOMM)

The evidence for equivalence of tele-assessment and face-to-face administration relevant to the Test of Memory Malingering (TOMM; Tombaugh, 1996) is reviewed in this section. Special administration considerations are discussed.

TOMM Equivalence Evidence

There have been no direct studies on the TOMM and tele-assessment; however, the basic input and output demands of the task have support. Rapid Reference 6.25 provides analysis of the input and output demands and lists relevant indirect evidence by age range.

≋ Rapid Reference 6.25

TOMM Input and Output Demands and Equivalence Evidence

Input	Output	Evidence[a] Citation: Task Abbreviation/ Ages
Brief spoken directions, picture stimuli, timed presentation	Multiple choice, spoken response	Dekhtyar et al., 2020/26–75, RPM
		Hildebrand et al., 2004/60+, MR
		Hodge et al., 2019/8–12, MR
		Wright 2018a/3–19, NM
		Wright 2020a/6–16, MR, PS

[a]**Evidence column task abbreviations:** MR = Matrix Reasoning, NM = Nonverbal Memory, PS = Picture Span, RPM = Raven's Progressive Matrices.

TOMM Administration Considerations

During the COVID-19 crisis, MHS gave permission to lay the TOMM physical stimulus book flat and display the stimuli on a document camera, or to position the stimulus book on an easel and display it on a web camera. We strongly recommend the former method (use of a document camera) rather than placing the stimulus book in front of a web camera, whenever possible, for higher quality visual stimuli. Using either of these methods, the test can be administered and scored as usual.

High quality audio and video is required. A headset with a microphone is recommended for both the examinee and examiner. Special administration considerations are listed in Rapid 6.26Reference.

≡Rapid Reference 6.26

TOMM Administration Considerations

Administration Considerations

- Requires examiner to have access to test directions through the manual
- During the COVID-19 crisis, MHS gave permission to lay physical stimulus book flat and display stimuli on a document camera, or to position stimulus book on an easel and display it on web camera. Ensure that permission remains in place at https://info.mhs.com/remote-tomm
- Do not share stimuli on camera when stimulus book cover is closed to ensure examinee cannot view test name or acronym at any time
- Scan area around examinee with camera to ensure no one else is present in room
- Seat examinee with their back to a closed door to ensure no one can enter room undetected
- Examinee should keep hands visible to protect from compromising test security and results (e.g., screen recording, pictures, recording)
- Examinee should verbally state number that corresponds to selected response so examiner can record it
- Alter verbal instructions to say "Tell me which picture I showed you before. Was it this one (point to top picture) or this one (point to bottom picture)?"

Wechsler Memory Scale, Fourth Edition (WMS-IV)

This section reviews the Wechsler Memory Scale, Fourth Edition (WMS-IV, Wechsler, 2009) evidence (direct and indirect) for equivalence of tele-assessment and face-to-face administration. Special administration considerations are discussed, as well as composite score selection, which varies related to the need for physical materials in examinee's location.

WMS-IV Equivalence Evidence

Because the WMS-IV age range is broad and the direct evidence only covered one of the tasks for a selective age range, a review of other tele-assessment equivalence studies with similar tasks and examinees of varied ages is helpful to inform interpretation. Rapid Reference 6.27 provides analysis of each subtest's input and output demands. It also lists both direct and indirect evidence of equivalence for each task, along with the age ranges studied.

≡ Rapid Reference 6.27

WMS-IV Input and Output Demands and Equivalence Evidence

Subtest(s)	Input	Output	Evidence[a] Citation: Task Abbreviation/ Ages
Brief Cognitive Status Exam	Brief spoken directions, gestured directions, picture stimuli, response booklet, spoken stimulus	Brief spoken response, open ended, task-level time limit, written or fine motor response	**Indirect evidence:** Brearly et al., 2017: MMSE/Adult Cullum et al., 2006: MMSE/51–84 Cullum et al., 2014: MMSE/46–90 Dekhtyar et al., 2020: CQ/26–75 Grosch et al., 2015: MMSE/67–85 Hildebrand et al., 2004: VC/60+ Hodge et al., 2019: SI, VC/8–12 Jacobsen et al., 2003: VC/adult Temple et al., 2010: VC/23–63 Turkstra et al., 2012: MDEP, ABD/21–69 Vahia et al., 2015: MMSE/65+ Wadsworth et al., 2018: MMSE/older adult Wright, 2018a: GW, VR/3–19 Wright, 2018b: OV, GI/5–16 Wright, 2020b: SI, VC, IN, CO/6–16

(continued)

Subtest(s)	Input	Output	Evidence[a] Citation: Task Abbreviation/ Ages
Designs I Designs II Spatial Addition	Brief spoken directions, gestured directions, motor demonstration, physical manipulatives, timed presentation	Fine motor response	**Indirect evidence:** Dekhtyar et al., 2020: BD/26–75 Hodge et al., 2019: BD/8–12 Jacobsen et al., 2003: BD, GP/adult Temple et al., 2010: BD/23–63 Vestal et al., 2006: TKT/68–78 Wright, 2018a: NM/3–19 Wright, 2020b: BD/6–16
Logical Memory I Logical Memory II	Brief spoken directions, spoken stimuli	Open ended, spoken response	**Direct evidence:** Jacobsen et al., 2003: LM/adult (not equivalent) Stain et al., 2011: LM/14–27 Indirect evidence: Galusha-Glasscock et al., 2016: SM/58–84 Wright, 2018a: VM/3–19 Wright, 2018b: SR/5–16
Verbal Paired Associates I Verbal Paired Associates II	Brief spoken directions, spoken stimuli	Brief spoken response, item-level time limit, open ended	**Indirect evidence:** Barcellos et al., 2017: CVLT/18–69 Brearly et al., 2017: LL/Adult Cullum et al., 2006: HVLT/51–84 (not equivalent) Cullum et al., 2014: HVLT/46–90 (not equivalent) Galusha-Glasscock et al., 2016: LL, LR, LRg/58–84 Hildebrand et al., 2004: RAVLT/60+ Vahia et al., 2015: HVLT/65+

Subtest(s)	Input	Output	Evidence[a] Citation: Task Abbreviation/ Ages
Symbol Span	Brief spoken directions, gestured directions, letters digits or symbols in print, timed presentation	Multiple choice, pointing or brief spoken response	**Indirect evidence:** Dekhtyar et al., 2020: RPM/26–75 Hildebrand et al., 2004: MR/60+ Hodge et al., 2019: VP, MR, FW, PS/8–12 Sutherland et al., 2017: CFD, WC/8–12 Vahia et al., 2015: BVMT/65+ Vestal et al., 2006: ACWP/68–78 Waite et al., 2010: CFD/5–9 Wright, 2018a: NM, OIO, WM/3–19 Wright, 2018b: CF, VZ/5–16 Wright, 2020b: VP, MR, FW, PC, PS/6–16
Visual Reproduction I Visual Reproduction II	Brief spoken directions, gestured directions, letters digits or symbols in print, response booklet *Immediate:* Timed presentation	Task-level time limit, written response	**Indirect evidence:** Dekhtyar et al., 2020: DR/26–75 Galusha-Glasscock et al., 2016: FD, FR/58–84 Hodge et al., 2019: CD, SS/8–12 Jacobsen et al., 2003: SDMT/adult Temple et al., 2010: BVMI/23–63 Vahia et al., 2015: BVMT/65+ Wright, 2018b: LPM, MFF/5–16 Wright, 2020b: CD, SS, CA/6–16

Note. Digital/paper format equivalence evidence is also available for the WMS-IV (Daniel, 2013b).

[a]Evidence column task abbreviations: ABD = AphasiaBank discourse tasks, BD = Block Design, BVMI = Beery Buktenica Developmental Test of Visual Motor Integration, BVMT = Brief Visuospatial Memory Test, CA = Cancellation, CD = Coding, CF = Concept Formation, CFD = Concepts and Following Directions, CO = Comprehension, CQ = Conversational Questions, CVLT = California Verbal Learning Test, DR = Drawing, FR = Figure Recall, FS = Formulated Sentences, FW = Figure Weights, GI = General Information, GP = Grooved Pegboard, GW = Guess What, HVLT = Hopkins Verbal Learning Test, IN = Information, LL = List Learning, LM = Logical Memory, LPM = Letter–Pattern Matching, LR = List Recall, LRg = List Recognition, MDEP = Mediated Discourse Elicitation Protocol, MFF = Math Facts Fluency, MR = Matrix Reasoning, NM = Nonverbal Memory, OIO = Odd-Item Out, OV = Oral Vocabulary, PC = Picture Concepts, PS = Picture Span, RAVLT = Rey Auditory Verbal Learning Test, RPM = Raven's Progressive Matrices, SDMT = Symbol Digit Modalities Test, SI = Similarities, SM = Story Memory, SR = Story Recall, SS = Symbol Search, TKT = Token Test, VC = Vocabulary, VM = Verbal Memory, VP = Visual Puzzles, VR = Verbal Reasoning, VZ = Visualization, WM = What's Missing.

WMS-IV Administration Considerations

The WMS-IV can be administered via tele-assessment using Q-global or Q-interactive. Physical manipulatives and paper response booklets are necessary regardless of which platform is used. A paper record form is necessary with Q-global.

Administering the WMS-IV via tele-assessment requires high quality audio and video for nearly all tasks. A headset with a microphone is recommended for both the examinee and examiner. Special administration considerations are listed by subtest in Rapid Reference 6.28.

≣Rapid Reference 6.28

WMS-IV Administration Considerations

Subtest(s)	Administration Considerations
Brief Cognitive Status Exam	• Ensure any analog clocks are removed from examinee's view • Examiner uses stopwatch and stops examinee at task time limit • Peripheral camera/device should be placed in a stable position that provides examiner a view of examinee's clock drawing
Logical Memory I Logical Memory II Verbal Paired Associates I Verbal Paired Associates II	• Do not repeat any item unless it was not heard due to technical problems, unless permitted in manual (i.e., recognition items)
Designs I Designs II Spatial Addition	• Onsite professional should assist with administration of these subtests • Train new onsite professionals until presentation of manipulatives during instructions and items is performed according to directions in Administration and Scoring Manual • Do not allow non-professionals to present manipulative stimuli nor attempt to have examinee set up or present their own stimuli • Onsite professional presents stimuli while *examiner* provides all verbal instructions

Subtest(s)	Administration Considerations
	• Examiner or facilitator can use stopwatch and time stimulus exposure; ensure lags in connectivity do not influence length of exposure time • Peripheral camera/device should be placed in a stable position to show examinee's card placements in grid • Requires a print stimulus book in examinee's location or digital stimulus book on a tablet • Stimuli should lay flat on table, not presented on vertical screen (impact of vertical presentation is unknown) • Train onsite professional to present stimuli facing correct direction, as items easily become rotated 180° • Do not allow examinee to rotate stimuli
Symbol Span	• Examiner uses mouse/cursor to point to stimuli on screen • Multiple choice item instructions may be altered to ask examinee to say number(s) or letter(s) of response to clarify if necessary • It is not recommended to allow examinee to use mouse/cursor to point at choices as intended responses cannot always be clearly determined • *Optional:* Peripheral camera/device can be placed in stable position that shows examinee's screen and provides a view of choices made nonverbally (e.g., pointing) • Examiner uses stopwatch to time stimuli exposure; ensure lags in connectivity do not influence length of exposure time
Visual Reproduction I Visual Reproduction II	• Peripheral camera/device should be placed in a stable position that shows examinee's response booklet and provides examiner a view of examinee's written responses • Examiner points to stimuli on screen • It may be helpful to have a printed copy of response booklet in examiner's location in order to help examinee find correct page if necessary

WMS-IV Score Selection Considerations

If available, the onsite professional can present the Designs and Spatial Addition cards and grids. Psychologists using this approach can obtain the typical composite scores that are available in face-to-face administrations.

If an onsite professional is not available, Designs and Spatial Addition are not feasible for tele-assessment. This impacts the session workflow and composite score selection.

Specifically, for anyone under the age of 70, composite scores that do not use Designs or Spatial Addition can be derived using different sets of WMS-IV subtests as shown in the WMS-IV Flexible Approach (Wechsler, 2009). These are the same sets of subtests typically used for composite scores for older adult examinees aged 70–90 for the Immediate Memory Index, Delayed Memory Index, Auditory Memory Index (AMI), and Visual Memory Index (VMI). The only composite score which cannot be obtained is the Visual WMI.

If response booklets are not used, the composite score options are limited to the AMI. Rapid Reference 6.29 presents the composite score selection, which varies according to manipulative and response booklet use and battery used (i.e., adult or older adult).

TELE-ASSESSMENT WITH NEUROPSYCHOLOGICAL TESTS

Bender Visual Motor Gestalt Test, Second Edition

This section reviews the Bender Visual Motor Gestalt Test, Second Edition (Bender-Gestalt; Brannigan & Decker, 2003) evidence for equivalence of tele-assessment and face-to-face administration. Special administration considerations are discussed.

Bender-Gestalt Equivalence Evidence
There have been no direct studies on the Bender-Gestalt and tele-assessment; however, the basic input and output demands of the task have support. Rapid Reference 6.30 provides analysis of the input and output demands and lists relevant indirect evidence by age range.

Rapid Reference 6.29

WMS-IV Composite Score Selection According to Manipulative and Response Booklet Use, by Battery

Composite Score	Full Administration		No Manipulatives		No Manipulatives or Response Booklets	
	Adult	Older Adult	Adult	Older Adult	Adult	Older Adult
			Typical Composite Score Available?			
Immediate Memory Index	✓	✓	No, use WMS-IV Flex approach (Logical Memory I + Visual Reproduction I)	✓	No	No
Delayed Memory Index	✓	✓	No, use WMS-IV Flex approach (Logical Memory II + Visual Reproduction II)	✓	No	No
AMI	✓	✓	✓	✓	✓	✓
VMI	✓	✓	No, use WMS-IV Flex approach (Visual Reproduction I + II)	✓	No	No
Visual WMI	✓		No		No	

≝Rapid Reference 6.30

Bender-Gestalt Input and Output Demands and Equivalence Evidence

Input	Output	Evidence[a] Citation: Task Abbreviation/Ages
Brief spoken directions, physical manipulatives, picture stimuli	Written response	**Indirect evidence:** Dekhtyar et al., 2020: DR/26–75 Galusha-Glasscock et al., 2016: FC, FR/58–84 Temple et al., 2010: BVMI/23–63 Vahia et al., 2015: BVMT/65+

[a]**Evidence column task abbreviations:** BVMI = Beery Buktenica Developmental Test of Visual Motor Integration, BVMT = Brief Visuospatial Memory Test, DR = Drawing, FC = Figure Copy, FR = Figure Recall.

Bender-Gestalt Administration Considerations

The Bender-Gestalt can be administered via tele-assessment with the help of an onsite professional, like the methodology used for many other tests with manipulative materials previously discussed in this chapter (see Rapid Reference 6.31 for administrative considerations). In this situation, the cards are presented by the onsite professional, while the psychologist gives instructions via video conferencing.

≝Rapid Reference 6.31

Bender-Gestalt Administration Considerations

Administration Considerations

- Onsite professional should assist with administration
- Onsite professional presents cards while examiner provides all verbal instructions
- Peripheral camera/device should be placed in stable position to show examinee's written responses

Conners Continuous Performance Tests (Conners CPTs)

The Conners suite of CPTs includes the Conners Kiddie Continuous Performance Test, Second Edition (Conners K-CPT 2; Conners, 2015), the Conners Continuous Performance Test, Third Edition (Conners CPT 3; Conners, 2008), and the Conners Continuous Auditory Test of Attention (Conners CATA; Conners, 2014). The publisher of the Conners suite of CPTs, Multihealth Systems (MHS), notes that these tests are *not appropriate for remote videoconferencing administration*. This is because the precise millisecond reaction time required for these tasks could be impacted by internet variability and speed. MHS is developing an online version of the CPT 3 that can be accessed online that would capture the reaction time responses locally. Psychologists should check the MHS website to see if those have been made available.

For these reasons, in order to administer the Conners CPTs via tele-assessment, an onsite professional must be available and trained to do so. In this case, the onsite professional should be trained in all aspects of administering the tests as usual. The psychologist can observe the examinee's behaviors through a webcam placed in a stable position behind the examinee. Teleconferencing platforms should not be active on the computer the examinee is using to take the current versions of the Conners CPT.

> ### CAUTION
> Many CPT tasks are not appropriate for remote administration because the capture of precise millisecond reaction time required for these tasks could be impacted by internet variability and speed. Reaction times must be captured on a local computer. One exception, the IVA-2, is discussed later in this section.

Delis–Kaplan Executive Function System (D–KEFS)

This section reviews the Delis–Kaplan Executive Function System (D–KEFS; Delis, Kaplan, & Kramer, 2001) evidence for equivalence of tele-assessment and face-to-face administration. Special administration considerations are discussed.

D–KEFS Equivalence Evidence

There have been no direct studies on the D–KEFS and tele-assessment; however, the basic input and output demands of the tasks have support. Rapid Reference 6.32 provides analysis of the input and output demands and lists relevant indirect evidence by age range.

Rapid Reference 6.32

D-KEFS Input and Output Demands and Equivalence Evidence

Test	Input	Output	Evidence[a] Citation: Task Abbreviation/Ages
Trail Making Design Fluency	Gestured directions, response booklet, spoken directions *Design Fluency:* Letters digits or symbols in print	Item-level time limit, simple written response	**Indirect evidence:** Galusha-Glasscock et al., 2016: CD/58–84 Hodge et al., 2019: CD, SS/8–12 Jacobsen et al., 2003: SDMT/adult Wright, 2018a: SPS/3–19 Wright, 2018b: LPM, MFF/5–16 Wright, 2020b: CD, SS, CA/6–16
Verbal Fluency	Brief spoken directions	Open ended, spoken response, task-level time limit	**Indirect evidence:** Brearly et al., 2017: SF/adult Dekhtyar et al., 2020: VVF/26–75 Galusha-Glasscock et al., 2016: SF/58–84 Hildebrand et al., 2004: CWAT/60+ Stain et al., 2011: CWAT/14–27 Wright, 2018b: PP/5–16

Color–Word Interference	Brief spoken directions, color-critical items, gestured directions, picture stimuli, words in print	Item-level time limit, open ended, spoken response	**Indirect evidence:** Wright, 2018a: SNT/7–19
Sorting	Brief spoken directions, motor demonstration, physical manipulatives, picture stimuli, words in print	Fine motor response, item-level time limit	**Indirect evidence:** Dekhtyar et al., 2020: BD/26–75 Hodge et al., 2019: BD/8–12 Jacobsen et al., 2003: BD, GP/adult Temple et al., 2010: BD/23–63 Vestal et al., 2006: TKT/68–78 Wright, 2020b: BD/6–16
Twenty Questions	Brief spoken directions, picture stimuli, spoken stimuli	Multiple choice, pointing or brief spoken response	**Indirect evidence:** Brearly et al., 2017: BNT/adult Cullum et al., 2006: BNT/51–84 Cullum et al., 2014: BNT/46–90 Dekhtyar et al., 2020: PD/26–75 Galusha-Glasscock et al., 2016: PN/58–84 Vestal et al., 2006: BNT, PD/68–78 Wadsworth et al., 2018: BNT/adult Waite et al., 2010: FS, WS/5–9

Test	Input	Output	Evidence[a] Citation: Task Abbreviation/Ages
Word Context Proverb	Spoken directions, spoken stimuli, words in print	Open ended, spoken response	**Indirect evidence:** Dekhtyar et al., 2020: CQ/26–75 Hildebrand et al., 2004: VC/60+ Hodge et al., 2019: SI, VC/8–12 Jacobsen et al., 2003: VC/adult Temple et al., 2010: VC/23–63 Turkstra et al., 2012: ABD, MDEP/21–69 Wright, 2018a: GW, VR/3–19 Wright, 2018b: OV, GI/5–16 Wright, 2020b: SI, VC, IN, CO/6–16
Tower	Gestured directions, motor demonstration, physical manipulatives, picture stimuli, spoken directions, words in print	Item-level time limit, fine motor response	**Indirect evidence:** Dekhtyar et al., 2020: BD/26–75 Hodge et al., 2019: BD/8–12 Jacobsen et al., 2003: BD, GP/adult Temple et al., 2010: BD/23–63 Vestal et al., 2006: TKT/68–78 Wright, 2020b: BD/6–16

Note. Digital/paper format equivalence evidence is also available for the D-KEFS (Daniel, 2012c).

[a]Evidence column task abbreviations: ABD = AphasiaBank discourse tasks; BD = Block Design; BNT = Boston Naming Test; CD = Coding; CO = Comprehension; CQ = Conversational Questions; CWAT = Controlled Word Association Test; FS = Formulated Sentences; GI = General Information; GP = Grooved Pegboard; GW = Guess What; IN = Information; LPM = Letter–Pattern Matching; MDEP = Mediated Discourse Elicitation Protocol; MFF = Math Facts Fluency; OV = Oral Vocabulary; PD = Picture Description; PP = Phonological Processing; SDMT = Symbol Digit Modalities Test; SF = Semantic Fluency; SI = Similarities; SNT = Speeded Naming Task; SPS = Speeded Picture Search; SS = Symbol Search; TKT = Token Test; VC = ocabulary; VR = Verbal Reasoning; WS = Word Structure.

D–KEFS Administration Considerations

The D–KEFS can be administered via tele-assessment in multiple ways. There are two platforms where the digital stimuli are available: Q-global and Q-interactive. Only a subset of the D–KEFS tasks are available on Q-interactive. Physical manipulatives (e.g., tower, cards) and response booklets are necessary. For Q-global, a paper record form is also necessary.

Administering the D–KEFS via tele-assessment requires high quality audio and video for nearly all tasks. A headset with a microphone is recommended for both the examinee and examiner. Special administration considerations are listed by test in Rapid Reference 6.33.

≡ Rapid Reference 6.33

D–KEFS Administration Considerations

Test	Administration Considerations
Trail Making Design Fluency	• Examiner should complete Design Fluency practice boxes and Trails demonstrations in examinee's response booklet prior to sending • Peripheral camera/device must be placed in a stable position that shows examinee's response booklets and provides examiner a view of examinee's written responses to allow feedback to be given in real time • Printed copies of response booklets in examiner's location needed in order to show on camera drawing demonstrations as outlined in test directions • Examiner uses stopwatch and must ensure examinee stops at task time limit • Ensure response booklet is opened only to correct page when directed
Verbal Fluency	• Examiner uses stopwatch or timer
Color–Word Interference	• Requires high quality audio and video for examinee and examiner • Examiner points to stimuli on screen • Examiner uses stopwatch and stops examinee at time limit

(continued)

Test	Administration Considerations
Sorting	• Onsite professional should assist with administration • Train new onsite professionals until presentation of cards during instructions and items is performed according to directions in manual • Do not allow non-professionals to present cards or record results nor attempt to have examinee present their own cards or record results • Onsite professional presents stimuli while examiner provides all verbal instructions • Peripheral camera/device should be placed in a stable position to show examinee's responses
Twenty Questions	• Examiner uses mouse/cursor to point to stimuli on screen • Examinee can say name of object or use mouse/cursor to point at choices • Optional: Peripheral camera/device can be placed in stable position that shows examinee's screen and provides a view of choices made nonverbally (e.g., pointing)
Word Context	• Items 1, 4, 7, and 10 may elicit pointing or gestured responses if examinee is in home environment; ask examinee to say answer using words
Tower	• Onsite professional should assist with administration of this task • Train new onsite professionals until presentation of manipulatives (base, disks) during instructions and items is performed according to directions • Do not allow non-professionals to present manipulatives nor attempt to have examinee present their own manipulatives • Onsite professional presents stimuli while *examiner* provides all verbal instructions • Examiner uses mouse/cursor to point to stimuli on screen • Examiner uses stopwatch and stops examinee at item time limit • Peripheral camera/device should be placed in a stable position to show examinee's responses
Proverb	Examiner displays and reads stimuli on screen

If available, the onsite professional can present manipulatives and response booklets. Psychologists using this approach can administer all tests that are available in face-to-face administrations.

If an onsite professional is not available, Tower is not feasible for tele-assessment. However, each test is independent, so this doesn't reduce or affect composite scores.

IVA-2

The Integrated Visual and Auditory Continuous Performance Test, Second Edition (IVA-2; Sandford & Sandford, 2015) *can be administered remotely.* This is because the precise millisecond reaction time required for these tasks is captured at the examinee's location on a computer or Apple device (e.g., iPad Air, iPad Mini, iPad Pro, or iPhone) and transmitted back to the psychologist. Therefore, the internet variability and speed do not impact the accuracy of the data.

In order to administer the IVA-2 via tele-assessment, the psychologist must purchase a remote license from the test publisher, BrainTrain. Only one test can be run at a time. The computer or Apple device in the examinee's location must have the Chrome browser installed.

The examiner instructs the examinee or another onsite individual in how to download the software to the computer or device in the examinee's location. Next, the examiner provides a test code and password so the examinee can log in and take the test. Teleconferencing software must include high speed connectivity, audio, and video, and the examiner must observe the administration.

If the examinee is taking the test on a computer, the mouse may be wireless or wired. A wired mouse is recommended.

If the examinee is taking the test on an Apple device, a separate license is necessary. The examinee must have a small wired speaker, ear buds, or headphones. The examinee must not use wireless devices to convey sound.

Special administration considerations are listed in Rapid Reference 6.34.

≡Rapid Reference 6.34

IVA-2 Administration Considerations

Administration Considerations

- If examinee is a minor, parent/guardian must be in the room to enter codes and access the test website
- Parent/guardian is to stay in room sitting behind examinee during administration in case guidance or intervention is needed (i.e., safety, compliance, stopping or restarting test if examiner directs)
- Provide test manual titled Dos and Don'ts to the parent/guardian and review with them during test setup
- It is critical to disable all notifications on the computer or Apple device that examinee uses to respond
- Disable examinee's computer screen saver and disable virus scan before testing session (enable again afterwards)
- Close all programs besides Chrome during testing session
- Examiner must be clearly heard by examinee
- Examinee uses left mouse button (if computer) or hand (if Apple device) to respond on screen
- Peripheral camera/device should be placed in a stable position to show examinee's hand as they enter responses
- Examinee must not remove hand from the specified position (i.e., on left mouse button if responding on computer, or off to side of the green Tap Here button but not touching the screen if responding on Apple device)
- Examiner must monitor administration through teleconferencing platform

Pediatric Performance Validity Test Suite (PdPVTs)

This section reviews the Pediatric Performance Validity Test Suite (PdPVTs; McCaffrey, Lynch, Leark, & Reynolds, 2019) evidence for equivalence of tele-assessment and face-to-face administration. Special administration considerations are discussed.

PdPVTs Equivalence Evidence

There have been no direct studies on the PdPVTs and tele-assessment; however, the basic input and output demands of the tasks have support. Rapid Reference 6.35 provides analysis of the input and output demands and lists relevant indirect evidence by age range.

≡ Rapid Reference 6.35
....

PdPVTs Input and Output Demands and Equivalence Evidence

Task	Input	Output	Evidence[a] Citation:Task Abbreviation/Ages
Find the Animal Matching Shape Learning Silhouettes	Brief spoken directions, picture stimuli *Matching and Shape Learning*: Timed presentation	Multiple choice *Find the Animal*: Pointing response *All tasks except Find the Animal*: Multiple choice	**Indirect evidence:** Dekhtyar et al., 2020: RPM/26–75 Hildebrand et al., 2004: MR/60+ Hodge et al., 2019:VP, MR, FW, PS/8–12 Sutherland et al., 2017: CFD, WC/8–12 Vahia et al., 2015: BVMT/65+ Vestal et al., 2006: ACWP/68–78 Waite et al., 2010: CFD/5–9 Wright, 2018a: NM, OIO, WM/3–19 Wright, 2018b: CF, VZ/5–16 Wright, 2020b: VP, MR, FW, PC, PS/6–16
Story Questions	Brief spoken directions, spoken stimuli	Open ended, spoken response	**Indirect evidence:** Jacobsen et al., 2003: LM/ adult (not equivalent) Stain et al., 2011: LM/14–27 Wright, 2018a: VM/3–19 Wright, 2018b: SR/5–16

[a]**Evidence column task abbreviations:** AWCP = Aural Comprehension of Words and Phrases; BVMT = rief Visuospatial Memory Test, CF = Concept Formation, CFD = Concepts and Following Directions, FW = Figure Weights, LM = Logical Memory, MR = Matrix Reasoning, NM = Nonverbal Memory, OIO = Odd-Item Out, PC = Picture Concepts, PS = Picture Span, RPM = Raven's Progressive Matrices, SM = Story Memory, SR = Story Recall, VM = Verbal Memory, VP = Visual Puzzles, VZ = Visualization, WM = What's Missing.

PdPVTs Administration Considerations

MHS Online Portals has an online app available for the PdPVTs. Psychologists can use the app as they usually do for face-to face assessment and videoconferencing software to share the visual and auditory stimuli.

High quality audio and video are required. A headset with a microphone is needed for both the examinee and examiner. Special administration considerations are listed in Rapid Reference 6.36.

≋Rapid Reference 6.36

PdPVTs Administration Considerations

Task	Administration Considerations
Find the Animal	• Examinee uses touchscreen device to touch a selection and a home button
Matching	• Multiple choice item instructions may be altered to ask examinee to say number of response
Shape Learning	
Silhouettes	• Examiner uses stopwatch
Story Questions	• Do not repeat any item unless it was not heard due to technical problems

If an onsite professional is available, all tasks can be administered. The onsite professional will need a touchscreen device to allow the child to complete Find the Animal, and all other tasks can be completed as usual. If an onsite professional is not available, all tasks except for Find the Animal can be administered via teleconferencing.

Repeatable Battery for the Assessment of Neuropsychological Status Update (RBANS Update)

This section reviews the Repeatable Battery for the Assessment of Neuropsychological Status Update (RBANS Update; Randolph, 2012) evidence for equivalence of tele-assessment and face-to-face administration. Special administration considerations are discussed.

RBANS Update Equivalence Evidence

Rapid Reference 6.37 provides analysis of the input and output demands. It also lists both direct and indirect evidence of equivalence, along with the age ranges studied. Because the test can be administered to a broad range and the direct evidence only covers ages 58–84 from a specific clinical population, a review of other tele-assessment equivalence studies with examinees of varied ages is helpful to inform interpretation.

≡ Rapid Reference 6.37

RBANS Update Input and Output Demands and Equivalence Evidence

Subtest	Input	Output	Evidence[a] Citation: Task Abbreviation/ Ages
List Learning List Recall List Recognition	Brief spoken directions, spoken stimuli	Open ended, spoken response *Recognition:* Brief spoken response, multiple choice	**Direct evidence:** Galusha-Glasscock et al., 2016: LL, LR, LRg/58–84 **Indirect evidence:** Barcellos et al., 2017: CVLT/18–69 Brearly et al., 2017: LL/Adult Cullum et al., 2006: HVLT/51–84 (not equivalent) Cullum et al., 2014: HVLT/46–90 (not equivalent) Hildebrand et al., 2004: RAVLT/60+ Vahia et al., 2015: HVLT/65+
Story Memory Story Recall	Brief spoken directions, spoken stimuli	Open ended, spoken response	**Direct evidence:** Galusha-Glasscock et al., 2016: SM/58–84 **Indirect evidence:** Jacobsen et al., 2003: LM/adult (not equivalent) Stain et al., 2011: LM/14–27 Wright, 2018a: VM/3–19 Wright, 2018b: SR/5–16

(continued)

Subtest	Input	Output	Evidence[a] Citation: Task Abbreviation/ Ages
Figure Copy Figure Recall	Brief spoken directions, letters digits or symbols in print, response booklet	Written or fine motor response	**Direct evidence:** Galusha-Glasscock et al., 2016: FC, FR/58–84 **Indirect evidence:** Dekhtyar et al., 2020: DR/26–75 Temple et al., 2010: BVMI/23–63 Vahia et al., 2015: BVMT/65+
Line Orientation	Brief spoken directions, letters digits or symbols in print	Item-level time limit, multiple choice, pointing or brief spoken response	**Direct evidence:** Galusha-Glasscock et al., 2016: LO/58–84
Picture Naming	Brief spoken directions, picture stimuli	Brief spoken response, item-level time limit, open ended	**Direct Evidence:** Galusha-Glasscock et al., 2016: PN/58–84 **Indirect Evidence:** Brearly et al., 2017: BNT/adult Cullum et al., 2006: BNT/51–84 Cullum et al., 2014: BNT/46–90 Dekhtyar et al., 2020: PD/26–75 Sutherland et al., 2017: FS, WS/8–12 Vestal et al., 2006: BNT, PD/68–78 Wadsworth et al., 2018: BNT/ adult Waite et al., 2010: FS, WS/5–9
Semantic Fluency	Brief spoken directions	Open ended, spoken response, task-level time limit	**Direct Evidence:** Galusha-Glasscock et al., 2016: SF/58–84 **Indirect evidence:** Brearly et al., 2017: SF/adult Dekhtyar et al., 2020: WF/26–75

Subtest	Input	Output	Evidence[a] Citation: Task Abbreviation/ Ages
			Hildebrand et al., 2004: CWAT/60+
			Stain et al., 2011: CWAT/14–27
			Wright, 2018b: PP/5–16
Digit Span	Brief spoken directions, spoken stimuli	Open ended, spoken response	**Direct Evidence:** Galusha-Glasscock et al., 2016: DS/58–84
			Indirect Evidence: Cullum et al., 2006: DS/51–84
			Cullum et al., 2014: DS/46–90
			Grosch et al., 2015: DS/67–85
			Hodge et al., 2019: DS/8–12
			Jacobsen et al., 2003: DS/adult
			Stain et al., 2011: DS/14–27
			Vahia et al., 2015: DS/65+
			Wadsworth et al., 2018: DS/adult
			Wright, 2020b: DS, LN/6–16 (LN not equivalent)
			Wright, 2018b: NR/5–16
Coding	Brief spoken directions, gestured directions, letters digits or symbols in print, motor demonstration, response booklet	Task-level time limit, written or fine motor response	**Direct Evidence:** Galusha-Glasscock et al., 2016: CD/58–84
			Indirect Evidence: Hodge et al., 2019: CD, SS/8–12
			Wright, 2020b: CD, SS, CA/6–16
			Jacobsen et al., 2003: SDMT/adult
			Wright, 2018a: SPS/3–19
			Wright, 2018b: LPM, MFF/5–16

[a]Evidence column task abbreviations: BNT = Boston Naming Test, BVMI = Beery Buktenica Developmental Test of Visual Motor Integration, BVMT = Brief Visuospatial Memory Test, CD = Coding, CVLT = California Verbal Learning Test, CWAT = Controlled Word Association Test, DR = Drawing, DS = Digit Span, FC = Figure Copy, FS = Formulated Sentences, HVLT = Hopkins Verbal Learning Test, LL = List Learning, LN = Letter–Number Sequencing, LO = Line Orientation, LM = Logical Memory, LR = List Recall, LRg = List Recognition, LPM = Letter–Pattern Matching, MFF = Math Facts Fluency, NR = Numbers Reversed, PD = Picture Description, PN = Picture Naming, PP = Phonological Processing, RAVLT = Rey Auditory Verbal Learning Test, SDMT = Symbol Digit Modalities Test, SF = Semantic Fluency, SM = Story Memory, SR = Story Recall, SPS = Speeded Picture Search, VM = Verbal Memory, WF = Word Fluency, WS = Word Structure.

RBANS Update Administration Considerations

RBANS Update can be administered via tele-assessment in multiple ways. There are two platforms where the digital stimuli are available: Q-global and Q-interactive. For Q-global, a paper record form is necessary in the examiner's location. Remember that the examinee needs to have a response booklet in their location prior to testing.

Administering the RBANS Update via tele-assessment requires high quality audio and video for nearly all tasks. A headset with a microphone is recommended for both the examinee and examiner. Special administration considerations are listed by subtest in Rapid Reference 6.38.

≡ Rapid Reference 6.38

RBANS Update Administration Considerations

Subtest(s)	Administration Considerations
List Learning List Recall List Recognition Digit Span	• Do not repeat any item unless it was not heard due to technical problems, unless permitted in manual (i.e., recognition items)
Story Memory Story Recall	• Do not repeat any item unless it was not heard due to technical problems, unless permitted in manual (i.e., recognition items)
Figure Copy Figure Recall	• Examinee uses response booklet • Peripheral camera/device should be placed in stable position to show examinee's written responses • Before administering Figure Recall, ensure Figure Copy responses are completely out of examinee's view • *Figure Copy:* Examiner uses stopwatch and must ensure examinee stops at task time limit
Line Orientation	• Examiner uses mouse/cursor to point to stimuli on screen • Examinee can use mouse/cursor to point at choices • Optional: Peripheral camera/device can be placed in stable position that shows examinee's screen and provides a view of choices made nonverbally (e.g., pointing) • Examiner uses stopwatch and must ensure examinee stops at task time limit

Subtest(s)	Administration Considerations
Picture Naming	• Examiner uses stopwatch and must ensure examinee stops at task time limit
Semantic Fluency	• Examiner uses stopwatch and must ensure examinee stops at task time limit
Coding	• Examinee uses response booklet • Peripheral camera/device should be placed in a stable position that shows examinee's response booklet and provides examiner a view of examinee's written responses • Examiner can complete demonstration items in examinee's response booklets prior to sending and can also demonstrate on screen during testing session • Examiner points to stimuli on screen and may fill in demonstration items on digital copy of response booklet displayed on screen with writing utensil tool (if a good one exists in teleconference platform) • Remove response booklet from screensharing display after demonstrating as examinees tend to look up at digital response booklet key instead of their own copy • Examiner uses stopwatch and must ensure examinee stops at task time limit

RBANS Update Composite Score Selection Considerations

If available, an onsite professional can present the response booklet. Psychologists using this approach can administer all subtests and obtain all typical composite scores that are available in face-to-face administrations. Be careful to ensure the examinee's Figure Copy drawing is not visible before administering Figure Recall.

CAUTION

Ensure the examinee's Figure Copy drawing is not visible before administering Figure Recall.

If the Coding subtest is not used, the Attention and Total Scale composite scores cannot be obtained. Rapid Reference 6.39 presents the RBANS Update composite score selection, which varies according to Coding use. Additionally, if Coding is not administered, this changes the distraction demands between the original stimuli presented (including the word list, story, and figure) and the recall task of the measure. This alters the amount and type of distraction between learning and recall, so recall data should be interpreted with caution.

≡ Rapid Reference 6.39

RBANS Update Composite Score Selection According to Coding Use

	Full Administration	No Response Booklet
Composite Score	Composite Score Available?	
Immediate Memory	✓	✓
Delayed Memory	✓	a
Attention	✓	No
Language	✓	✓
Visuospatial/ Constructional	✓	b✓
Total Scale	✓	No

[a]This score can be obtained, but should be interpreted with caution, as not as much distraction has occurred as in the normative sample.

[b]If the response booklet is not available in the examinee's location a sheet of blank paper can be used in lieu of the response booklet for Figure Copy and Figure Recall.

Test of Variables of Attention (TOVA)

The Test of Variables of Attention (TOVA; TOVA Company, 2020) is not appropriate for remote videoconferencing administration for the same reasons as the Conners CPTs, which has already been discussed in this section. In order to administer the TOVA via tele-assessment, an onsite professional must be available and trained in all aspects of administering the test as usual. The psychologist can observe the examinee's behaviors through a webcam placed in a stable position behind the examinee. Teleconferencing platforms should not be active on the computer the examinee is using to take the TOVA.

Wisconsin Card Sorting Test (WCST)

This section reviews the Wisconsin Card Sorting Test (WCST; Grant & Berg, 1948) evidence for equivalence of tele-assessment and face-to-face administration. Special administration considerations are discussed.

WCST Equivalence Evidence

There have been no direct studies on the WCST and tele-assessment; however, the basic input and output demands of the task have support. Rapid Reference 6.40 provides analysis of the input and output demands and lists relevant indirect evidence by age range.

≡Rapid Reference 6.40

WCST Card Format Input and Output Demands and Equivalence Evidence

Input	Output	Evidence[a] Citation: Task Abbreviation/Ages
Brief spoken directions, motor demonstration, physical manipulatives, picture stimuli	Fine motor response	**Indirect evidence:** Dekhtyar et al., 2020: BD/26–75 Hodge et al., 2019: BD/8–12 Jacobsen et al., 2003: BD, GP/adult Temple et al., 2010: BD/23–63 Vestal et al., 2006: TKT/68–78 Wright, 2020b: BD/6–16

[a]**Evidence column task abbreviations:** BD = Block Design, GP = Grooved Pegboard, TKT = Token Test.

WCST Administration Considerations

There are several administration considerations, by format, as shown in Rapid Reference 6.41.

Card Format. The WCST can be administered via tele-assessment with the help of an onsite professional, like the methodology used for many other tests with physical manipulatives discussed in this chapter. In this situation, the cards are presented and results recorded by the onsite professional, while the psychologist gives instructions via videoconferencing.

Computerized Format. Another option is to administer the computerized format. The Wisconsin Card Sorting Test Computer Version 4 Research Edition (WCST-CV4) software can be purchased from PAR and downloaded then administered via videoconferencing software. The product page indicates that although the computerized version has been available for many years, it is considered a

≋Rapid Reference 6.4 l

WCST Administration Considerations, by Format

Format	Administration Considerations
Cards	• Onsite professional should assist with administration • Train new onsite professionals until presentation of cards during instructions and items is performed according to directions in manual • Do not allow non-professionals to present cards or record results nor attempt to have examinee present their own cards or record results • Onsite professional presents stimuli while examiner provides all verbal instructions • Peripheral camera/device should be placed in a stable position to show examinee's responses
Computerized	• Examiner streams and shares computer's video and audio from online platform • Examiner must pass control of mouse to examinee • Examinee responds using mouse/cursor

research edition because the norms were collected via the traditional card-based method. The equivalence studies on the card-based and computer-administered formats have mixed outcomes, with some studies indicating they are equivalent (Artiola I Fortuny & Heaton, 1996; Wagner & Trentini, 2009) and others suggesting the formats produce different results (Coelho, Rosário, Mastrorosa, Miranda, & Bueno, 2012; Feldstein et al., 1999; Steinmetz, Brunner, Loarer, & Houssemand, 2010).

TELE-ASSESSMENT WITH LANGUAGE TESTS

Clinical Evaluation of Language Fundamentals, Fifth Edition (CELF-5)

This section reviews the Clinical Evaluation of Language Fundamentals, Fifth Edition (CELF-5; Wiig, Semel, & Secord, 2013) evidence for equivalence of tele-assessment and face-to-face administration. Special administration considerations are discussed.

CELF-5 Equivalence Evidence

Multiple studies have been conducted to examine equivalence of the CELF in tele-assessment and face-to-face conditions (Sutherland et al., 2017; Waite et al., 2010). Equivalence was supported for all subtests and composites that have been examined. However, these studies are among those that received a rating of "3" in our *Tele-Assessment Equivalence Study Database* because they evaluated only interrater reliability of an examiner in person and an examiner in a remote location. The studies also did not examine all CELF-5 tasks. Therefore, a review of other tele-assessment equivalence studies with examinees of varied ages is helpful to inform interpretation.

Rapid Reference 6.42 provides analysis of each subtest's input and output demands. It also lists both direct and indirect evidence of equivalence for each task, along with the age ranges studied.

CELF-5 Administration Considerations

The CELF-5 can be administered via tele-assessment in multiple ways. There are two platforms where the digital stimuli are available: Q-global and Q-interactive.

Administering the CELF-5 via tele-assessment requires high quality audio and video for nearly all tasks. A headset with a microphone is recommended for both the examinee and examiner. Special administration considerations are listed by subtest in Rapid Reference 6.43.

≡ Rapid Reference 6.42

CELF-5 Input and Output Demands and Equivalence Evidence

Subtest(s)	Input	Output	Evidence[a] Citation: Task Abbreviation/Ages
Sentence Comprehension Linguistic Concepts Following Directions	Brief spoken directions, picture stimuli, spoken stimuli *Following Directions*: Color-critical items	Multiple choice, pointing response	**Direct evidence:** Sutherland et al., 2017: CFD/8–12 **Indirect evidence:** Vestal et al., 2006: ACWP/68–78

(continued)

Subtest(s)	Input	Output	Evidence[a] Citation: Task Abbreviation/Ages
Word Structure	Brief spoken directions, picture stimuli, spoken stimuli	Brief spoken response, multiple choice	**Direct evidence:** Sutherland et al., 2017: WS/8–12 Waite et al., 2010: WS/5–9 **Indirect evidence:** Brearly et al., 2017: BNT/adult Cullum et al., 2006: BNT/51–84 Cullum et al., 2014: BNT/46–90 Dekhtyar et al., 2020: PD/26–75 Galusha-Glasscock et al., 2016: PN/58–84 Sutherland et al., 2017: FS/8–12 Vestal et al., 2006: BNT, PD/68–78 Wadsworth et al., 2018: BNT/adult Waite et al., 2010: FS/5–9
Sentence Assembly Semantic Relationships	Brief spoken directions, spoken stimuli, words in print	Sentence Assembly: Spoken response Semantic Relationships: Pointing or brief spoken response	**Indirect evidence:** Dekhtyar et al., 2020: RCS/26–75 Wright, 2018b: LWI, PCO, PP, SWF, WSp/5–16 Stain et al., 2011: WTAR/14–27
Word Classes	Brief spoken directions, picture stimuli, spoken stimuli	Brief spoken response, multiple choice	**Direct evidence:** Sutherland et al., 2017: WC/8–12 **Indirect evidence:** Hodge et al., 2019: SI/8–12 Wright, 2018a: VR/3–19 Wright, 2020b: SI, PC/6–16

Subtest(s)	Input	Output	Evidence[a] Citation: Task Abbreviation/Ages
Formulated Sentences	Brief spoken directions, picture stimuli, spoken stimuli	Spoken response	**Direct evidence:** Sutherland et al., 2017: FS, WS/8–12 Waite et al., 2010: FS, WS/5–9 **Indirect evidence:** Dekhtyar et al., 2020: PD/26–75 Vestal et al., 2006: PD/68–78 Wright, 2018b: PP/5–16
Recalling Sentences Understanding Spoken Paragraphs	Brief spoken directions, spoken stimuli	Open ended, spoken response	**Direct evidence:** Sutherland et al., 2017: RS/8–12 Waite et al., 2010: RS/5–9 **Indirect evidence:** Cullum et al., 2006: DS/51–84 Cullum et al., 2014: DS/46–90 Dekhtyar et al., 2020: CS/26–75 Galusha-Glasscock et al., 2016: DS/58–84 Grosch et al., 2015: DS/67–85 Hodge et al., 2019: DS/8–12 Jacobsen et al., 2003: DS/adult Stain et al., 2011: DS/14–27 Vahia et al., 2015: DS/65+ Wadsworth et al., 2018: DS/adult Wright, 2018b: NR/5–16 Wright, 2020b/6–16 (LN not equivalent)
Word Definitions	Brief spoken directions, spoken stimuli	Open ended, spoken response	**Indirect evidence:** Dekhtyar et al., 2020: CQ/26–75 Hildebrand et al., 2004: VC/60+ Hodge et al., 2019: SI, VC/8–12 Jacobsen et al., 2003: VC/adult Temple et al., 2010: VC/23–63 Turkstra et al., 2012: MDEP, ABD/21–69 Wright, 2018a: GW, VR/3–19 Wright, 2018b: GI, OV/5–16 Wright, 2020b: SI, VC, IN, CO/6–16

(continued)

Subtest(s)	Input	Output	Evidence[a] Citation: Task Abbreviation/Ages
Reading Comprehension	Brief spoken directions, words in print	Open ended, spoken response	**Indirect evidence:** Dekhtyar et al., 2020: RCd, RCS/26–75 Wright, 2018b: PCO/5–16
Structured Writing	Brief spoken directions, response booklet, spoken stimuli, words in print	Open ended, written response	**Indirect evidence:** Dekhtyar et al., 2020: WO/26–75 Wright, 2018b: SW, SWF/5–16

Note. Digital/paper format equivalence evidence is also available for the CELF-5 (Daniel, Wahlstrom, & Zhou, 2014).

[a]**Evidence column task abbreviations:** ABD = AphasiaBank discourse tasks, ACWP = Aural Comprehension of Words and Phrases, BNT = Boston Naming Test, CFD = Concepts and Following Directions, CO = omprehension, CQ = Conversational Questions, DS = Digit Span, FS = Formulated Sentences, GI = General Information, GW = Guess What, IN = Information, LWI = Letter–Word Identification, NR = Numbers Reversed, LN = Letter–Number Sequencing, MDEP = Mediated Discourse Elicitation Protocol, OV = Oral Vocabulary, PC = Picture Concepts, PCO = Passage Comprehension, PD = Picture Description, PP = Phonological Processing, PN = Picture Naming, RCd = Reading Commands, RCS = Reading Comprehension of Sentences, RS = Recalling Sentences, SI = Similarities, SWF = Sentence Writing Fluency, VC = Vocabulary, VR = Verbal Reasoning, WC = Word Classes, WO = Writing Output, WS = Word Structure, WSp = Writing Samples, WTAR = Wechsler Test of Adult Reading.

≡ Rapid Reference 6.43

CELF-5 Administration Considerations

Subtest(s)	Administration Considerations
Observational Rating Scale	• Cannot be administered via tele-assessment as full, traditional in-person observation of child is required
Sentence Comprehension Linguistic Concepts Following Directions	• Examiner uses mouse/cursor to point to stimuli on screen • Examinee can use mouse/cursor to point at choices • Multiple choice item instructions may be altered to ask examinee to say number(s) or letter(s) of response to clarify if necessary • Optional: Peripheral camera/device can be placed in stable position that shows examinee's screen and provides a view of choices made nonverbally (e.g., pointing)

Subtest(s)	Administration Considerations
Word Structure Sentence Assembly Semantic Relationships	• Examiner uses mouse/cursor to point to stimuli on screen
Word Classes	• For picture items, examiner uses mouse/cursor to point to stimuli on screen • Some items may elicit pointing or gestured responses if examinee is in home environment; ask examinee to say answer using words
Formulated Sentences	• Examiner displays and point to stimuli projected on examinee's monitor
Recalling Sentences Understanding Spoken Paragraphs	• Do not repeat stimuli unless it was not heard due to technical problems
Word Definitions	• Some items may elicit pointing or gestured responses if examinee is in home environment; ask examinee to say answer using words
Reading Comprehension	• Examiner shares print paragraph stimuli on screen
Structured Writing	• Peripheral camera/device should be placed in a stable position that shows examinee's response booklet and provides examiner a view of examinee's written responses • It may be helpful to have a printed copy of response booklets in examiner's location also in order to show briefly on camera additional response booklet pages if applicable or how to turn to correct item for cancellation when giving test item directions • Ensure response booklet is opened only to correct page when directed
Pragmatics Profile	• May require additional information gathered from informants
Pragmatics Activities Checklist	• Cannot be administered via tele-assessment as observation of child is required

Expressive Vocabulary Test (EVT-3)

This section reviews the Expressive Vocabulary Test (EVT-3; Williams, 2018) evidence for equivalence of tele-assessment and face-to-face administration. Special administration considerations are discussed.

EVT-3 Equivalence Evidence

There have been no direct studies on the EVT-3 and tele-assessment; however, the basic input and output demands of the task have support. Rapid Reference 6.44 provides analysis of the input and output demands and lists relevant indirect evidence by age range.

EVT-3 Administration Considerations

The EVT-3 can be administered via tele-assessment using Q-global or Q-interactive. A paper record form is necessary if Q-global is used.

Administering the EVT-3 via tele-assessment requires high quality audio and video. A headset with a microphone is recommended for both the examinee and examiner. Special administration considerations are listed in Rapid Reference 6.45.

≋ Rapid Reference 6.44

EVT-3 Input and Output Demands and Equivalence Evidence

Input	Output	Evidence[a] Citation: Task Abbreviation/Ages
Brief spoken directions, picture stimuli	Brief spoken response, open ended	**Indirect evidence:**
		Brearly et al., 2017: BNT/adult
		Cullum et al., 2006: BNT/51–84
		Cullum et al., 2014: BNT/46–90
		Dekhtyar et al., 2020: PD/26–75
		Galusha-Glasscock et al., 2016: PN/58–84
		Sutherland et al., 2017: FS, WS/8–12
		Vestal et al., 2006: BNT, PD/68–78
		Wadsworth et al., 2018: BNT/adult
		Waite et al., 2010: FS, WS/5–9

[a]Evidence column task abbreviations: BNT = Boston Naming Test, FS = Formulated Sentences, PD = Picture Description, PN = Picture Naming, WS = Word Structure.

≡ Rapid Reference 6.45

· ·

EVT-3 Administration Considerations

Administration Considerations

- Examiner uses mouse/cursor to point to stimuli on screen
- Some items may elicit pointing or gestured responses if examinee is in home environment; ask examinee to say answer using words

Ortiz Picture Vocabulary Acquisition Test (Ortiz PVAT)

This section reviews the Ortiz Picture Vocabulary Acquisition Test (Ortiz PVAT; Ortiz, 2018) evidence for equivalence of tele-assessment and face-to-face administration. Special administration considerations are discussed.

Ortiz PVAT Equivalence Evidence

There have been no direct studies on the Ortiz PVAT and tele-assessment; however, the basic input and output demands of the tasks have support. Rapid Reference 6.46 provides analysis of the input and output demands and lists relevant indirect evidence by age range.

Ortiz PVAT Administration Considerations

The Ortiz PVAT can be administered via the MHS Online Portals app. Psychologists can use the app as they usually do for face-to-face assessment and videoconferencing software to share the visual and auditory stimuli.

Administering the Ortiz PVAT via tele-assessment requires high quality audio and video. A headset with a microphone is recommended for both the examinee and examiner. Special administration considerations are listed in Rapid Reference 6.47. Examinees should verbally state the number that corresponds to the response so the examiner can record it.

Peabody Picture Vocabulary Test, Fifth Edition (PPVT-5)

This section reviews the Peabody Picture Vocabulary Test, Fifth Edition (PPVT–5; Dunn, 2018) evidence for equivalence of tele-assessment and face-to-face administration. Special administration considerations are discussed.

≡ Rapid Reference 6.46

Ortiz PVAT Input and Output Demands and Equivalence Evidence

Input	Output	Evidence[a] Citation: Task Abbreviation/Ages
Brief spoken directions, gestured directions, picture stimuli, timed presentation	Multiple choice, pointing or brief spoken response	**Indirect evidence:** Dekhtyar et al., 2020: RPM/26–75 Hildebrand et al., 2004: MR/60+ Hodge et al., 2019: VP, MR, FW, PS/8–12 Sutherland et al., 2017: CFD, WC/8–12 Vahia et al., 2015: BVMT/65+ Vestal et al., 2006: ACWP/68–78 Waite et al., 2010: CFD/5–9 Wright, 2018a: NM, OIO, WM/3–19 Wright, 2018b: CF, VZ/5–16 Wright, 2020b: VP, MR, FW, PC, PS/6–16

[a]**Evidence column task abbreviations:** ACWP = Aural Comprehension of Words and Phrases, BVMT = Brief Visuospatial Memory Test, CF = Concept Formation, CFD = Concepts and Following Directions, FW = Figure Weights, MR = Matrix Reasoning, NM = Nonverbal Memory, OIO = Odd-Item Out, PC = Picture Concepts, PS = Picture Span, VP = Visual Puzzles, VZ = Visualization, WC = Word Classes, WM = What's Missing.

≡ Rapid Reference 6.47

Ortiz PVAT Administration Considerations

Administration Considerations

- Examiner uses mouse/cursor to point to stimuli on screen
- Multiple choice item instructions should be altered to ask examinee to say number of response
- Optional: Peripheral camera/device can be placed in stable position that shows examinee's screen and provides a view of choices made nonverbally (e.g., pointing)
- Examiner uses stopwatch to time stimuli exposure; ensure lags in connectivity do not influence length of exposure time

☰ Rapid Reference 6.48

PPVT-5 Input and Output Demands and Equivalence Evidence

Input	Output	Evidence[a] Citation: Task Abbreviation/Ages
Brief spoken directions, picture stimuli, spoken stimuli	Multiple choice, pointing or brief spoken response	**Indirect evidence:** Sutherland et al., 2017: WC/8–12 Vestal et al., 2006: ACWP/68–78 Wright, 2020b: PCO/5–16

[a]**Evidence column task abbreviations:** ACWP = Aural Comprehension of Words and Phrases, PCO = Passage Comprehension, WC = Word Classes.

PPVT-5 Equivalence Evidence

There have been no direct studies on the PPVT-5 and tele-assessment; however, the basic input and output demands of the tasks have support. Rapid Reference 6.48 provides analysis of the input and output demands and lists relevant indirect evidence by age range.

PPVT-5 Administration Considerations

The PPVT-5 can be administered via tele-assessment using Q-global or Q-interactive. A paper record form is necessary if Q-global is used.

Administering the PPVT-5 via tele-assessment requires high quality audio and video. A headset with a microphone is recommended for both the examinee and examiner. Special administration considerations are listed in Rapid Reference 6.49.

☰ Rapid Reference 6.49

PPVT-5 Administration Considerations

Administration Considerations

- Examiner uses mouse/cursor to point to stimuli on screen
- Examinee can use mouse/cursor to point at choices
- Multiple choice item instructions may be altered to ask examinee to say number of response to clarify if necessary
- Optional: Peripheral camera/device can be placed in stable position that shows examinee's screen and provides a view of choices made nonverbally (e.g., pointing)

CONCLUSION

Test publishers have made digital stimuli of cognitive tests widely available to psychologists. There are a variety of tools and platforms where the stimuli can be obtained for use in tele-assessment.

Every cognitive task administered via tele-assessment has specific considerations that should be prepared for and attended to. These issues add a layer of complexity relative to face-to-face administration. Psychologists should thoroughly review these issues and practice all items of any task before administering it via tele-assessment in a clinical context.

Many tests have been examined for equivalence between face-to-face and tele-assessment modes. However, many have not yet been studied specifically, but have similar input and output demands to other tasks that have been. Many types of tasks have research that supports their equivalence in face-to-face and remote tele-assessment contexts, either directly or indirectly.

Psychologists are encouraged to know the state of the literature supporting the tasks they are using clinically and interpret accordingly. As noted throughout this book, supporting clinical decisions through convergence of data across methods helps account for the error that exists in psychological tests, especially when engaging in tele-assessment.

Seven

ACADEMIC ACHIEVEMENT TELE-ASSESSMENT

With Katy Genseke

A cademic achievement testing is frequently used in the context of evaluations targeting learning difficulties and school-related problems. Much of the detailed footwork and notes needed to prepare for academic achievement via tele-assessment are provided in this chapter. This chapter can be used as a training reference as you practice, as well as to refresh and remind yourself of requirements prior to beginning a tele-assessment session.

Much of the information in this chapter is predicated on understanding the information in Chapter 6. Chapter 6 introduced many aspects of tele-assessment with performance-based tests, including how to access digital stimuli, which test publishers and platforms provide it, and how they work.

Before you administer a performance-based test via tele-assessment, you should be aware of the evidence that supports its use in the new mode. Chapter 6 introduced a method to examine equivalence evidence, both direct and indirect, and to apply the evidence to individual tasks to inform interpretation.

This chapter and Chapter 6 reference equivalence evidence by task, much of which was discussed broadly in Chapter 1. The references are drawn from both *direct evidence* (i.e., drawn directly from research on the listed task or measure) and *indirect evidence* (i.e., drawn from research based on other tasks

Essentials of Psychological Tele-Assessment, First Edition.
A. Jordan Wright and Susan Engi Raiford
© 2021 John Wiley & Sons, Inc. Published 2021 by John Wiley & Sons, Inc.

DON'T FORGET

Some tests, measures, and tasks have *direct evidence* of equivalence between tele-assessment methods and traditional in-person methods. This means that they have specifically been studied and shown to be equivalent, to not have a significant method effect that affects the data. Other tasks have *indirect evidence* of equivalence, such that measures with similar or nearly identical *input demands* (delivery of stimuli to the examinee) and *output demands* (delivery of responses from the examinee) have shown equivalence in research.

CAUTION

There is very little evidence on tele-assessment and face-to-face equivalence of performance-based tests with young children. Pay close attention to the age ranges examined for each study in the Rapid Reference that corresponds to a test used with young children. *Proceed with great caution when interpreting results obtained with young children via tele-assessment.*

with similar or identical input and output demands) of tele-assessment and face-to-face administration mode equivalence, as discussed in Chapters 1, 5, and 6.

Some tasks discussed in this chapter and in Chapter 6 are supported with both direct and indirect evidence, and other tasks are supported with only indirect evidence. As you review the evidence supporting a task, pay close attention to the age ranges that have been studied. *Note that very few studies have been conducted on tele-assessment with very young children.*

Refer to Chapter 1 and to the online resource that accompanies this book, the *Tele-Assessment Equivalence Study Database*, for more in-depth information about each tele-assessment equivalence study and the input and output demands of each researched task. The contents of the database and its potential uses are discussed in Chapter 6. The studies and information in the database are referred to throughout this chapter and Chapter 6.

TELE-ASSESSMENT WITH ACADEMIC ACHIEVEMENT TESTS

Kaufman Test of Educational Achievement, Third Edition (KTEA-3)

The Kaufman Test of Educational Achievement, Third Edition (KTEA-3; Kaufman & Kaufman, 2014) is a widely used measure to evaluate academic performance. This section introduces the indirect equivalence evidence, as well as considerations for administering it in a tele-assessment context.

KTEA-3 Equivalence Evidence

There have been no direct studies on the KTEA-3 and tele-assessment; however, the basic input and output demands of the tasks have support. Rapid Reference 7.1 provides analysis of the input and output demands and lists relevant indirect evidence by age range.

≣ Rapid Reference 7.1

KTEA-3 Input and Output Demands and Equivalence Evidence

Subtest(s)	Input	Output	Evidence[a] Citation: Task Abbreviation/Ages
Listening Comprehension	Audio recorded stimuli, spoken directions, spoken stimuli	Multiple choice, open ended, spoken response	**Indirect evidence:** Wright, 2018a: VM/3–19 Wright, 2018b: SR, VA/5–16
Math Fluency	Letters digits or symbols in print, response booklet, spoken directions	Open ended, task-level time limit, written response	**Indirect evidence:** Dekhtyar et al., 2020: CL/26–75 Wright, 2018b: CL, MFF/5–16
Math Concepts & Applications	Brief spoken directions, color critical items, letters digits or symbols in print, spoken stimuli, tables and graphs in print, words in print	Brief spoken response, multiple choice, open ended, pointing response, written response	**Indirect evidence:** Dekhtyar et al., 2020: CL, MC/26–75 Wright, 2018b: AP Wright, 2020b: AR/6–16
Math Computation	Brief spoken directions, letters digits or symbols in print, response booklet	Open ended, written response	**Indirect evidence:** Dekhtyar et al., 2020: CL/26–75 Wright, 2018b: CL, MFF/5–16
Oral Expression	Brief spoken directions, picture stimuli, spoken stimuli, words in print	Open ended, spoken response	**Indirect evidence:** Wright, 2018b: GI, OV/5–16 Wright, 2020b: SI, VC, IN, CO: 6–16

(continued)

Subtest(s)	Input	Output	Evidence[a] Citation: Task Abbreviation/Ages
Associational Fluency	Brief spoken directions	Open ended, spoken response, task-level time limit	**Indirect evidence:** Brearly et al., 2017: SF/adult Dekhtyar et al., 2020: WF/26–75 Galusha-Glasscock et al., 2016: SF/58–84 Hildebrand et al., 2004: CWAT/60+ Stain et al., 2011: CWAT/14–27
Object Naming Facility	Brief directions, picture stimuli	Spoken response, task-level time limit	**Indirect Evidence:** Wright, 2018a: SNT/7–19
Decoding Fluency Letter Naming Facility Word Recognition Fluency	Brief spoken directions *Letter Naming Facility:* Letters digits or symbols in print *Decoding and Word Recognition:* Words in print	Spoken response, task-level time limit	**Indirect evidence:** Dekhtyar et al., 2020: RCd, RCS, RIW, RNW/26–75 Stain et al., 2011: WTAR/14–27 Wright, 2018b: LWI, NS, OR, PCO, WA/5–16
Phonological Processing	Brief spoken directions, picture stimuli, spoken stimuli	Multiple choice, open ended, pointing response, spoken response	**Indirect evidence:** Brearly et al., 2017: SF/adult Dekhtyar et al., 2020: WF/26–75 Galusha-Glasscock et al., 2016: SF/58–84 Hildebrand et al., 2004: CWAT/60+ Stain et al., 2011: CWAT/14–27 Wright, 2018b: PP/5–16

Subtest(s)	Input	Output	Evidence[a] Citation: Task Abbreviation/Ages
Nonsense Word Decoding	Brief spoken directions, words in print	Open ended, spoken response	**Indirect evidence:** Dekhtyar et al., 2020: RCd, RCS, RIW, RNW/26–75 Stain et al., 2011: WTAR/14–27 Wright, 2018b: LWI, NS, OR, PCO, WA/5–16
Reading Vocabulary	Picture stimuli, spoken directions, words in print	Pointing or brief spoken response	**Direct evidence:** Sutherland et al., 2017: FS, WS/8–12 Waite et al., 2010: FS, WS/5–9
Reading Comprehension	Brief spoken directions, picture stimuli, spoken stimuli, words in print	Gross motor response, multiple choice, open ended, pointing response, spoken response	**Indirect evidence:** Dekhtyar et al., 2020: RCd, RCS, RIW, RNW/26–75 Stain et al., 2011: WTAR/14–27 Wright, 2018b: LWI, NS, OR, PCO, WA/5–16
Written Expression	Picture stimuli, response booklet, spoken directions, words in print	Open ended, written response, task-level time limit (essay)	**Indirect evidence:** Dekhtyar et al., 2020: WDW, WID, WND, WO/26–75 Wright, 2018b: SWF, WSp/5–16
Writing Fluency	Brief spoken directions, picture stimuli, response booklet	Open ended, task-level time limit, written response	**Indirect evidence:** Dekhtyar et al., 2020: WDW, WID, WND, WO/26–75 Wright, 2018b: SWF, WSp/5–16

Subtest(s)	Input	Output	Evidence[a] Citation: Task Abbreviation/Ages
Silent Reading Fluency	Brief spoken directions, response booklet, words in print	Multiple choice, simple written response, task-level time limit	**Indirect evidence:** Dekhtyar et al., 2020: RCd, RCS, RIW, RNW/26–75 Stain et al., 2011: WTAR/14–27 Wright, 2018b: LWI, NS, OR, PCO, WA/5–16 Wright, 2020b: SS, CA/6–16
Spelling	Brief spoken directions, response booklet, spoken stimuli	Written response	**Indirect evidence:** Dekhtyar et al., 2020: SP, WDW, WID, WND/26–75 Wright, 2018b: SP/5–16
Letter & Word Recognition	Brief spoken directions, letters digits or symbols in print, spoken stimuli, words in print	Multiple choice, open ended, pointing response, spoken response	**Indirect evidence:** Dekhtyar et al., 2020: RCd, RCS, RIW, RNW/26–75 Stain et al., 2011: WTAR/14–27 Wright, 2018b: LWI, NS, OR, PCO, WA/5–16

[a]**Evidence column task abbreviations:** AP = Applied Problems, AR = Arithmetic, CD = Coding, CL = Calculation, CO = Comprehension, CWAT = Controlled Word Association Test, FS = Formulated Sentences, GI = General Information, IN = Information, LWI = Letter–Word Identification, MC = Math Calculation, MFF = Math Facts Fluency, NS = Number Series, OR = Oral Reading, OV = Oral Vocabulary, PCO = Passage Comprehension, PP = Phonological Processing, RCd = Reading Commands, RCS = Reading Comprehension of Sentences, RIW = Reading Irregular Words, RNW = Reading Nonwords, SF = Semantic Fluency, SI = Similarities, SNT = Speeded Naming Test, SP = Spelling, SR = Story Recall, SS = Symbol Search, SWF = Sentence Writing Fluency, VA = Verbal Attention, VC = Vocabulary, VM = Verbal Memory, WA = Word Attack, WDW = Writing Dictated Words, WF = Word Fluency, WID = Writing Irregular Words to Dictation, WND = Writing Nonwords to Dictation, WO = Writing Output, WS = Word Structure, WSp = Writing Samples, WTAR = Wechsler Test of Adult Reading.

KTEA-3 Administration Considerations

The KTEA-3 can be administered via tele-assessment in multiple ways. There are two platforms where the digital stimuli are available: Q-global and Q-interactive. Paper response booklets are necessary with both platforms, and a paper record form is necessary with Q-global.

Administering the KTEA-3 via tele-assessment requires high-quality audio and video for nearly all tasks, and that both examiner and examinee can clearly view one another's mouths when speaking as well. A headset with a microphone is recommended for both the examinee and examiner.

Special administration considerations are listed by subtest in Rapid Reference 7.2.

≋ Rapid Reference 7.2

KTEA-3 Administration Considerations

Subtest(s)	Administration Considerations
Associational Fluency	• Audio recording examinee's responses is recommended to provide clarity for scoring
Letter & Word Recognition	• Examiner uses mouse/cursor to point to stimuli on screen • Examinee uses mouse to point to some items • *Optional:* peripheral camera/device can be positioned in stable position for items involving pointing to show examinee's screen and provide view of responses given nonverbally through pointing • Audio recording examinee's responses is recommended to provide clarity for scoring
Listening Comprehension	• Requires examiner to stream audio then read questions aloud • Do not repeat audio stimuli
Math Computation	• Requires response booklet • Requires examinee to have pencil • Peripheral camera/device should be placed in a stable position that shows examinee's response booklet and provides examiner a view of examinee's written and pointing responses • Examiner can point to or write on digital response booklet on screen during testing session

(continued)

Subtest(s)	Administration Considerations
Math Concepts and Applications	• Examiner uses mouse/cursor to point to stimuli on screen • Examinee uses mouse to point to several items • *Optional*: peripheral camera/device can be positioned in stable position for items involving pointing to show examinee's screen and provide view of responses given nonverbally through pointing • Examiner needs to see examinee's scratch paper for several items; view requires peripheral device to be correctly positioned or scratch paper can be held up to camera
Nonsense Word Decoding	• Examiner uses mouse/cursor to point to stimuli on screen • If using speed process scores examiner must immediately navigate to next page • Audio recording examinee's responses is recommended to provide clarity for scoring
Letter Naming Facility Object Naming Facility	• Examiner uses mouse/cursor to point to stimuli on screen • Examinee uses mouse to point to several items • Peripheral camera/device should be placed in a stable position that shows examinee's pointing responses • Examiner uses stopwatch
Oral Expression	• Examiner uses mouse/cursor to point to stimuli on screen • Audio recording examinee's responses is recommended to provide clarity for scoring
Phonological Processing	• Examiner uses mouse/cursor to point to stimuli on screen • Examinee uses mouse to point to some items • *Optional*: peripheral camera/device can be positioned in stable position for items involving pointing to show examinee's screen and provide view of responses given nonverbally through pointing • Optional puppet cannot be used for Section 5 (Segmenting)
Reading Comprehension	• Examiner accesses and displays stimuli and asks questions while examinee responds • Examiner uses mouse/cursor to point to stimuli on screen • Examinee uses mouse to point to some items • *Optional*: peripheral camera/device can be positioned in stable position for items involving pointing to show examinee's screen and provide view of responses given nonverbally through pointing

Subtest(s)	Administration Considerations
Reading Vocabulary	• Examiner uses mouse/cursor to point to stimuli on screen • Examinee must have choice of saying or pointing to response using mouse • Peripheral camera/device should be placed in a stable position that shows examinee's pointing responses
Decoding Fluency Word Recognition Fluency	• Examiner accesses and displays stimuli while examinee responds orally • Examiner uses mouse/cursor to point to stimuli on screen • Examiner uses stopwatch and must ensure examinee stops at task time limit • Audio recording examinee's responses is recommended to provide clarity for scoring
Math Fluency Silent Reading Fluency Spelling Writing Fluency Written Expression	• Requires response booklet • Requires examinee to have pencil • Peripheral camera/device should be placed in a stable position that shows examinee's response booklet and provides examiner a view of examinee's written responses • Examiner can point to digital response booklet on screen during testing session • Examiner can do what is necessary to help the examinee to understand instructions (e.g., holding up and pointing at a paper response booklet, demonstrating on screen during the testing session, pointing to or marking on the digital copy of the response booklet displayed onscreen with the writing utensil tool) • *Written Expression, Math Fluency, Writing Fluency, Silent Reading Fluency:* Examiner uses stopwatch; examiner must ensure the examinee stops at time limit

KTEA-3 Composite Score Considerations

If available, an onsite professional can present response booklets. Psychologists using this approach can administer all subtests and obtain all typical composite scores that are available in face-to face administrations.

It is recommended if possible that psychologists use response booklets when administering the KTEA-3. If response booklets are not used, it impacts the composite score selection. Many KTEA-3 subtests require use of a response booklet. Rapid Reference 7.3 describes the KTEA-3 composite score selection, which varies if response booklets are not used.

≋ Rapid Reference 7.3

KTEA-3 Composite Score Selection According to Response Booklet Use

Composite Score	Full Administration	No Response Booklets
	Composite Score Available?	
Reading	✔	✔
Written Language	✔	No
Math	✔	No
Academic Skills Battery Composite	✔	No
Sound-Symbol	✔	✔
Decoding	✔	✔
Reading Fluency	✔	No
Reading Understanding	✔	✔
Oral Language	✔	✔
Oral Fluency	✔	✔
Comprehension	✔	✔
Expression	✔	No
Orthographic Processing	✔	No
Academic Fluency	✔	No

WECHSLER INDIVIDUAL ACHIEVEMENT TEST, FOURTH EDITION (WIAT-4)

This section reviews the Wechsler Individual Achievement Test, Fourth Edition (WIAT-4; Pearson, 2020) evidence for equivalence of tele-assessment and face-to-face administration. Special administration considerations are discussed, as is composite score selection related to the need for response booklets in the examinee's location.

WIAT-4 Equivalence Evidence

There have been no direct studies on the WIAT-4 and tele-assessment; however, the basic input and output demands of the tasks have support. Rapid Reference 7.4 provides analysis of the input and output demands and lists relevant indirect evidence by age range.

≡ Rapid Reference 7.4

WIAT-4 Input and Output Demands and Equivalence Evidence

Subtest(s)	Input	Output	Evidence[a] Citation: Task Abbreviation/Ages
Alphabet Writing Fluency	Brief spoken directions, response booklet	Simple written response, task-level time limit	**Indirect evidence:** Dekhtyar et al., 2020: AN, WDW, WID, WND, WO/26–75 Wright, 2018b: SWF, WSp/5–16
Essay Composition	Response booklet, spoken directions	Open ended, task-level time limit, written response	**Indirect evidence:** Dekhtyar et al., 2020: WDW, WID, WND, WO/26–75 Wright, 2018b: SWF, WSp/5–16
Listening Comprehension Receptive Vocabulary	Brief spoken directions, picture stimuli	Multiple choice, pointing or brief spoken response	**Indirect evidence:** Sutherland et al., 2017: WC/8–12 Vestal et al., 2006: ACWP/68–78
Listening Comprehension Oral Discourse Comprehnsion	Audio recorded stimuli, spoken directions, spoken stimuli	Open ended, spoken response	**Indirect evidence:** Wright, 2018a: VM/3–19 Wright, 2018b: SR, VA/5–16
Math FluencyAddition, Subtraction, and Multiplication	Letters digits or symbols in print, response booklet, spoken directions	Open ended, task-level time limit, written response	**Indirect evidence:** Dekhtyar et al., 2020: CL/26–75 Wright, 2018b: CL, MFF/5–16

(continued)

Subtest(s)	Input	Output	Evidence[a] Citation: Task Abbreviation/Ages
Math Problem Solving	Brief spoken directions, letters digits or symbols in print, spoken stimuli, tables and graphs in print, words in print	Brief spoken response, multiple choice, open ended, pointing response	**Indirect evidence:** Dekhtyar et al., 2020: CL, MC/26–75 Wright, 2018b: AP/5–16 Wright, 2020b: AR/6–16
Numerical Operations	Brief spoken directions, letters digits or symbols in print, response booklet, words in print	Open ended, written response	**Indirect evidence:** Dekhtyar et al., 2020: CL/26–75 Wright, 2018b: CL, MFF/5–16
Oral Expression Expressive Vocabulary	Brief spoken directions, picture stimuli, spoken stimuli	Brief spoken response	**Indirect evidence:** Brearly et al., 2017: BNT/adult Cullum et al., 2006: BNT/51–84 Cullum et al., 2014: BNT/46–90 Dekhtyar et al., 2020: PD/26–75 Galusha-Glasscock et al., 2016: PN/58–84 Sutherland et al., 2017: FS, WS/8–12 Vestal et al., 2006: BNT, PD/68–78 Wadsworth et al., 2018: BNT/adult Waite et al., 2010: FS, WS/5–9
Oral Expression Oral Word Fluency	Brief spoken directions	Open ended, spoken response, task-level time limit	**Indirect evidence:** Brearly et al., 2017: SF/adult Dekhtyar et al., 2020: WF/26–75 Galusha-Glasscock et al., 2016: SF/58–84 Hildebrand et al., 2004: CWAT/60+ Stain et al., 2011: CWAT/14–27 Wright, 2018b: PP/5–16

Subtest(s)	Input	Output	Evidence[a] Citation: Task Abbreviation/Ages
Oral Expression Sentence Repetition	Brief spoken directions, spoken stimuli	Spoken response	**Indirect evidence:** Cullum et al., 2006: DS/51–84 Cullum et al., 2014: DS/46–90 Dekhtyar et al., 2020: DS/26–75 Galusha-Glasscock et al., 2016: DS/58–84 Grosch et al., 2015: DS/67–85 Hodge et al., 2019: DS/8–12 Jacobsen et al., 2003: DS/adult Stain et al., 2011: DS/14–27 Sutherland et al., 2017: RS/8–12 Vahia et al., 2015: DS/65+ Wadsworth et al., 2018: DS/adult Waite et al., 2010: RS/5–9 Wright, 2019b: NR/5–16 Wright, 2020b: DS, LN/6–16 (LN not equivalent)
Decoding Fluency Oral Reading Fluency Orthographic Fluency	Brief spoken directions, words in print	Item-level time limit, spoken response	**Indirect evidence:** Dekhtyar et al., 2020: RCd, RCS, RIW, RNW/26–75 Stain et al., 2011: WTAR/14–27 Wright, 2018b: LWI, NS, OR, PCO, WA/5–16
Orthographic Choice	Brief spoken directions, words in print	Pointing response	**Indirect evidence:** Dekhtyar et al., 2020: RCd, RCS, RIW, RNW/26–75 Stain et al., 2011: WTAR/14–27 Wright, 2018b: LWI, NS, OR, PCO, WA/5–16

(continued)

Subtest(s)	Input	Output	Evidence[a] Citation: Task Abbreviation/Ages
Phonemic Proficiency	Audio recorded stimuli, brief spoken directions	Brief spoken response	**Indirect evidence:** Brearly et al., 2017: SF/adult Dekhtyar et al., 2020: WF/26–75 Galusha-Glasscock et al., 2016: SF/58–84 Hildebrand et al., 2004: CWAT/60+ Stain et al., 2011: CWAT/14–27 Wright, 2018b: PP/5–16
Pseudoword Decoding	Brief spoken directions, words in print	Open ended, spoken response	**Indirect evidence:** Dekhtyar et al., 2020: RCd, RCS, RIW, RNW/26–75 Stain et al., 2011: WTAR/14–27 Wright, 2018b: LWI, NS, OR, PCO, WA/5–16
Reading Comprehension	Brief spoken directions, words in print	Open ended, spoken response	**Indirect evidence:** Dekhtyar et al., 2020: RCd, RCS, RIW, RNW/26–75 Stain et al., 2011: WTAR/14–27 Wright, 2018b: LWI, NS, OR, PCO, WA/5–16
Sentence Composition	Response booklet, spoken directions, words in print	Open ended, written response	**Indirect evidence:** Dekhtyar et al., 2020: WDW, WID, WND, WO/26–75 Wright, 2018b: SWF, WSp/5–16
Sentence Writing Fluency	Brief spoken directions, gestured directions, response booklet	Task-level time limit, written response	**Indirect evidence:** Dekhtyar et al., 2020: WDW, WID, WND, WO/26–75 Wright, 2018b: SWF, WSp/5–16
Spelling	Brief spoken directions, response booklet, spoken stimuli	Written response	**Indirect evidence:** Dekhtyar et al., 2020: SP, WDW, WID, WND/26–75 Wright, 2018b: SP/5–16

Subtest(s)	Input	Output	Evidence* Citation: Task Abbreviation/Ages
Word Reading	Brief spoken directions, words in print	Open ended, spoken response	**Indirect evidence:** Dekhtyar et al., 2020: RCd, RCS, RIW, RNW/26–75 Stain et al., 2011: WTAR/14–27 Wright, 2018b: LWI, NS, OR, PCO, WA/5–16

Note. In-person digital/paper format equivalence evidence for the WIAT: Daniel (2013a).

*Evidence column task abbreviations: ACWP = Aural Comprehension of Words and Phrases, AN = Alphabet and Numbers, AP = Applied Problems, AR = Arithmetic, BNT = Boston Naming Test, CL = Calculation, CWAT = Controlled Word Association Test, DS = Digit Span, FS = Formulated Sentences, LN = Letter–Number Sequencing, LWI = Letter–Word Identification, MC = Math Calculation, MFF = Math Facts Fluency, NR = Numbers Reversed, NS = Number Series, OR = Oral Reading, PCO = Passage Comprehension, PD = Picture Description, PN = Picture Naming, PP = Phonological Processing, RCd = Reading Commands, RCS = Reading Comprehension of Sentences, RIW = Reading Irregular Words, RNW = Reading Nonwords, RS = Recalling Sentences, SF = Semantic Fluency, SP = Spelling, SR = Story Recall, SWF = Sentence Writing Fluency, VA = Verbal Attention, VM = Verbal Memory, WA = Word Attack, WC = Word Classes, WDW = Writing Dictated Words, WF = Word Fluency, WID = Writing Irregular Words to Dictation, WND = Writing Nonwords to Dictation, WO = Writing Output, WS = Word Structure, WSp = Writing Samples, WTAR = Wechsler Test of Adult Reading.

WIAT-4 Administration Considerations

The WIAT-4 can be administered via tele-assessment in multiple ways. There are two platforms where the digital stimuli are available: Q-global and Q-interactive. Paper response booklets are necessary with both platforms, and a paper record form is necessary with Q-global.

Administering the WIAT-4 via tele-assessment requires high-quality audio and video for nearly all tasks, and that both examiner and examinee can clearly view one another's mouths when speaking as well. A headset with a microphone is recommended for both the examinee and examiner.

Special administration considerations are listed by subtest in Rapid Reference 7.5.

≡ Rapid Reference 7.5

WIAT-4 Administration Considerations

Subtest(s)	Administration Considerations
Listening Comprehension Oral Discourse Comprehension	• Requires examiner to stream audio then read questions aloud • Do not repeat audio stimuli
Listening ComprehensionReceptive Vocabulary	• Examiner uses mouse/cursor to point to stimuli on screen • Examinee can use mouse/cursor to point at choices • Multiple choice item instructions may be altered to ask examinee to say number(s) or letter(s) of response to clarify if necessary • Optional: Peripheral camera/device can be placed in stable position that shows examinee's screen and provides a view of choices made nonverbally (e.g., pointing)
Alphabet Writing Fluency Essay Composition Math Fluency Sentence Composition Spelling	• Requires response booklet • Requires examinee to have pencil • Peripheral camera/device should be placed in a stable position that shows examinee's response booklet and provides examiner a view of examinee's written responses • Examiner can point to digital response booklet on screen during testing session • Examiner can do what is necessary to help the examinee to understand instructions (e.g., holding up and pointing at a paper response booklet, demonstrating on screen during the testing session, pointing to or marking on the digital copy of the response booklet displayed onscreen with the writing utensil tool) • *Math Fluency, Essay Composition, and Alphabet Writing Fluency*: Examiner uses stopwatch; examiner must ensure the examinee stops at time limit

Subtest(s)	Administration Considerations
Math Problem Solving	• Examiner uses mouse/cursor to point to stimuli on screen • Examinee uses mouse to point to some items • *Optional:* peripheral camera/device can be positioned in stable position for items involving pointing to show examinee's screen and provide view of responses given nonverbally through pointing • Examiner notes for qualitative purposes if examinee uses scratch paper; view may require peripheral device to be correctly positioned
Numerical Operations	• Requires response booklet • Requires examinee to have pencil • Peripheral camera/device should be placed in a stable position that shows examinee's response bookletlet and provides examiner a view of examinee's written and pointing responses • Examiner can point to digital response booklet on screen during testing session
Oral Expression Expressive Vocabulary	• Examiner uses mouse/cursor to point to stimuli on screen
Oral Expression Oral Word Fluency	• Audio recording examinee's responses is recommended to provide clarity for scoring • Examiner uses stopwatch
Oral Expression Sentence Repetition	• Do not repeat stimuli unless it was not heard due to technical problems, except for Sample A
Oral Reading Fluency Decoding Fluency	• Examiner accesses and displays stimuli while examinee responds orally • Examiner uses mouse/cursor to point to stimuli on screen • Examiner uses stopwatch and must ensure examinee stops at task time limit • Audio recording examinee's responses is recommended to provide clarity for scoring

(continued)

Subtest(s)	Administration Considerations
Orthographic Choice	• This subtest can only be administered on Q-interactive • iPad with stimuli can be displayed onscreen • Peripheral camera/device should be placed in a stable position that shows examinee's pointing responses • Examiner enters examinee's responses into iPad with stimuli
Phonemic Proficiency	• Examiner streams and shares audio from online platform
Pseudoword Decoding	• Examiner uses mouse/cursor to point to stimuli on screen • If using speed process scores examiner must immediately navigate to next page • Audio recording examinee's responses is recommended to provide clarity for scoring • Examiner uses stopwatch
Reading Comprehension	• Examiner accesses and displays stimuli and asks questions while examinee responds
Word Reading	• Examiner uses mouse/cursor to point to stimuli on screen

WIAT-4 Composite Score Considerations

If available, an onsite professional can present response booklets. Psychologists using this approach can administer all subtests and obtain all typical composite scores that are available in face-to face administrations.

It is recommended if possible that psychologists use response booklets when administering the WIAT-4. Many WIAT-4 subtests require use of a response booklet. Rapid Reference 7.6 describes the WIAT-4 composite score selection, which varies if response booklets are not used.

≡ Rapid Reference 7.6

WIAT-4 Composite Score Selection According to Response Booklet Use

	Full Administration	No Response Booklets
Composite Score	Composite Score Available?	
Reading	✔	✔
Written Expression	✔	No

Composite Score	Full Administration	No Response Booklets
	Composite Score Available?	
Mathematics	✔	No
Total Achievement	✔	No
Basic Reading	✔	✔
Decoding	✔	✔
Reading Fluency	✔	✔
Math Fluency	✔	No
Writing Fluency	✔	No
Oral Language	✔	✔
Phonological Processing	✔	No
Orthographic Processing	✔	✔
Dyslexia Index	✔	✔

WOODCOCK–JOHNSON, FOURTH EDITION TESTS OF ACHIEVEMENT (WJ-IV-ACH)

This section reviews the WJ-IV Tests of Achievement (WJ-IV-Ach; Schrank, Mather, & McGrew, 2014a) evidence for equivalence of tele-assessment and face-to-face administration. Special administration considerations are discussed, as is composite score selection related to the need for response books in the examinee's location. The WJ-IV ECAD (Schrank, McGrew, & Mather, 2015) information appears in Chapter 6 of this book along with the WJ-IV-Cog.

> **DON'T FORGET**
> ·····································
> The information relevant to the WJ-IV ECAD appears in Chapter 6 of this book along with the WJ-IV-Cog.

WJ-IV-Ach Equivalence Evidence

A study was conducted to examine equivalence of the first 11 tests of the WJ-IV-Ach in tele-assessment and face-to-face conditions for ages 5–16 (Wright, 2018b).

Equivalence was supported for all subtest and composite scores that were studied.

Because the WJ-IV-Ach can be used with a wide age range and the age range for Wright's (2018b) equivalence study was only 5–16, a review of other tele-assessment equivalence studies with examinees of varied ages is helpful to inform interpretation. Rapid Reference 7.7 provides analysis of each test's input and output demands. It lists both direct and indirect evidence of equivalence for each task, along with the age ranges studied.

≣Rapid Reference 7.7

WJ-IV-Ach Input and Output Demands and Equivalence Evidence

Test(s)	Input	Output	Evidence[a] Citation: Task Abbreviation/Ages
ACH 1: Letter–Word Identification	Brief spoken directions, gestured directions, letters digits or symbols in print, words in print	Pointing response	**Direct Evidence:** Wright, 2018b: LWI/5–16 **Indirect Evidence:** Dekhtyar et al., 2020: RCd, RCS, RIW, RNW/26–75 Stain et al., 2011: WTAR/14–27 Wright, 2018b: NS, OR, PCO, WA/5–16
ACH 2: Applied Problems	Brief spoken directions, gestured directions, response book, spoken stimuli	Brief spoken response, open ended	**Direct Evidence:** Wright, 2018b: AP/5–16 **Indirect Evidence:** Dekhtyar et al., 2020: CL, MC/26–75 Wright, 2020b: AR/6–16
ACH 3: Spelling	Brief spoken directions, response book, spoken stimuli	Open ended, written response	**Direct Evidence:** Wright, 2018b: SP/5–16 **Indirect Evidence:** Dekhtyar et al., 2020: SP, WDW, WID, WND/26–75

Test(s)	Input	Output	Evidence[a] Citation: Task Abbreviation/Ages
ACH 4: Passage Comprehension	Brief spoken directions, picture stimuli, spoken stimuli, words in print	Brief spoken response, multiple choice, pointing or brief spoken response	**Direct evidence:** Wright, 2018b: PCO/5–16 **Indirect evidence:** Dekhtyar et al., 2020: RCd, RCS, RIW, RNW/26–75 Stain et al., 2011: WTAR/14–27 Wright, 2018b: LWI, NS, OR, WA/5–16
ACH 5: Calculation ACH 10: Math Facts Fluency	Brief spoken directions, letters digits or symbols in print, response book	Written response *Math Facts Fluency:* Task level time limit	**Direct evidence:** Wright, 2018b: CL, MFF/5–16 **Indirect evidence:** Dekhtyar et al., 2020: CL/26–75
ACH 6: Writing Samples ACH 11: Sentence Writing Fluency	Brief spoken directions, gestured directions, response book	Written response Sentence Writing Fluency: Task-level time limit	**Direct evidence:** Wright, 2018b: SWF, WSp/5–16 **Indirect evidence:** Dekhtyar et al., 2020: WDW, WID, WND, WO/26–75
ACH 7: Word Attack	Brief spoken directions, gestured directions, letters digits or symbols in print, words in print	Brief spoken response	**Direct evidence:** Wright, 2018b: WA/5–16 **Indirect evidence:** Dekhtyar et al., 2020: RCd, RCS, RIW, RNW/26–75 Stain et al., 2011: WTAR/14–27 Wright, 2018b: LWI, NS, OR, PCO/5–16
ACH 8: Oral Reading	Brief spoken directions, words in print	Open ended, spoken response	**Direct evidence:** Wright, 2018b: OR/5–16 **Indirect evidence:** Dekhtyar et al., 2020: RCd, RCS, RIW, RNW/26–75 Stain et al., 2011: WTAR/14–27 Wright, 2018b: LWI, NS, PCO, WA/5–16

(continued)

Test(s)	Input	Output	Evidence[a] Citation: Task Abbreviation/Ages
ACH 9: Sentence Reading Fluency	Brief spoken directions, gestured directions, response book, words in print	Simple written response, task-level time limit	**Direct evidence:** Wright, 2018b: SRF/5–16 **Indirect evidence:** Dekhtyar et al., 2020: RCd, RCS, RIW, RNW/26–75 Stain et al., 2011: WTAR/14–27 Wright, 2018b: LWI, NS, OR, PCO, WA/5–16
ACH 12: Reading Recall	Brief spoken directions, spoken stimuli, words in print	Spoken response	**Indirect evidence:** Galusha-Glasscock et al., 2016: SM, SR/58–84 Jacobsen et al., 2003: LM/adult (not equivalent) Stain et al., 2011: LM/14–27 Wright, 2018a: VM/3–19 Wright, 2018b: SR/5–16
ACH 13: Number Matrices	Brief spoken directions, gestured directions, response book, letters digits or symbols in print	Brief spoken response, item-level time limit, open ended	**Indirect evidence:** Dekhtyar et al., 2020: CL, MC/26–75 Wright, 2018b: AP, NS/5–16 Wright, 2020b: AR, CD, SS/6–16
ACH 14: Editing	Brief spoken directions, words in print	Spoken response	**Indirect evidence:** Wright, 2018b: OR/5–16
ACH 15: Word Reading Fluency	Brief spoken directions, response book, words in print	Simple written response, task-level time limit	**Indirect Evidence:** Dekhtyar et al., 2020: RCd, RCS, RIW, RNW/26–75 Stain et al., 2011: WTAR/14–27 Wright, 2018b: LWI, NS, OR, PCO, WA/5–16
ACH 16: Spelling of Sounds	Audio recorded stimuli, brief spoken directions, response book	Written response	Dekhtyar et al., 2020: SP, WDW, WID, WND/26–75 Wright, 2018b: SP/5–16

Test(s)	Input	Output	Evidence[a] Citation: Task Abbreviation/Ages
ACH 17: Reading Vocabulary	Brief spoken directions, words in print, spoken stimuli	Open ended, spoken response	**Indirect Evidence:** Dekhtyar et al., 2020: RCd, RCS, RIW, RNW/26–75 Hildebrand et al., 2004: VC/60+ Hodge et al., 2019: SI, VC/8–12 Jacobsen et al., 2003: VC/adult Stain et al., 2011: WTAR/14–27 Temple et al., 2010: VC/23–63 Wright, 2018a: GW, VR/3–19 Wright, 2018b: LWI, NS, OV, PCO/5–16 Wright, 2020b: VC/6–16
ACH 18: Science ACH 19: Social Studies ACH 20: Humanities	Brief spoken directions, picture stimuli	Spoken response	**Indirect Evidence:** Brearly et al., 2017: BNT/adult Cullum et al., 2006: BNT/51–84 Cullum et al., 2014: BNT/46–90 Dekhtyar et al., 2020: PD/26–75 Galusha-Glasscock et al., 2016: PN/58–84 Sutherland et al., 2017: FS, WS/8–12 Vestal et al., 2006: BNT, PD/68–78 Wadsworth et al., 2018: BNT/adult Waite et al., 2010: FS, WS/5–9

[a]**Evidence column task abbreviations:** AP = Applied Problems, AR = Arithmetic, BNT = Boston Naming Test, CD = Coding, CL = Calculation, FS = Formulated Sentences, LM = Logical Memory, LWI = Letter–Word Identification, MC = Math Calculation, MFF = Math Facts Fluency, NS = Number Series, OR = Oral Reading, PCO = Passage Comprehension, PD = Picture Description, PN = Picture Naming, RCd = Reading Commands, RCS = Reading Comprehension of Sentences, RIW = Reading Irregular Words, RNW = Reading Nonwords, SI = Similarities, SM = Story Memory, SP = Spelling, SR = Story Recall, SRF = Sentence Reading Fluency, SS = Symbol Search, SWF = Sentence Writing Fluency, VC = Vocabulary, VM = Verbal Memory, WA = Word Attack, WDW = Writing Dictated Words, WID = Writing Irregular Words to Dictation, WND = Writing Nonwords to Dictation, WO = Writing Output, WS = Word Structure, WSp = Writing Samples, WTAR = Wechsler Test of Adult Reading.

WJ-IV-Ach Administration Considerations

The WJ-IV-Ach can be administered via tele-assessment using the stimuli on the Riversidescore.com platform. The WJ-IV-Ach requires high quality audio and video and a headset with a microphone for both the examinee and examiner for nearly all tasks. The examiner and examinee should almost always be positioned to see one another's mouths. The examiner must have access to test directions through the physical test book easels. Special administration considerations are listed by test in Rapid Reference 7.8.

≡ Rapid Reference 7.8

WJ IV Ach Administration Considerations

Test(s)	Administration Considerations
ACH 1: Letter-Word Identification	• Examiner uses mouse/cursor to point to stimuli on screen • Examinee points to Items 1–6; 11–13 • *Optional*: peripheral camera/device can be positioned in stable position for Items 1–6; 11–13 to show examinee's screen and provide view of responses given nonverbally through pointing
ACH 2: Applied Problems	• Examiner uses mouse/cursor to point to stimuli on screen • Examinee points to Items 3, 5, 12, 13, 16, and 21 • *Optional*: peripheral camera/device can be positioned in stable position for Items 3, 5, 12, 13, 16, and 21 to show examinee's screen and provide view of responses given nonverbally through pointing • Requires response book or blank sheet of paper • Requires examinee to have pencil
ACH 3: Spelling	• Requires response book or blank sheet of paper • Examiner should have a printed copy of response books in examiner's location in order demonstrate test Items 1–3 • Examiner can complete demo of test Items 1–3 in examinee's response books prior to sending and should also demonstrate on peripheral camera during testing session • Requires examinee to have pencil • Computer camera or peripheral camera/device should be placed in a stable position that shows examinee's response book and provides examiner a view of examinee's written responses

Test(s)	Administration Considerations
ACH 4: Passage Comprehension	• Examiner uses mouse/cursor to point to stimuli on screen during administration of Items 1–11 • *Optional*: peripheral camera/device can be positioned in stable position for Items 1–11 to show examinee's screen and provide view of responses given nonverbally through pointing
ACH 5: Calculation ACH 6: Writing Samples	• Requires response book • Requires examinee to have pencil • Computer camera or peripheral camera/device should be placed in a stable position that shows examinee's response book and provides examiner a view of examinee's written responses
ACH 7: Word Attack	• Examiner uses mouse/cursor to point to stimuli on screen • Examinee points to Items 1–5 • *Optional*: peripheral camera/device can be positioned in stable position for Items 1–5 to show examinee's screen and provide view of responses given nonverbally through pointing
ACH 8: Oral Reading	• Examiner accesses and displays stimuli while examinee responds orally
ACH 9: Sentence Reading Fluency ACH 10: Math Facts Fluency ACH 11: Sentence Writing Fluency ACH 15: Word Reading Fluency	• Requires response book • Requires examinee to have pencil • Computer camera or peripheral camera/device should be placed in a stable position that shows examinee's response book and provides examiner a view of examinee's written responses • Examiner monitors examinee's responses • Examiner uses stopwatch and must ensure examinee stops at task time limit
ACH 12: Reading Recall ACH 14: Editing	• Examiner accesses and displays stimuli while examinee responds
ACH 13: Number Matrices	• Examiner uses mouse/cursor to point to stimuli on screen • Requires response book • Requires examinee to have pencil

(continued)

Test(s)	Administration Considerations
ACH 16: Spelling of Sounds	• Requires response book or blank sheet of paper • Requires examinee to have pencil • Computer camera or peripheral camera/device should be placed in a stable position that shows examinee's response book and provides examiner a view of examinee's written responses • Examiner presents Sample Items A–D and Items 1–5 orally • Requires examiner to stream audio from online platform for Items 6–30 • If streaming audio from platform does not produce best quality audio, follow guidance in Examiner's Manual for presenting items orally
ACH 17A: Reading Vocabulary— Synonyms ACH 17B: Reading Vocabulary— Antonyms	• Examiner accesses and displays stimuli while examinee responds
ACH 18: Science ACH 19: Social Studies ACH 20: Humanities	• Examiner uses mouse/cursor to point to stimuli on screen

WJ-IV-Ach Composite Score Considerations

If available, an onsite professional can present response books. Psychologists using this approach can administer all tests and obtain all typical composite scores that are available in face-to face administrations.

It is recommended if possible that psychologists use response books when administering the WJ-IV-Ach. If response books are not used, the Selective Testing Tables in the Test Books and Examiner Manual can help determine which composite scores can and cannot be obtained.

For the WJ-IV-Ach, many tests require use of a response book. However, for a few subtests (i.e., Applied Problems, Spelling for children aged 5 and up, and Basic Writing Skills), a sheet of blank paper will suffice. In general, if a response book is not used, the Brief Achievement composite can be obtained, along with Reading, Basic Reading, and Reading Comprehension composites. Rapid Reference 7.9 describes the WJ-IV-Ach composite score selection, which varies if response books are not used.

≡ Rapid Reference 7.9

WJ IV Ach Composite Score Selection According to Response Booklet Use

	Full Administration	No Response Booklets
Composite Score	*Composite Score Available?*	
Reading	✔	✔
Broad Reading	✔	No
Basic Reading Skills	✔	✔
Reading Comprehension	✔	✔
Reading Fluency	✔	No
Reading Rate	✔	No
Mathematics	✔	No
Broad Mathematics	✔	No
Math Calculation Skills	✔	No
Math Problem Solving	✔	✔
Written Language	✔	No
Broad Written Language	✔	No
Basic Writing Skills	✔	Ages 5 and up only
Written Expression	✔	No
Academic Skills	✔	No
Academic Fluency	✔	No
Academic Applications	✔	No
Academic Knowledge	✔	✔

(continued)

Composite Score	Full Administration	No Response Booklets
	Composite Score Available?	
Phoneme-Grapheme Knowledge	✔	✔
Brief Achievement	✔	Ages 5 and up only
Broad Achievement	✔	No

TELE-ASSESSMENT WITH BRIEF AND TARGETED ACHIEVEMENT TESTS

Comprehensive Test of Phonological Processing, Second Edition (CTOPP-2)

The evidence for equivalence of tele-assessment and face-to-face administration relevant to the Comprehensive Test of Phonological Processing, Second Edition (CTOPP-2; Wagner, Torgesen, Rashotte, & Pearson, 1999) is reviewed in this section. Special administration considerations are discussed.

CTOPP-2 Equivalence Evidence

There have been no direct studies on the CTOPP-2 and tele-assessment; however, the basic input and output demands of the tasks have support. Rapid Reference 7.10 provides analysis of the input and output demands and lists relevant indirect evidence by age range.

≡Rapid Reference 7.10

CTOPP-2 Input and Output Demands and Equivalence Evidence

Subtest(s)	Input	Output	Evidence[a] Citation: Task Abbreviation/Ages
Elison Blending Words Phoneme Isolation Blending Nonwords Segmenting Nonwords	Brief spoken directions, spoken stimuli	Brief spoken response, open ended	**Indirect evidence:** Wright, 2018b: PP/5–16

Subtest(s)	Input	Output	Evidence[a] Citation: Task Abbreviation/Ages
Sound Matching	Brief spoken directions, picture stimuli, spoken stimuli	Brief spoken response, multiple choice	**Indirect evidence:** Wright, 2018b: PP/5–16
Memory for Digits Nonword Repetition	Brief spoken directions, spoken stimuli	Open ended, spoken response	**Direct Evidence: Indirect Evidence:** Cullum et al., 2006: DS/51–84 Cullum et al., 2014: DS/46–90 Galusha-Glasscock et al., 2016: DS/58–84 Grosch et al., 2015: DS/67–85 Hodge et al., 2019: DS/8–12 Jacobsen et al., 2003: DS/adult Stain et al., 2011: DS/14–27 Vahia et al., 2015: DS/65+ Wadsworth et al., 2018: DS/adult Wright, 2018b: NR/5–16 Wright, 2020b: DS, LN/6–16 (LN not equivalent)
Rapid Digit Naming Rapid Letter Naming	Brief spoken directions, letters digits or symbols in print	Spoken response	**Indirect evidence:** Wright, 2018b: LWI/5–16
Rapid Color Naming Rapid Object Naming	Brief spoken directions, picture stimuli	Spoken response	**Indirect evidence:** Wright, 2018a: SNT/7–19

[a]**Evidence column task abbreviations:** DS = Digit Span, LN = Letter–Number Sequencing, LWI = Letter–Word Identification, NR = Numbers Reversed, PP = Phonological Processing, SNT = Speeded Naming Task.

CTOPP-2 Administration Considerations

The CTOPP-2 can be administered via tele-assessment using the virtual picture book, which is available from the test's publisher, Pro-Ed, and delivered by RedShelf. Administering the CTOPP-2 via tele-assessment requires high quality audio and video. A headset with a microphone is recommended for both the examinee and examiner. Recording the examinee's responses throughout the test is recommended for later review and scoring clarity. Special administration considerations are listed in Rapid Reference 7.11.

≡ Rapid Reference 7.11

CTOPP-2 Administration Considerations

Subtest(s)	Administration Considerations
Elison Blending Words Phoneme Isolation Blending Nonwords Segmenting Nonwords	• Examiner provides spoken stimuli and examinee response verbally
Sound Matching	• Examiner uses mouse/cursor to point to virtual picture book on screen
Memory for Digits Nonword Repetition	• Do not repeat stimuli unless it was not heard due to technical problems
Rapid Digit Naming Rapid Letter Naming Rapid Color Naming Rapid Object Naming	• Examiner points to virtual picture book on screen • Examiner uses stopwatch

GRAY ORAL READING TESTS, FIFTH EDITION (GORT-5)

The evidence for equivalence of tele-assessment and face-to-face administration relevant to the Gray Oral Reading Tests, Fifth Edition (GORT-5; Wiederholt & Bryant, 2012) is reviewed in this section. Special administration considerations are discussed.

GORT-5 Equivalence Evidence

There have been no direct studies on the GORT-5 and tele-assessment; however, the basic input and output demands of the task have support. Rapid Reference 7.12 provides analysis of the input and output demands and lists relevant indirect evidence by age range.

≋ Rapid Reference 7.12

GORT-5 Input and Output Demands and Equivalence Evidence

Input	Output	Evidence[a] Citation: Task Abbreviation/Ages
Brief spoken directions, words in print	Open ended, spoken response	**Indirect evidence:** Dekhtyar et al., 2020: RCd, RCS, RIW, RNW/26–75 Stain et al., 2011: WTAR/14–27 Wright, 2018b: LWI, NS, OR, PCO, WA/5–16

[a]**Evidence column task abbreviations:** LWI = Letter–Word Identification, NS = Number Series, OR = Oral Reading, PCO = Passage Comprehension, RCd = Reading Commands, RCS = Reading Comprehension of Sentences, RIW = Reading Irregular Words, RNW = Reading Nonwords, WA = Word Attack, WTAR = Wechsler Test of Adult Reading.

GORT-5 Administration Considerations

The GORT-5 can be administered via tele-assessment using the virtual student's book, which is available from the test's publisher, Pro-Ed, and delivered by RedShelf. The examiner will need a record booklet.

Administering the GORT-5 via tele-assessment requires high quality audio and video. A headset with a microphone is recommended for both the examinee and examiner. Special administration considerations are listed in Rapid Reference 7.13.

≋ Rapid Reference 7.13

GORT-5 Administration Considerations

Administration Considerations

- Examiner uses mouse/cursor to point to stimuli on screen
- Audio recording examinee's responses is recommended to provide clarity for scoring
- Examiner uses stopwatch

GRAY SILENT READING TESTS (GSRT)

The evidence for equivalence of tele-assessment and face-to-face administration relevant to the Gray Silent Reading Tests (GRST; Wiederholt & Blalock, 2000) is reviewed in this section. Special administration considerations are discussed.

GRST Equivalence Evidence

There have been no direct studies on the GRST and tele-assessment; however, the basic input and output demands of the task have support. Rapid Reference 7.14 provides analysis of the input and output demands and lists relevant indirect evidence by age range.

≣ Rapid Reference 7.14

GRST Input and Output Demands and Equivalence Evidence

Input	Output	Evidence[a] Citation: Task Abbreviation/ Ages
Brief spoken directions, words in print	Multiple choice, simple written response	**Indirect evidence:** Dekhtyar et al., 2020: RCS/26–75 Wright, 2018b: PCO/5–16

[a]**Evidence column task abbreviations:** PCO = Passage Comprehension, RCS = Reading Comprehension of Sentences.

GRST Administration Considerations

The GRST can be administered via tele-assessment using the virtual reading book, which is available from the test's publisher, Pro-Ed, and delivered by RedShelf.

Administering the GRST via tele-assessment requires high quality audio and video. A headset with a microphone is recommended for both the examinee and examiner. Special administration considerations are listed in Rapid Reference 7.15.

≣ Rapid Reference 7.15

GRST Administration Considerations

Administration Considerations

* Examiner displays virtual reading book on screen
* Examiner uses mouse/cursor to point to stimuli on screen

MATHEMATICS FLUENCY AND CALCULATION TESTS (MFACTS)

The evidence for equivalence of tele-assessment and face-to-face administration relevant to the Mathematics Fluency and Calculation Tests (MFaCTs; Reynolds, Voress, & Kamphaus, 2014) is reviewed in this section. Special administration considerations are discussed.

MFaCTs Equivalence Evidence

There have been no direct studies on the MFaCTs and tele-assessment; however, the basic input and output demands of the tasks have support. Rapid Reference 7.16 provides analysis of the input and output demands and lists relevant indirect evidence by age range.

≣ Rapid Reference 7.16

MFaCTs Input and Output Demands and Equivalence Evidence

Subtest	Input	Output	Evidence[a] Citation: Task Abbreviation/Ages
Fluency	Brief spoken directions, letters digits or symbols in print, record sheet	Task-level time limit; written response	**Indirect evidence:** Dekhtyar et al., 2020: CL, MC/26–75 Wright, 2018b: CL, MFF/5–16

(continued)

Subtest	Input	Output	Evidence[a] Citation: Task Abbreviation/Ages
Calculation	Brief spoken directions, letters digits or symbols in print, record booklet	Written response	**Indirect evidence:** Dekhtyar et al., 2020: CL, MC/26–75 Wright, 2018b: CL, MFF/5–16

[a]Evidence column task abbreviations: CL = Calculation, MC = Math Calculation, MFF = Math Facts Fluency.

MFaCTs Administration Considerations

The MFaCTs can be administered via tele-assessment using the virtual examiner's manual, which is available from the test's publisher, Pro-Ed, and delivered by RedShelf. It can also be administered using the paper manual, if one is available. A record sheet and a record booklet are needed in the examinee's location.

Administering the MFaCTs via tele-assessment requires high quality audio and video. A headset with a microphone is recommended for both the examinee and examiner. Special administration considerations are listed in Rapid Reference 7.17.

≋ Rapid Reference 7.17

MFaCTs Administration Considerations

Administration Considerations

- Examiner provides brief verbal instructions
- *Optional*: Peripheral camera/device can be placed in stable position that shows examinee's record sheet and record booklet and provides a view of examinee's written responses

RAPID AUTOMATIZED NAMING AND RAPID ALTERNATING STIMULUS TESTS (RAN/RAS)

The evidence for equivalence of tele-assessment and face-to-face administration relevant to the Rapid Automatized Naming and Rapid Alternating Stimulus Tests

(RAN/RAS; Wolf & Denckla, 2005) is reviewed in this section. Special administration considerations are discussed.

RAN/RAS Equivalence Evidence

There have been no direct studies on the RAN/RAS and tele-assessment; however, the basic input and output demands of the tasks have support. Rapid Reference 7.18 provides analysis of the input and output demands and lists relevant indirect evidence by age range.

≡ Rapid Reference 7.18

RAN/RAS Input and Output Demands and Equivalence Evidence

Input	Output	Evidence Citation: Task/Ages
Brief spoken directions, gestured directions, letters numbers or symbols in print, picture stimuli	Open ended, spoken response, task-level time limit	**Indirect Evidence:** Wright, 2018a: Speeded Naming Task/7–19

RAN/RAS Administration Considerations

The RAN/RAS can be administered via tele-assessment using the virtual card pack, which is available from the test's publisher, Pro-Ed, and delivered by RedShelf.

Administering the RAN/RAS via tele-assessment requires high quality audio and video. A headset with a microphone is recommended for both the examinee and examiner. Special administration considerations are listed in Rapid Reference 7.19.

≡ Rapid Reference 7.19

RAN/RAS Administration Considerations

Administration Considerations

- Examiner uses mouse/cursor to point to stimuli on screen
- Audio recording examinee's responses is recommended to provide clarity for scoring
- Examiner uses stopwatch

TEST OF PRESCHOOL EARLY LITERACY (TOPEL)

The evidence for equivalence of tele-assessment and face-to-face administration relevant to the Test of Preschool Early Literacy (TOPEL; Lonigan, Wagner, Torgesen, & Rashotte, 2007) is reviewed in this section. Special administration considerations are discussed.

TOPEL Equivalence Evidence

There have been no direct studies on the TOPEL and tele-assessment; however, the basic input and output demands of the tasks have support. Rapid Reference 7.20 provides analysis of the input and output demands and lists relevant indirect evidence by age range. However, because the age range of the TOPEL is 3 to 5–11, there is only even indirect support for using this test for those age 5 to 5–11. Using this test in a tele-assessment context with children younger than 5 should be approached with extreme caution.

≋ Rapid Reference 7.20

TOPEL Input and Output Demands and Equivalence Evidence

Subtest	Input	Output	Evidence[a] Citation: Task Abbreviation/Ages
Print Knowledge	Brief spoken directions, letters digits or symbols in print, spoken stimuli, words in print	Brief spoken response, pointing response	**Indirect Evidence:** Wright, 2018b: LWI/5–16 Wright, 2018b: NS, OR, PCO, WA/5–16
Definitional Vocabulary	Brief spoken directions, picture stimuli	Brief spoken response, open ended	**Indirect Evidence:** Sutherland et al., 2017: FS, WS/8–12 Waite et al., 2010: FS, WS/5–9
Phonological Awareness	Brief spoken directions, spoken stimuli	Open ended, spoken response	**Indirect evidence:** Wright, 2018b: PP/5–16

[a]**Evidence column task abbreviations:** BNT = Boston Naming Test, FS = Formulated Sentences, LWI = Letter–Word Identification, NS = Number Series, OR = Oral Reading, PCO = Passage Comprehension, PD = Picture Description, PN = Picture Naming, PP = Phonological Processing, WA = Word Attack, WS = Word Structure.

TOPEL Administration Considerations

The TOPEL can be administered via tele-assessment using the virtual picture book, which is available from the test's publisher, Pro-Ed, and delivered by RedShelf. Administering the TOPEL via tele-assessment requires high quality audio and video. A headset with a microphone is recommended for both the examinee and examiner. Recording the examinees responses throughout the test is recommended for later review and scoring clarity. Special administration considerations are listed in Rapid Reference 7.21.

≡ Rapid Reference 7.21

TOPEL Administration Considerations

Subtest	Administration Considerations
Print Knowledge	• Examiner uses mouse/cursor to point to virtual picture book on screen
Definitional Vocabulary	• Examiner uses mouse/cursor to point to virtual picture book on screen
Phonological Awareness	• Examiner provides verbal stimuli and examinee responds verbally

TEST OF WRITTEN LANGUAGE, FOURTH EDITION (TOWL-4)

The evidence for equivalence of tele-assessment and face-to-face administration relevant to the Test of Written Language, Fourth Edition (TOWL-4; Hammill & Larsen, 2009) is reviewed in this section. Special administration considerations are discussed.

TOWL-4 Equivalence Evidence

There have been no direct studies on the TOWL-4 and tele-assessment; however, the basic input and output demands of the tasks have support. Rapid Reference 7.22 provides analysis of the input and output demands and lists relevant indirect evidence by age range.

≡ Rapid Reference 7.22

....

TOWL-4 Input and Output Demands and Equivalence Evidence

Subtest	Input	Output	Evidence[a] Citation: Task Abbreviation/Ages
Vocabulary	Brief spoken directions, response booklet, spoken stimuli	Written response	**Indirect evidence:** Dekhtyar et al., 2020: SP, WDW, WID, WND, WTD/26–75 Wright, 2018b: SP/5–16
Spelling	Brief spoken directions, response booklet, spoken stimuli	Written response	**Indirect evidence:** Dekhtyar et al., 2020: SP, WDW, WID, WND, WTD/26–75 Wright, 2018b: SP/5–16
Punctuation	Brief spoken directions, response booklet, spoken stimuli	Written response	**Indirect evidence:** Dekhtyar et al., 2020: SP, WDW, WID, WND, WTD/26–75 Wright, 2018b: SP/5–16
Logical Sentences	Brief spoken directions, response booklet, words in print	Written response	**Indirect evidence:** Dekhtyar et al., 2020: SP, WDW, WID, WND, WTD/26–75 Wright, 2018b: SP/5–16
Sentence Combining	Brief spoken directions, response booklet, words in print	Written response	**Indirect evidence:** Dekhtyar et al., 2020: SP, WDW, WID, WND, WTD/26–75 Wright, 2018b: SP/5–16
Contextual Conventions	Brief spoken directions, picture stimuli, response booklet	Written response	**Indirect evidence:** Dekhtyar et al., 2020: WO/26–75 Wright, 2018b: WSp/5–16

Subtest	Input	Output	Evidence[a] Citation: Task Abbreviation/Ages
Story Composition	Brief spoken directions, response booklet	Written response	**Indirect evidence:** Dekhtyar et al., 2020: WO/26–75 Wright, 2018b: WSp/5–16

[a]**Evidence column task abbreviations:** SP = Spelling, SWF = Sentence Writing Fluency, WDW = Writing Dictated Words, WF = Word Fluency, WID = Writing Irregular Words to Dictation, WND = Writing Nonwords to Dictation, WTD = Writing to Dictation, WO = Writing Output, WSp = Writing Samples.

TOWL-4 Administration Considerations

The TOWL-4 can be administered via tele-assessment using the virtual stimuli (picture cards), which are available from the test's publisher, Pro-Ed, and delivered by RedShelf. A response booklet is needed in the examinee's location. Without the response booklet, very little in the way of administration can be completed, so this is required.

Administering the TOWL-4 via tele-assessment requires high quality audio and video. A headset with a microphone is recommended for both the examinee and examiner. Special administration considerations are listed in Rapid Reference 7.23.

≋ Rapid Reference 7.23

TOWL-4 Administration Considerations

Subtests	Administration Considerations
Vocabulary Spelling Punctuation Logical Sentences Spelling	• Requires response booklet • Requires examinee to have pencil • Peripheral camera/device should be placed in a stable position that shows examinee's response booklet and provides examiner a view of examinee's written responses • Examiner should do what is necessary to help the examinee to understand instructions (e.g., holding up and pointing at a paper response booklet, demonstrating on screen during the testing session)

Subtests	Administration Considerations
Contextual Conventions Story Composition	• Examiner uses mouse/cursor to point to virtual picture cards on screen • Requires response booklet • Requires examinee to have pencil • Peripheral camera/device should be placed in a stable position that shows examinee's response booklet and provides examiner a view of examinee's written responses • Examiner should do what is necessary to help the examinee to understand instructions (e.g., holding up and pointing at a paper response booklet, demonstrating on screen during the testing session)

TEST OF WORD READING EFFICIENCY, SECOND EDITION (TOWRE-2)

The evidence for equivalence of tele-assessment and face-to-face administration relevant to the Test of Word Reading Efficiency, Second Edition (TOWRE-2; Torgesen, Wagner, & Rashotte, 2012) is reviewed in this section. Special administration considerations are discussed.

TOWRE-2 Equivalence Evidence

There have been no direct studies on the TOWRE-2 and tele-assessment; however, the basic input and output demands of the task have support. Rapid Reference 7.24 provides analysis of the input and output demands and lists relevant indirect evidence by age range.

≡ Rapid Reference 7.24

TOWRE-2 Input and Output Demands and Equivalence Evidence

Input	Output	Evidence[a] Citation: Task Abbreviation/Ages
Brief spoken directions, words in print	Open ended, spoken response	**Indirect evidence:** Dekhtyar et al., 2020: RCd, RCS, RIW, RNW/26–75 Stain et al., 2011: WTAR/14–27 Wright, 2018b: LWI, NS, OR, WA/5–16

[a]**Evidence column task abbreviations:** LWI = Letter–Word Identification, NS = Number Series, OR = Oral Reading, RCd = Reading Commands, RCS = Reading Comprehension of Sentences, RIW = Reading Irregular Words, RNW = Reading Nonwords, WA = Word Attack, WTAR = Wechsler Test of Adult Reading.

TOWRE-2 Administration Considerations

The TOWRE-2 can be administered via tele-assessment using the virtual word cards, which are available from the test's publisher, Pro-Ed, and delivered by RedShelf. The examiner will need a record booklet.

Administering the TOWRE-2 via tele-assessment requires high quality audio and video. A headset with a microphone is recommended for both the examinee and examiner. Special administration considerations are listed in Rapid Reference 7.25.

≝ Rapid Reference 7.25

TOWRE-2 Administration Considerations

Administration Considerations

- Examiner uses mouse/cursor to point to stimuli on screen
- Audio recording examinee's responses is recommended to provide clarity for scoring
- Examiner uses stopwatch

WIDE RANGE ACHIEVEMENT TEST, FIFTH EDITION (WRAT5)

This section reviews the Wide Range Achievement Test, Fifth Edition (WRAT5; Wilkinson & Robertson, 2017) evidence for equivalence of tele-assessment and face-to-face administration. Special administration considerations are discussed.

WRAT5 Equivalence Evidence

There have been no direct studies on the WRAT5 and tele-assessment; however, the basic input and output demands of the tasks have support. Rapid Reference 7.26 provides analysis of the input and output demands and lists relevant indirect evidence by age range.

≡ Rapid Reference 7.26

WRAT5 Input and Output Demands and Equivalence Evidence

Subtest(s)	Input	Output	Evidence[a] Citation: Task Abbreviation/Ages
Word Reading	Brief spoken directions, letters in print, words in print	Open ended, spoken response	**Indirect evidence:** Dekhtyar et al., 2020: RCd, RCS, RIW, RNW/26–75 Stain et al., 2011: WTAR/14–27 Wright, 2018b: LWI, OR, PCO, WA/5–16
Math Computation	Letters digits or symbols in print, response booklet, spoken directions	Brief spoken response, gestured response, open ended, pointing response, task-level time limit, written response	**Indirect evidence:** Dekhtyar et al., 2020: CL, MC/26–75 Wright, 2018b: AP, CL, MFF/5–16 Wright, 2020b: AR/6–16
Sentence Comprehension	Brief spoken directions, words in print	Open ended, brief spoken response	**Indirect evidence:** Dekhtyar et al., 2020: RCd, RCS, RIW, RNW/26–75 Stain et al., 2011: WTAR/14–27 Wright, 2018b: LWI, OR, PCO, WA/5–16
Spelling	Brief spoken directions, response booklet, spoken stimuli	Written response	**Indirect evidence:** Dekhtyar et al., 2020: SP, WDW, WID, WND/26–75 Wright, 2018b: SP/5–16

[a]**Evidence column task abbreviations:** AR = Arithmetic, CL = Calculation, LWI = Letter–Word Identification, MC = Math Calculation, MFF = Math Facts Fluency, OR = Oral Reading, PCO = Passage Comprehension, RCd = Reading Commands, RCS = Reading Comprehension of Sentences, RIW = Reading Irregular Words, RNW = Reading Nonwords, SP = Spelling, WA = Word Attack, WDW = Writing Dictated Words, WID = Writing Irregular Words to Dictation, WND = Writing Nonwords to Dictation, WTAR = Wechsler Test of Adult Reading.

WRAT5 Administration Considerations

The WRAT5 can be administered via tele-assessment in multiple ways. There are two platforms where the digital stimuli are available: Q-global and Q-interactive. A paper response booklet is necessary with both platforms, and a paper record form is necessary with Q-global.

Administering the WRAT5 via tele-assessment requires high quality audio and video for nearly all tasks, and that both examiner and examinee can clearly view one another's mouths when speaking as well. A headset with a microphone is recommended for both the examinee and examiner.

Special administration considerations are listed by subtest in Rapid Reference 7.27.

≡ Rapid Reference 7.27

WRAT5 Administration Considerations

Subtest	Administration Considerations
Word Reading	• Examiner uses mouse/cursor to point to stimuli on screen
Math Computation	• Requires response booklet • Requires examinee to have pencil • Examiner uses mouse/cursor to point to stimuli on screen • Examinee uses mouse to point to some items • Peripheral camera/device should be placed in a stable position that shows examinee's response booklet and provides examiner a view of examinee's written and pointing responses • Examiner can point to digital response booklet on screen during testing session
Sentence Comprehension	• Examiner accesses and displays stimuli
Spelling	• Requires response booklet • Requires examinee to have pencil • Peripheral camera/device should be placed in a stable position that shows examinee's response booklet and provides examiner a view of examinee's written responses • Examiner can point to digital response booklet on screen during testing session • Examiner can do what is necessary to help the examinee to understand instructions (e.g., holding up and pointing at a paper response booklet, demonstrating on screen during the testing session, pointing to or marking on the digital copy of the response booklet displayed onscreen with the writing utensil tool)

WOODCOCK READING MASTERY TEST, THIRD EDITION (WRMT-III)

This section reviews the Woodcock Reading Mastery Test, Third Edition (WRMT-III; Woodcock, 2011) evidence for equivalence of tele-assessment and face-to-face administration. Special administration considerations are discussed.

WRMT-III Equivalence Evidence

There have been no direct studies on the WRMT-III and tele-assessment; however, the basic input and output demands of the tasks have support. Rapid Reference 7.28 provides analysis of the input and output demands and lists relevant indirect evidence by age range.

≡ Rapid Reference 7.28

WRMT-III Input and Output Demands and Equivalence Evidence

Subtest(s)	Input	Output	Evidence[a] Citation: Task Abbreviation/Ages
Letter Identification Word Identification	Brief spoken directions, letters digits or symbols in print	Open ended, spoken response	**Indirect Evidence:** Dekhtyar et al., 2020: RCd, RCS, RIW, RNW/26–75 Stain et al., 2011: WTAR/14–27 Wright, 2018b: NS, OR, PCO, WA/5–16 Wright, 2018b: LWI/5–16
Phonological Awareness	Brief spoken directions, picture stimuli, spoken stimuli, words in print	Multiple choice, open ended, pointing response, spoken response	**Indirect Evidence:** Brearly et al., 2017: SF/adult Dekhtyar et al., 2020: WF/26–75 Galusha-Glasscock et al., 2016: SF/58–84 Hildebrand et al., 2004: CWAT/60+ Stain et al., 2011: CWAT/14–27 Wright, 2018b: LWI, PP/5–16

Subtest(s)	Input	Output	Evidence[a] Citation: Task Abbreviation/Ages
Rapid Picture Naming	Brief spoken directions, gestured directions, picture stimuli	Open ended, spoken response, task-level time limit	**Indirect Evidence:** Wright, 2018a: SNT/7–19
Word Attack	Brief spoken directions, words in print	Brief spoken response, open ended	**Indirect evidence:** Dekhtyar et al., 2020: RCd, RCS, RIW, RNW/26–75 Stain et al., 2011: WTAR/14–27 Wright, 2018b: LWI, NS, OR, PCO/5–16 Wright, 2018b: WA/5–16
Listening Comprehension	Audio recorded stimuli, picture stimuli, spoken directions, spoken stimuli	Multiple choice, open ended, pointing response, spoken response	**Indirect evidence:** Wright, 2018a: VM/3–19 Wright, 2018b: SR, VA/5–16
Word Comprehension: Antonyms, Synonyms, & Analogies	Spoken directions, words in print	Open ended, spoken response	**Indirect Evidence:** Dekhtyar et al., 2020: CQ/26–75 Hildebrand et al., 2004: VC/60+ Hodge et al., 2019: SI, VC/8–12 Jacobsen et al., 2003: VC/adult Temple et al., 2010: VC/23–63 Turkstra et al., 2012: MDEP, ABD/21–69 Wright, 2018a: GW, VR/3–19 Wright, 2018b: OV, GI/5–16 Wright, 2020b: SI, VC, IN, CO/6–16
Passage Comprehension	Brief spoken directions, picture stimuli, spoken stimuli, words in print	Open ended, spoken response	**Indirect evidence:** Dekhtyar et al., 2020: RCd, RCS, RIW, RNW/26–75 Stain et al., 2011: WTAR/14–27 Wright, 2018b: LWI, NS, OR, PCO, WA/5–16

(continued)

Subtest(s)	Input	Output	Evidence[a] Citation: Task Abbreviation/Ages
Oral Reading Fluency	Brief spoken directions, words in print	Item-level time limit, spoken response	**Indirect evidence:** Dekhtyar et al., 2020: RCd, RCS, RIW, RNW/26–75 Stain et al., 2011: WTAR/14–27 Wright, 2018b: LWI, NS, OR, PCO, WA/5–16

[a]**Evidence column task abbreviations:** ABD = Aphasia Bank Discourse, CO = Comprehension, CQ = Conversational Questions, CWAT = Controlled Word Association Test, GI = General Information, GW = Guess What, IN = Information, LWI = Letter–Word Identification, MDEP = Mediated Discourse Elicitation Protocol, NS = Number Series, OV = Oral Vocabulary, OR = Oral Reading, PCO = Passage Comprehension, PP = Phonological Processing, RCd = Reading Commands, RCS = Reading Comprehension of Sentences, RIW = Reading Irregular Words, RNW = Reading Nonwords, SF = Semantic Fluency, SI = Similarities, SNT = Speeded Naming Task, SR = Story Recall, VA = Verbal Attention, VC = Vocabulary, VM = Verbal Memory, VR = Verbal Reasoning, WA = Word Attack, WF = Word Fluency, WTAR = Wechsler Test of Adult Reading.

WRMT-III Administration Considerations

The WRMT-III can be administered via tele-assessment using the stimuli on Q-global. The WRMT-III requires high-quality audio and video and a headset with a microphone for both the examinee and examiner for nearly all tasks. The examiner and examinee should almost always be positioned to see one another's mouths. The examiner must have access to test directions through the physical test book easels. Special administration considerations are listed by test in Rapid Reference 7.29.

≡ Rapid Reference 7.29
· ·

WRMT-III Administration Considerations

Subtest(s)	Administration Considerations
Letter Identification Word Identification	• Examiner uses mouse/cursor to point to stimuli on screen • *Word Identification:* Audio recording examinee's responses is recommended to provide clarity for scoring

Subtest(s)	Administration Considerations
Phonological Awareness	• *First-Sound Matching and Last Sound Matching*: Examiner uses mouse/cursor to point to stimuli on screen • Examinee points to or says name of correct answer on screen • *Optional*: peripheral camera/device can be positioned in stable position to show examinee's screen and provide view of responses given nonverbally through pointing
Rapid Automatic Naming	• Examiner uses mouse/cursor to point to stimuli on screen • Audio recording examinee's responses is recommended to provide clarity for scoring • Examiner uses stopwatch
Word Attack	• Examiner uses mouse/cursor to point to stimuli on screen • Audio recording examinee's responses is recommended to provide clarity for scoring
Listening Comprehension	• Requires examiner to stream audio from online platform • Do not repeat any stimuli unless they were not heard due to technical problems; questions may be repeated once
Word Comprehension	• Examiner uses mouse/cursor to point to stimuli on screen • Audio recording examinee's responses is recommended to provide clarity for scoring
Passage Comprehension	• Examiner uses mouse/cursor to point to stimuli on screen
Oral Reading Fluency	• Examiner uses mouse/cursor to point to stimuli on screen • Audio recording examinee's responses is recommended to provide clarity for scoring • Examiner uses stopwatch

CONCLUSION

Digital stimuli for a wide variety of academic achievement tests are available to psychologists. There are a variety of tools and platforms where the stimuli can be obtained for use in tele-assessment. Psychologists should have an easy time finding digital stimuli for almost any achievement-related skill they wish to appraise.

While achievement tests have specific considerations related to tele-assessment that should be prepared for and attended to, and there are many similarities across these tasks. However, there is still an added layer of complexity relative to face-to-face administration. Psychologists should thoroughly review these issues and practice all items of any task before administering it via tele-assessment in a clinical context. It is particularly important with achievement tasks to manage response sheets and booklets and ensure they are all returned, as many of these measures require written responses of some fashion.

Relative to cognitive tasks, there are fewer studies on equivalence between face-to-face and tele-assessment modes on achievement tests. Many have not yet been studied specifically, but the input and output demands are very similar to those of other tasks that have been. Many types of tasks have research that supports their equivalence in face-to-face and remote, tele-assessment context, either directly or indirectly.

There is a great deal of redundancy in the achievement tests available for tele-assessment. This is good news for psychologists wishing to test in this mode, because any subtest, test, or task that gets spoiled somehow (e.g., because of technology issues) can be supplemented by another, very similar task from another measure. Psychologists are encouraged to know the state of the literature supporting the achievement tests they are using clinically and interpret accordingly.

Eight

PERSONALITY, EMOTIONAL, AND BEHAVIORAL TELE-ASSESSMENT

In general, personality, emotional, and behavioral assessment (most often called "personality assessment" for short, but also directly related to the assessment of psychopathology) is significantly less affected by the switch to tele-assessment procedures than are cognitive, neuropsychological, and academic achievement tests. Assessment of personality and psychopathology has heavily relied on multiple methods and multiple informants, and the overwhelming modalities employed have generally not been performance-based (i.e., requiring interaction between the psychologist, client, and stimulus materials). There are certainly exceptions, as will be discussed in the sections on performance-based measures of psychopathology and behavioral assessment, but in general interviews, rating forms, questionnaires, and other methods that are less susceptible to method effects when moved into a tele-assessment framework are the foundation of the work.

MULTI-METHOD ASSESSMENT

As pointed out by the Society for Personality Assessment (COVID-19 Task Force to Support Personality Assessment, 2020), best practice in evidence-based psychological assessment, especially of psychopathology, is to collect and integrate information from multiple measures, methods, and (when appropriate) reporters (Bornstein, 2017; De Los Reyes et al., 2015; Hunsley & Mash, 2007; Youngstrom, Choukas-Bradley, Calhoun, & Jensen-Doss, 2015). This approach acknowledges the limitations of any test to reflect precisely the underlying construct it is meant to assess, for multiple test error reasons (AERA, APA, & NCME, 2014). For example, clinical interviews are limited by insight; self-report measures are subject to response bias; collateral-report measures are

Essentials of Psychological Tele-Assessment, First Edition.
A. Jordan Wright and Susan Engi Raiford
© 2021 John Wiley & Sons, Inc. Published 2021 by John Wiley & Sons, Inc.

also subject to response bias, as well as limited to the traits and behaviors observed by the collateral source; and performance-based methods have built-in test error. All of this (and more) error is the consequence of trying to assess underlying traits, functioning, and abilities that are not directly accessible (rather than, say, cholesterol or body mass index, which *are* directly accessible via medical assessment techniques).

Psychological assessment, and indeed psychological tele-assessment, requires the triangulation of data—scrutinizing data that emerge from different sources, measures, and methods for convergence of information—in order to build confidence in clinical assertions. As varied and increasing data support a clinical conclusion, confidence in that conclusion is strengthened. In a tele-assessment situation, confirming data from altered administration procedures (such as performance-based personality measures) using methods and measures that have not been altered significantly or at all (like self- and collateral-report interviews and questionnaires) can validate the information that emerges.

> **DON'T FORGET**
> ....
> Psychological assessment, and indeed psychological tele-assessment, requires the integration of data that emerge from different sources, measures, and methods in order to build confidence in clinical assertions.

CLINICAL INTERVIEWS

Clinical interviews are perhaps the most widely used methodology in clinical (and most other) assessment, widely taught across graduate programs (Mihura, Roy, & Graceffo, 2017) as a foundational step in the assessment process. Clinical interviews, however, have significant problems associated with the quality of data they elicit (e.g., Orbach & Lamb, 2001; Ramsden, 2018). Regardless, clinical interviews are important for determining specific assessment questions, understanding any presenting problems and functional impairment, situating current functioning within appropriate context (cultural, historical, and current), and ultimately developing hypotheses for what is likely occurring for an individual. Psychological tests and measures can rule out or support these hypotheses (Wright, 2020a). The major issue to grapple with in tele-assessment is whether or not information elicited from a clinical interview over videoconferencing technology is generally as reliable and valid (and imperfect) as in face-to-face interviewing situations.

In general, research definitely supports the adequacy of data that emerge from tele-assessment clinical interviews (Schopp, Johnstone, & Merrell, 2000; Singh, Arya, & Peters, 2007). SPA (COVID-19 Task Force to Support Personality Assessment, 2020) notes that a major contributing factor to the usability of data from clinical interviews has to do with a positive therapeutic alliance, which has been shown to be a strength of tele-assessment and tele-health services in general (Bouchard et al., 2000; Germain, Marchand, Bouchard, Guay, & Drouin, 2010; Morgan, Patrick, & Magaletta, 2008; Simpson, 2001). Additionally, as with any clinical interview data, psychologists need to determine the likelihood of misinformation being reported due to lack of insight and understanding, clinical or cognitive issues (like problems with memory), or motivated skewed reporting (e.g., for secondary gain).

In traditional assessment practice, structured and even semi-structured clinical interviews have emerged as superior for diagnostic accuracy when compared to unstructured clinical interviews (Sternberg, Lamb, Esplin, Orbach, & Hershkowitz, 2002). This is especially true regarding the detection of comorbid disorders and other difficulties not directly related to the primary presenting problem (Zimmerman, 2016). However, a very small proportion of clinicians uses structured clinical interviews, opting instead for much broader use of unstructured clinical interviews (Bruchmüller, Margraf, Suppiger, & Schneider, 2011). The transition to tele-assessment may spur clinicians to transition to more empirically supported structured, standardized methodologies, such as structured clinical interviews.

The research provides reasonably strong support for structured clinical interviews in a tele-assessment context for diagnostic purposes (Hyler, Gangure, & Batchelder, 2005; Malhotra et al., 2017; Ruskin et al., 1998; Shore, Savin, Orton, Beals, & Manson, 2007). In general, most research has found no significant difference between diagnostic decisions made in tele-assessment and in-person contexts using structured and semi-structured clinical interviews. This finding is true both for broad diagnostic interviews (like the Structured Clinical Interview for DSM Disorders [SCID; current version First, Williams, Karg, & Spitzer, 2015] and the Diagnostic Interview for Anxiety, Mood, and OCD and Related Neuropsychiatric Disorders [DIAMOND; Tolin et al., 2018]) and for more targeted structured diagnostic interviews (like the Yale–Brown Obsessive-Compulsive Scale [YBOCS; Goodman et al., 1989]). In general, the data elicited in a tele-assessment context from structured clinical interviews seems to be largely intact and as usable as those from a traditional, in-person assessment.

COMPONENTS THAT DO NOT CHANGE MUCH

SPA's guidance document (COVID-19 Task Force to Support Personality Assessment, 2020) highlights that there are some components of psychological assessment that do not change at all in a tele-assessment context. Specifically, reviews of records are widely used to collect especially historical context and data in order to take advantage of any documented information that can help elucidate a client's current functioning. This information can be invaluable and an integral part of the assessment process (Braden, 2003; Fink, 2017). The process for reviewing records does not change significantly in a tele-assessment context. The one consideration to attend to is the data security of records, which are most likely to be sent in electronic format in a tele-assessment (rather than physical paper records, which may be provided in an in-person assessment). Psychologists need to discuss risks to data privacy when clients email records to them, for example, which can be easily intercepted (if not using an encrypted system or password protecting the documents themselves, which may be beyond the ability of many clients). Other than these privacy concerns, the actual process of reviewing records is identical in tele-assessment and traditional assessment.

The other component of psychological tele-assessment that remains almost entirely the same is the use of survey questionnaires to collect collateral-report information. There are some collateral-report measures that are only available in pencil-and-paper format, and these may not be available for use in tele-assessment (you should not use these in a digital format without the explicit permission from the test publishers to do so). The most widely used collateral-report measures, though, including teacher, parent, and caregiver/caretaker reports, were already being administered via email link, with no live monitoring. These procedures can continue in the exact same format as they are typically conducted.

It is important to note that if there are contextual circumstances that both require the use of tele-assessment and are likely impacting a client's functioning, you may need to be more explicit than usual in the instructions to collateral reporters about what their responses should reflect. For example, if a pandemic has required the use of tele-assessment and has also kept a child client physically away from their school for months, it will be important to instruct teachers about what they should be referring to in their report. Teachers can report on the client from the last time they were physically in school together, or they can report on the client based on their current circumstances. Some psychologists may choose to include two different versions of the teacher-report scale, such that the psychologist can compare and use both pieces of information (prior to the pandemic and during the pandemic) to contextualize any other findings. It should be precisely clear to the psychologist what the results of a collateral-report measure reflect, though, so being more specific and directive about how teachers and other collateral reporters approach these measures can be extremely useful. Other than these extra assessment variables, though, the tele-assessment process for collecting and using collateral-informant survey questionnaire data is completely unchanged from traditional, in-person assessment.

SELF-REPORT MEASURES

SPA (COVID-19 Task Force to Support Personality Assessment, 2020) discusses the strong research base showing equivalence between self-report measures administered online via tele-assessment procedures and those administered in the traditional in-office mode. Included in these self-report measures are specific, targeted, brief survey questionnaires focused on specific symptoms and disorders (e.g., Buchanan, 2003; Kobak, 2004; Kobak, Williams, & Engelhardt, 2008), as well as some of the most widely used personality inventories (Barak & English, 2002; Barak, Hen, Boniel-Nissim, & Shapira, 2008; Buchanan, 2002; Finger & Ones, 1999; Menton et al., 2019; Naglieri et al., 2004; Roper, Ben-Porath, & Butcher, 1995). Although there are some considerations around ensuring test security and integrity when an examinee completes a self-report measure from a distance, in general the data collected are equivalent to those elicited by traditional self-report procedures.

Corey and Ben-Porath (2020) published some practical guidance on administering the Minnesota Multiphasic Personality Inventory (MMPI)—and by extension all self-report measures—at a distance in a tele-assessment context. None of the guidance is surprising to clinicians already engaging in tele-assessment. However, their guidance is practical and useful, and thus it is summarized here. The authors highlight that while self-report measures are generally entirely self-administered (clients read the instructions, read the stimuli, and respond completely independently), they should be supervised by a professional throughout. Supervision is important for two overarching purposes: to maintain an environment and context that is conducive to clients providing the best possible information, and to identify any anomalies in behavior or environment that can later help contextualize findings from the measures. As a side note, this also works toward protecting test security and integrity, as the observer should be able to tell if the client is copying down test items, looking up information on the internet, or engaging in some other problematic approach to the self-report measure. Thus, even in tele-assessment, self-report measures should be observed by a professional.

Corey and Ben-Porath (2020) state that the best practice is to have an on-site proctor—a disinterested party—observing the client taking the test. If or when this is not possible, they suggest that proctoring can occur over a tele-assessment platform, as long as both video and audio are enabled throughout. With video trained on the client, the psychologist can scan visually for environmental disruptions or client behaviors that appear abnormal. With audio enabled, the client and psychologist can communicate if needed, and any noises or other disruptions or abnormalities can be detected. The tele-assessment test-taking observation should be *synchronous*; that is, the psychologist should proctor the client filling out the self-report measure *in real time*, not delayed on a recording. Abnormalities and disruptions should be addressed while the client is engaged with the self-report measure just as they would be in traditional test-taking in an office, not after the fact.

The authors further recommend that you confirm that you can adequately observe (via audio and video) the client before providing access (e.g., sending a link) to the self-report measure itself. They provide a checklist of five components (Rapid Reference 8.1) to confirm before beginning remote test administration: confirm the client's identity so that you are sure the correct person is taking the test; ensure that you can tell that the client will be completing the measure on their own; ensure that you can observe the client's environment for abnormalities throughout test-taking; confirm that the client's environment is conducive to eliciting valid information from the client; and monitor test security. Once those five conditions have been met, you can send the self-report measure's link to the remote administration.

Corey and Ben-Porath (2020) make other recommendations, which are aligned with many of the recommendations in other chapters of this book and so will not be addressed here. However, they do recommend that you embrace the use of checklists, especially when there are multiple steps, things to consider, and possibilities to forget an aspect of practice. They provide one such checklist specific to

≡ Rapid Reference 8.1

There are five conditions to ensure before sending the link to a remote administration of a self-report measures (Corey & Ben-Porath, 2020):

1. Verify the client's identity, to ensure they are the correct person to be taking the test
2. Ensure that you will be able to tell that the client is completing the measure on their own
3. Ensure that you can observe the environment well enough to identify any abnormalities (in client behavior or in the client's environment) throughout test-taking
4. Confirm that the client's environment is conducive to eliciting valid data from the client
5. Monitor test security throughout the self-report test administration

the MMPI, broken down into steps to take before the testing session, at the beginning of the testing session, during the testing session, and after the testing session. We also encourage the use of checklists (which is why several are included in this book), and adapting theirs or any of ours can help you ensure that you do not forget a component or a step in preparation for the ethical and valid administration of self-report and other measures.

PERFORMANCE-BASED PERSONALITY, EMOTIONAL, AND PSYCHOPATHOLOGY MEASURES

There are generally two types of performance-based measures of personality, emotional functioning, and psychopathology: performance-based measures and projective techniques. While both are performance-based (i.e., they require an interaction typically between an examiner, a client, and some kind of stimulus in the moment), projective measures are typically less rigorously standardized and less often used in structured ways in psychological assessment.

This is not true across the board. For example, the Wartegg Drawing Completion Test has been overlaid with a complex administration and coding procedure (Crisi & Palm, 2018), though the projective test established a long time ago has struggled to find a strong foothold for multiple reasons (Soilevuo Grønnerød & Grønnerød, 2012), and is not widely used. Similarly, the Thematic Apperception Test (TAT), widely used as a projective technique, has had many attempts at standardizing administration, coding, and interpretation. Perhaps the most empirically successful is Westen's (1995; Stein, Hilsenroth, Slavin-Mumford, & Pinsker, 2011) Social Cognition and Object Relations Scale (SCORS) system for coding the projective stories. While many practicing clinicians use the TAT, very few use an empirically supported coding and interpretive system like the SCORS. For whatever reason, only the Rorschach (Exner, 2003; Meyer, Viglione, Mihura, Erard, & Erdberg, 2011) has emerged as a widely taught and used performance-based measure of functioning with a standardized, rigorous, empirically-supported administration, coding, and interpretive system (two similar but competing systems at the moment, actually).

Some guidance is provided for the use of the Rorschach in tele-assessment practice by the Rorschach Performance Assessment System (R-PAS) developers, authors, and researchers (Meyer et al., 2020). While the guidance they provide is specific to the Rorschach, it applies to any performance-based or projective measure that requires clients to interact with physical stimulus cards (such as the TAT or the Tell-Me-A-Story [TEMAS] assessment [Costantino, Dana, & Malgady, 2007]).

The R-PAS team notes that important to the tasks is the ability for clients to take the cards in their hands, move them around, and reorient them in three dimensions; as such, it is not appropriate to hold the stimulus cards up to a camera or use a document camera to project the cards onto a client's screen. They offer an option of mailing the stimulus cards to clients with specific instructions about how to engage with them (not to open the package before test administration, etc.); however, they note two major flaws with this procedure. First, the cards are expensive, and mailing them out to a client means the distinct possibility of never getting them back. Second, they discuss test security. They acknowledge that the Rorschach cards specifically are widely available to view on the internet, so the issue of test security is minimized. This is also true for the TAT, but it would not hold true for another test whose stimulus materials are not widely available. As such, mailing out cards to a client is generally not a viable option.

The R-PAS team (Meyer et al., 2020) goes on to recommend a facilitator of some sort, either on-site or in-room. Specifically, the facilitator is primarily present to maintain oversight of the stimulus cards. If the client is able to manage altered administration procedures (i.e., following instructions for when to turn a card over and look at it, etc.), then the facilitator does not need to do much else. If a client is unable to follow the altered administration procedures, then the facilitator needs to remain in the room with the client to handle the cards as instructed by the examiner. While the authors discuss drawbacks to using a resident, in-room facilitator (i.e., someone who lives with the client, and thus has a relationship with them), they do not outright state that one should not be used. Instead, they recommend careful accommodations like, "the assessor will want to encourage the facilitator to remain neutral and avoid reacting to the cards or to the respondent's responses" (p. 4). And while they note that psychologists practicing therapeutic assessment have successfully used family members as facilitators (e.g., Tharinger et al., 2012), this constitutes a significant and notable deviation from the standardized administration, which can have consequences for coding and ultimately interpretation. With the many psychological processes involved in how a client interacts with and responds to ambiguous stimuli, we do not recommend the use of a family member or other known facilitator; even their presence may alter how a client responds aloud to the stimuli.

Perhaps most notable from the aforementioned guidance on performance-based measures utilizing stimuli that clients typically engage with physically (e.g., holding cards, turning them in a three-dimensional plane), such as the Rorschach and the TAT, these methods cannot be administered in a purely tele-assessment context unless there is a cooperating onsite professional to secure and administer the physical cards or you mail the stimuli to the client. That is, there is currently no way for clients to interact with these stimuli unless they physically have the cards. So, unless you provide onsite stimulus cards (and, again, you need to think about test security if doing direct-to-home tele-assessment), tele-assessments will have to do without these kinds of measures. There may be some similar tasks, such as the Adult Attachment Projective Picture System (AAP; George & West, 2012), that include stimuli that are less nuanced (the AAP uses line drawings of people in situations) and thus may be acceptable for presentation on a screen. However, there is no such guidance or supportive evidence for this test currently, and standard practice is still to hand clients the physical cards.

Regarding other types of projective techniques, the primary question is what kind of input (stimulus) is required for administration, as well as the output (response) from the client. For example, any type of projective drawing task will require minimal input (although the Wartegg system requires drawing stimuli on paper), but you need to be able to see in fine detail the output. This may be accomplished by having clients mail their drawings back to you, or capturing them on camera and taking screenshots (if the client's camera's resolution is high enough). Assuming you can get the materials back to interpret, though, projective drawing tasks should be accomplishable in tele-assessment.

Similarly, administering sentence completion tasks may be feasible, depending on the particular types of stimuli that are used. Many use written sentence stems, and clients respond in writing on a response form. This requires providing the stimulus materials to the client (which may be as easy as having the client print them out if test security is not an issue) and having the client return the materials to you (so that you can interpret the responses). Another version of the test involves verbally administered sentence stems with verbal responses. This is likely to be the easiest to administer and use in a tele-assessment context.

Performance-based and especially projective techniques have their share of psychometric controversy (e.g., Frick, Barry, & Kamphaus, 2020; Lilienfeld, Wood, & Garb, 2000; Miller & Nickerson, 2007). Psychologists who use them "psychometrically" (i.e., administer, code, score, and interpret them in a standardized manner that is supported by the empirical literature) should take caution when doing so in a tele-assessment context. However, their "clinical" use (i.e., administering in a less standard way and interpreting based on common clinical practice, rather than rigorous and standardized empirical support) may certainly be used to provide additional information in a psychological tele-assessment. Psychologists are encouraged to know and understand the differences between these techniques and uses of measures, though, and interpret accordingly.

DEVELOPMENTAL/BEHAVIORAL ASSESSMENT

The bulk of behavioral assessment relies on interviews and rating forms, with some using behavioral (such as classroom) observations. It should be noted that in child and adolescent assessment, *naturalistic observations* have shown extremely limited incremental validity (that is, they do not add very much information above and beyond teacher and parent reports), at times even contaminating other data (Johnston & Murray, 2003). However, naturalistic observation (though expensive, time consuming, and difficult to standardize) may add some information, especially for behaviors that teachers and parents are unlikely to observe on a regular basis (Johnston & Murray, 2003; McConaughy et al., 2010). The reality is, though, that naturalistic behavioral observation is generally not amenable to tele-assessment.

However, the field of teacher education has researched video classroom observation (e.g., Horsley & Walker, 2006; Liang, 2015), which may serve the purpose. Unfortunately, video classroom observation has some significant barriers. First, recording a single child in a classroom effectively is extremely difficult; while a teacher may primarily "live" in a single spot at the front of a class (at least for older grades), children travel throughout a classroom during the day (and even within a single class period). Second, and perhaps most importantly, is the issue of privacy for every other child in the classroom. There are ethical issues related to video recording an entire class of children, even if it is primarily to observe a single child. Getting informed consent for this is likely prohibitive. As such, naturalistic observation is quite difficult to achieve in tele-assessment.

Again, though, the bulk of behavioral assessment tends to come from *self-report and collateral-report questionnaires*, from parents, teachers, caregivers, spouses, and even therapists. Self-report and collateral-report questionnaires, as discussed in Chapter 1, are generally negligibly affected by changing the mode to tele-assessment. This is especially true of collateral-report measures, most of which already employ a distance, unmonitored format. Behavioral sampling based on teacher report seems to be especially useful in assessment (e.g., Atiken, Martinussen, & Tannock, 2017), though a multi-informant method is generally the most sensitive to problem behaviors (e.g., Shemmassian & Lee, 2016). As such, when doing behavioral assessments via tele-assessment, these forms of collateral-report questionnaire surveys add important information and do not veer from traditional administration procedures.

When it comes to *ASD assessments*, no professional organization has yet (as of the time of writing this book) made a statement or offered guidance on developmental tele-assessment. This is especially notable as the ADOS-2 (Lord, Rutter, DiLavore, Risi, Gotham, & Bishop, 2012) is widely accepted as a gold-standard assessment of ASD. The ADOS-2 includes so many physical toys and manipulatives and so much specific interaction that it is nearly impossible to complete via tele-assessment (with the possible exception of some of the interview prompts in Module 4, for older clients).

While the ADOS-2 is the most widely used performance-based measure to evaluate ASD, there are certainly many other measures, including interview measures (that primarily focus on parent/caregiver report) and holistic clinician rating measures (that are meant to account for amassed evidence from different sources). The Monteiro Interview Guidelines for Diagnosing the Autism Spectrum, Second Edition (MIGDAS-2; Monteiro, 2018), for example, is also an interactive interview and observation protocol, but is much more flexible than the ADOS-2. It has not been evaluated for tele-assessment procedures, but the procedure itself (including more flexibility with which toys are used, etc.) makes it slightly more amenable to tele-assessment than the ADOS-2. Additionally, it is used more often as an information gathering tool to build evidence that an individual's behaviors are consistent with or inconsistent with those linked to ASD, rather than as a rigorous diagnostic algorithm. So again, it may be able to elicit some behavioral evidence even through an unresearched methodology like tele-assessment.

Recently, however, there has been some headway into observational (somewhat performance-based) measures for ASD that specifically utilize tele-assessment methods, which are helpful when a psychologist cannot perform an ADOS-2 or MIGDAS-2. One such measure is the Brief Observation of Social Communication Change (BOSCC; Grzadzinski et al., 2016). The BOSCC includes very brief, guided tasks between parent and child being assessed (such as free play, bubbles, shared play with a toy, and conversation for those with language abilities) that are rated using some relevant codes from the ADOS-2. While the scores cannot be added and calculated like in an ADOS-2, the information can certainly build evidence for elicited behaviors that are and are not consistent with an ASD diagnosis. The BOSCC has gained some empirical support with videotaped observation (Frost, Russell, & Ingersoll, 2020; Kim, Grzadzinski, Martinez, & Lord, 2019; Kitzerow, Teufel, Wilker, & Freitag, 2016; Pijl et al., 2018).

Another measure that was developed specifically for tele-assessment practice is the Naturalistic Observation Diagnostic Assessment (NODA) for ASD (Smith et al., 2017). This measure guides families to create specific videos that can be coded for ASD-consistent and ASD-inconsistent behaviors in the home. The NODA also has some empirical support (Illingworth, Thomas, Rozga, & Smith, 2017; Nazneen et al., 2015),

For very young children, the Systematic Observation of Red Flags (SORF) for ASD (Dow, Guthrie, Stronach, & Wetherby, 2017) offers a screening instrument that can be administered via tele-assessment for ages 2 and under which has some empirical support (Dow, Day, Uutta, Nottke, & Wetherby, 2020). The TELE-ASD-PEDS (Corona et al., 2020a) offers another brief guided interaction between parent and child (ages 3 and under and without flexible phrase speech) that is coded for ASD-consistent and ASD-inconsistent behaviors, which has some support for parental acceptance of the process (Corona et al., 2020b) but no empirical support for its psychometrics or utility yet. Similarly, an adult tele-assessment for ASD was developed, but it has only to date been evaluated for acceptability of the process to clients (Parmanto, Pulantara, Schutte, Saptono, & McCue, 2013).

Finally, there is a measure/method that has been recently developed called the CLEAR Autism Diagnostic Evaluation (CADE; Willard, Kroncke, & Harrison, 2019). Like the other measures developed specifically for online use, the empirical support for the CADE is thin (with no peer-reviewed articles). However, similar to the other measures, there is some promising information. The measure itself is primarily a lengthy, guided questionnaire for multiple raters that is available online. It is guided by specific visual and written descriptions about how to rate each individual question. For children aged 3 and above, the 80 ratings assessing 11 domains yield an autism score (situating the child within levels of ASD), as well as descriptive information across domains. The CADE authors have an unpublished white paper (Willard et al., 2019) that claims, with a sample size of 191 participants (ages unknown), the clinician-rated CADE has 98% agreement with ADOS-2 diagnostic decisions, 96% consistency with "expert diagnosis," and an internal consistency (alpha) of .95. However, there are significant methodological problems with the study, including non-independent ratings (those clinicians who rated the children on the CADE used the ADOS-2 to inform their CADE ratings, so correlations between the ADOS-2 and the CADE are artificially high), and the paper itself presents some confusing statistics. While this measure is promising in the tele-assessment of ASD, it is not yet ready for clinical use as a quantitative tool. It can serve to provide some qualitative data about raters' (including parents') perception of a child's development and ASD symptoms, though.

Currently, there are a few promising methods for systematic observation and performance-based assessment of ASD through tele-assessment methods. Those that are available require further empirical evaluation.

CONCLUSION

A large proportion of personality, emotional, and behavioral assessment is achieved in typical (in-person) practice through the use of methods and measures that do not alter data quality much in a tele-assessment context. Interviews, records reviews, and survey measures (of clients and collateral reporters) can all be easily accomplished in a way that makes the likelihood of method effects on the data that emerge quite low. The major exceptions are performance-based—including projective—measures, which require more interaction between the psychologist, the client, and stimulus materials. To date, none of these measures that use physical stimuli (generally pictures printed on cards) has been evaluated for equivalence or validity in a remote, tele-assessment context. As such, using them as psychometric tests in a psychological tele-assessment generally is not feasible.

However, for those psychologists who use projective tests clinically (in a non-standardized way to collect more clinical information less formally), some may still be able to be utilized in psychological tele-assessment. Psychologists are encouraged to know and thoroughly understand the difference between using these measures psychometrically (for the ones that have standardized systems with empirical support) and using them clinically. Ultimately, the key to the assessment of personality and psychopathology (including emotional and behavioral assessment) is in the integration of data across multiple methods and (when appropriate and available) informants. Basing clinical decisions on convergence of data across methods helps account for the error that exists in every single psychological measure (whether administered in person or at a distance), and psychologists are encouraged to be especially methodical about aligning and finding convergent data, as well as reconciling discrepant data. This is especially necessary in psychological tele-assessment, where some error may exist that we have not yet accounted for.

Nine

CASE STUDIES IN PSYCHOLOGICAL TELE-ASSESSMENT

The following case examples of psychological tele-assessment in action were crowdsourced and collected from psychologists who are actually doing this work. They have been organized into domains by "lessons learned" (and most have been simplified in order to illustrate a single point at a time). While the transition from traditional, in-person assessment to tele-assessment is a complex one, these case examples illustrate some of the many pitfalls, barriers, difficulties, and ultimately solutions that can ensure valid and useful assessment in this context. Although they are not exhaustive (there is no way to include every single potential difficulty that could arise during an assessment, traditional or tele-assessment!), they highlight some of the major difficulties that can arise in a tele-assessment, how these difficulties can impact the process, and how psychologists can creatively and effectively deal with them. We are grateful to all those who submitted case examples, and, while we could not include all of them, we opted to include a selection that highlight the myriad considerations necessary in conducting psychological tele-assessment.

PROBLEMS WITH TECHNOLOGY

Technology problems are likely the most salient and anxiety-producing issues facing those engaging in psychological tele-assessment. Some problems with technology can frustrate clients and psychologists alike, negatively affect rapport, and even spoil tests and subtests. Here are some examples of moments when technology failed and workarounds were needed.

Essentials of Psychological Tele-Assessment, First Edition.
A. Jordan Wright and Susan Engi Raiford
© 2021 John Wiley & Sons, Inc. Published 2021 by John Wiley & Sons, Inc.

Lisa Michelle Griffiths, PsyD
Colorado Licensed Psychologist
Center for Valued Living, PLLC (C4VL)

"Tracy" was an African-American female in her mid-40s, who came in for a vocational rehabilitation evaluation. The objective of the evaluation was to identify any potential learning disabilities and a possible mood disorder. Additionally, her vocational rehabilitation counselor wanted assistance in defining a strategy for Tracy to be successful in a work environment. We conducted the assessment in two separate offices, but entirely remotely.

In general, the assessment proceeded well, and it was helpful not to have to rely on Tracy to set up the technology in her home. She and I were able to establish rapport very well for the interview portion over teleconference. However, despite practicing and getting it to work before, on the day of, the document camera would not connect; only the web camera would. Rather than abort testing for the day and frustrate both of us, I instructed Tracy to put the camera on her face when she was doing verbal tasks and then put it down to see either the iPad or response booklets when applicable.

Although this was not ideal, I was comfortable that test security was a nonissue, as the evaluation was happening in my office. Additionally, it did not seem to affect the processes engaged in the tests themselves. Aside from the camera needing to move up and down, I felt that the IQ test was not all that much different from an in-person administration, though I had to explain certain subtests slightly off standardization, as the instructions written in the manual are really written for in-person administration. The academic testing was a little more cumbersome, but it still felt like a valid administration, though it took somewhat longer than usual. The actual "work" Tracy did throughout the evaluation was extremely consistent with what she would have done in a traditional administration of the tests, even though she was being asked to perform some additional tasks throughout (including moving the camera up and down).

Raja M. David, PsyD, ABPP
Licensed Psychologist
Minnesota Center for Collaborative/Therapeutic Assessment

"Hudson" was a male in his mid-20s who had been referred for a therapeutic assessment (TA) by his individual therapist. He reportedly had a history of anxiety, depression, and relationship issues, and he was an active participant in trying to understand himself more. We had met three times virtually, with me in my home office and the client in his apartment. Our first appointments went well from both clinical and technological perspectives.

During our fourth session, I had planned on him completing two brief self-report measures of anxiety and depression and reviewing the items with him to explore his symptom picture. Almost immediately after we started, something occurred with my camera; while I could be heard, all Hudson saw was a white box where my picture should have been. Thankfully, the client was understanding as I initially tried to solve the issue. Eventually, after my problem-solving was not working, I told Hudson that I would end our video session, he should work on the self-report measures, and I would join again from another computer. I reconnected just as he was finishing the measures, and we continued our discussion.

While this technology issue did not seem to have a significant impact on our process, it was quite abrupt and caught me off guard. I had not had any such problem with my camera before that session (though it happened again after this session, so I eventually purchased a new camera). The timing was fortunate actually, as I could easily transition Hudson to completing tasks he needed to do independently anyway while I logged off, started the new computer, and logged back on. However, what Hudson did not see or know was that I had to make a mad dash to another part of the house to find a laptop to use. When I got back on, he was just completing the measures, so it worked out ok. I now make sure that I have both an additional laptop in the office and, when possible, some backup measures/tasks for clients to complete independently, in the case of a similar technological failing.

A. Jordan Wright, PhD, ABAP
Faculty and Director, Center for Counseling and Community Wellbeing
New York University

"Matt" was referred for an evaluation to evaluate some problems he was having in school, specifically around reading and reading comprehension. He was 14 years old and was getting really frustrated at school. He had asked his mother if he could be evaluated, because even getting extra informal support and engaging in a tutoring program after school were not making his work any easier.

During the tele-assessment, the clinical and collateral interviews went well. Rapport was easily established, and Matt genuinely seemed to want to figure out why he was struggling so much in reading. He reported that he had significant difficulty finishing any book assigned in school. We completed multiple measures, including a measure of intelligence, relatively seamlessly. When engaging in a task of oral reading fluency as part of a broad academic achievement measure, though, the internet became a bit spotty (it was unclear if the problem was on Matt's side or my side of the tele-assessment), and I could not hear him reading the passage aloud. Coding and scoring this task, which is extremely important in a reading evaluation, requires hearing exactly how he reads aloud, and so this task was ruined and unusable.

This was a moment I was glad we have multiple competing tests to evaluate most constructs in psychology. Although that task was ruined, I was able to use a nearly identical task from a different measure and get a picture of Matt's oral reading fluency. We decided to abort the session with the spotty internet connection, because I felt it would impede pretty much any task we could complete. During the next session, I made sure that the internet connection was consistent and solid before attempting the replacement oral reading fluency task (and other tasks). In the final report, I did not use the spoiled task.

PROBLEMS CONTROLLING THE CLIENT'S ENVIRONMENT

Whether conducting psychological tele-assessments in a remote, office-to-office context or between the psychologist and the client's home (or some other setting), we have significantly less control over the client's environment in tele-assessments than in traditional, in-office assessments. The difficulties controlling the environment can include random interruptions, intrusion by others who are present in the client's location, and issues with stimulus and response materials used physically by the client, among other things. There are ways to minimize the likelihood of intrusion and disruption (discussed in Chapter 3), but there are certainly moments where having less control over the client's environment leads to significant disruption (and interruption of standardized administration procedures). Some psychologists (as will be illustrated) have gotten creative about ways to gain more control over the situation though.

Stephanie Tabashnek, PsyD, JD
Forensic Psychologist
Wellesley, MA

"Abby" was a 33-year-old Latina woman referred for a forensic substance use and mental health evaluation that arose out of a child protection matter. Abby had three children who had been removed from the home after concerns about her alcohol use. Abby had a history of childhood trauma, alcohol use disorder, and post-traumatic stress disorder, as well as various unexplained somatic issues. At the time of the evaluation, Abby had reportedly been sober for over a year.

During the psychological tele-assessment, Abby was participating in a clinical interview on a videoconferencing platform, and after approximately an hour, the interview had shifted to the topic of childhood sexual abuse, a particularly sensitive topic. Suddenly, I noticed that the camera had moved and Abby appeared to be in a new location. I asked her about this and she informed me that she had just gotten into a car but that it was fine and that I could continue to ask her questions. I gently pressed her to clarify the details of why she had decided to get into a car. She reported that her tooth hurt and that she needed to go to the pharmacy to obtain pain medicine. I noticed that it did not seem that Abby was driving, and she reported that she actually was a passenger in the car. When I asked who was in the car with her, she reported that she was in an Uber and said that the drive to the pharmacy would take about 30 minutes.

I decided at that moment that, even if the client was perfectly comfortable talking about childhood sexual abuse issues in an Uber, I of course was not comfortable with the lack of privacy and how the presence of a third party could a) influence the client's responses and b) destroy attorney–client privilege (the client was referred by her attorney and the evaluation fell under attorney–client privilege). I conveyed to Abby that I was sorry that she was experiencing pain and indicated that we should reschedule the interview at a time when she felt better and could be in a private place without anyone else present. Abby seemed to understand the rationale and had no problem rescheduling. While somewhat of an inconvenience, the client's unexpected decision to enter a rideshare vehicle in the middle of the evaluation provided data about the client's judgment, planning, and interpersonal skills. The situation also highlighted areas in tele-assessment we have less control over as compared to traditional assessment, as well as the need to be explicit with clients about what we expect from them as they prepare to engage in an evaluation.

Nancy Corral Ziebert, PhD
Partner, Clinical Psychologist
Positive Developments, LLC

"Violet" was a 10-year-old girl who was referred for a neuropsychological assessment by her parents and treating psychologist. She had been exhibiting bouts of emotional dysregulation at home for at least two years and could be quite challenging to her parents, but at school she had always been "delightful" and very well-behaved. She was a good student with many friends. Violet's brother, who was also noncompliant and challenging with his parents, had ADHD (diagnosed by this evaluator a few years ago). Thus, Violet's parents sought an assessment to clarify whether her behavioral and emotional difficulties might be due to ADHD. In addition, Violet's parents noted that she very often expressed a wish to spend time with her mother, who worked long hours. During the initial parent meeting, Violet's mother shared her guilt over working such long days outside of the home, but she also stated that it was difficult for her to tolerate Violet's intense outbursts and that she often left the house when Violet became upset, which only intensified Violet's negative emotions.

Violet's remote assessment began with a "meet & greet" session because her parents were not convinced that she would be cooperative. During this initial meeting, we chatted in order to build rapport, and I introduced some sample activities via screen share. Violet was polite and answered questions, although she did seem somewhat reserved. After the meeting, she told her parents that she enjoyed our conversation and felt comfortable participating in the evaluation. The first two testing sessions proceeded uneventfully; Violet was highly cooperative, engaged, attentive, and able to work for 90-minute sessions without needing a break or appearing fatigued. She became more friendly and talkative as she became more comfortable with me and with the process.

During the third session, however, we were interrupted by an uninvited visitor—a wasp had entered the office in which Violet was working—and she became visibly anxious. Although she did not make any sudden moves, she verbalized feeling nervous and was carefully watching the wasp as it buzzed alongside the windowsill. Fortunately, we were working on an untimed math test, and so we simply paused test administration, and Violet went to retrieve her parents from the other room. When they arrived (both parents for one wasp), I was treated to a glimpse into their own self-regulation skills. While Violet's father danced around the room, rolled newspaper in hand, swatting at the air, her mother screamed, "Violet! Get back to your test! Sit back down! Work! Focus, focus! Just ignore us!" I tried to tell them it was alright and that the testing process was not being ruined in any way that could not be repaired after the chaos had subsided, but they could not hear me over the noise of their own yelling.

Violet stood off to the side, next to the computer, and watched the scene, much as I was watching through my own computer screen. After several minutes, they realized the wasp had outsmarted them and was hiding somewhere. They were beside themselves with distress—what should they do? I encouraged them to relocate Violet and the laptop to another room and resume the video call in 5 minutes. Of course, I could not imagine that we would be able to continue, but when Violet reappeared on my screen (sans frantic parents), she was her usual calm, poised, focused self, and we were able to continue working for another hour. In fact, two subtests later, Violet was asked to read a long passage about bees, and we laughed about the funny coincidence.

This intrusion could have absolutely also occurred in the idealized sanctity of an office, and I would have handled it in much the same way—pause the test, address the situation, and try to resume test administration after assessing if the child had fully recovered. Additionally, it highlights what I would not have been able to observe in my office—the parents' wonderfully natural reaction. This child's daily experience of parental intensity, anxiety, unrealistic expectations, and, most importantly, lack of attunement (asking her to do math while under perceived attack by a wasp) could not have been captured by any standardized measure, nor was it as clear to me from their verbal description of family life as it was from seeing it with my own eyes. In the end, this vignette helped me to understand that Violet and her parents likely become dysregulated *together*, and, probably often, her parents contribute in myriad ways to her outbursts, while all the while thinking she is driving the situation. In the end, I did not conclude that she had ADHD, but my feedback to Violet and her parents reinvigorated their commitment to therapy and helped the therapist to shift the focus more toward family communication and dynamics and away from Violet as the "identified patient."

Silva Hassert, PhD
California Licensed Psychologist
Mind Rising Psychological Assessment

"Jeremy" was a middle school student who attended private school. His parents wished to have his learning style assessed given specific struggles in math. He was highly motivated and eager to go through with the assessment.

Because in-person evaluation was not possible, I arranged to conduct an in-office, remote assessment, in which the student came to my office but tested in a separate room with the aid of Bluetooth technology and a document camera. During mock trials prior to testing, I recognized a need for test materials to be organized in a way that differed from an in-person evaluation. There were occasions where the student would be managing his response booklets and other stimulus materials as I provided instructions to him via the internet. To simulate in-person testing, it was important that he was not exposed to the test materials until the appropriate time during the evaluation. Particular thought was given to tasks that included a delay and recognition condition for instance. Prior to Jeremy entering the room, I organized the test materials in different colored folders and placed them around the testing room (e.g., on the table, chair, and shelf). The colored folders also included words that made them easier to describe and helped me remember my setup. For example, I separated the pages of a drawing and recall task and wrote "<u>C</u>at," "<u>I</u>guana," and "<u>D</u>og" on the folders that contained the <u>C</u>opy, <u>I</u>mmediate recall, and <u>D</u>elayed recall conditions.

During the evaluation, the colored folders opened the door for conversations with Jeremy, while staying focused on testing. He responded positively to having the materials arranged in different places. The setup was a bit like a treasure hunt that allowed for a short break while he looked for a folder. Moreover, in having him move away from his chair, I gleaned useful behavioral observations and witnessed how he followed multi-step instructions in real time. The process gave me the opportunity to critique the way I had been routinely administering psychological measures, while making necessary changes for tele-assessment to go more smoothly. Tele-assessment modifications are sometimes seen as just another box for a good evaluator to "check off." However, they actually give us an opportunity to be creative and continue to evaluate clients in new ways.

REDUCED ABILITY TO OBSERVE CLIENTS

In addition to not being able to control the environment and context of the tele-assessment client as closely, there is also a reduction in the ability to observe the whole client closely and monitor and redirect their behaviors as easily as in traditional, in-person assessment. Clients can find new and creative ways to be resistant, to disengage, to be nonresponsive, and even to cheat on measures. Introducing limits to the physical amount of the client that the psychologist can see and monitor closely opens up even more possibilities. We have to be extremely vigilant with clients, especially in cases in which there may be some motivation for them to either disengage or look for advantages for themselves. The following cases illustrate just two of many examples of a psychologist needing to be on their toes.

Rebecca MurrayMetzger PsyD
Licensed Psychologist, Owner
San Francisco Mind Matters

"Darcy," an 11-year-old girl, was referred for an assessment for language, attention, and peer relationships. Reportedly, she had an "independent streak." I planned to conduct the assessment entirely through tele-assessment, with an in-office setup (the child in one room with the necessary technology and stimulus materials, and me in another office conducting the assessment). Included in the client room is a camera pointed toward the side of the client, for a full side view.

Darcy was quite cooperative and friendly, and the first few subtests of the WISC-V went well. However, at some point during the test, the side-view camera clicked off, and I was unable to reboot it from my office. I decided to proceed with the next subtest, Digit Span, as it did not require that I see her workspace and I wanted to complete one more subtest before a break. During the administration of Digit Span Forward, I could see she was looking down when I said the numbers. I encouraged her to look up at me and listen closely, but she continued to put her head down whenever I said the numbers. I asked, "Are you writing?" She said, "Yes, but just with my finger." I complimented her strategy but reminded her that she was just supposed to listen and try to remember them in her head. Still, she kept looking down each time, despite continued requests not to do so. Her performance was extremely impressive, as she was able to continue to the very last string, making only a few mistakes on the way, and earning a scaled score of 14.

At the break (while she was in the waiting room), I went into her office to troubleshoot the camera. I noticed tiny eraser shavings all over the table and thought "hmmmmm." I fixed the camera so that I was able to see her from the side angle again. When testing resumed and I introduced Digit Span Backward, I could see her pull out a small sticky note and ready herself to write the numbers as I spoke. The side-view camera caught this behavior clearly. I asked her to put the sticky note away, and she complied. Not surprisingly, her performance on Digit Span Backward and Digit Span Sequencing were much lower (around a 7).

Based on this experience, I've learned the additional camera to provide a side-view angle of the client is key. In fact, it has allowed me to see some under-the-table behavior in other children that I never would have noticed sitting directly across from them. Additionally, with the in-office, remote setup, there are at least some ways to limit access to extra materials (like scrap paper), but even in this context clients can find ways to get them! For Darcy, at this point, I decided to substitute Letter–Number Sequencing for Digit Span when calculating the Full Scale IQ score. While her Digit Span Forward score cannot be considered valid, it will make a useful comparison to her Digit Span Backward and Digit Span Sequencing scores when talking to her parents, particularly when I try to reframe her "independent streak" as an effort on her part to compensate for her challenges.

Dustin B. Wygant, PhD
Professor of Psychology
Director of Clinical Training
Eastern Kentucky University

I was asked to evaluate the competency to stand trial of a 13-year old Latino male, "Ryan." He faced serious charges that included the theft of an automobile, wanton endangerment of others, and destruction of property. His defense counsel and mother, both of whom I interviewed over the telephone, noted that Ryan had a longstanding history of behavioral problems, emotional immaturity, and symptoms of severe mental illness, including a previous psychiatric hospitalization for suicidal ideation.

Ryan was at a juvenile residential facility when the evaluation took place. The remote assessment was conducted using a HIPAA-compliant telehealth platform. Staff from the facility used a conference room with a laptop for Ryan to complete the assessment in private. After signing onto the remote assessment session, I verified Ryan's identity, and the facility staff left the room. During the assessment, I emailed a link for Ryan to complete a self-report measure of behavioral and emotional functioning. Ryan was able to successfully open the link and begin the test. This allowed the test to be viewed on his screen while I was able to maintain visual contact. However, it became apparent rather quickly that Ryan was not actively engaged in the test. I noticed that Ryan was looking at the screen and typing, which of course would not be needed to complete the true/false measure. I attempted to ask him about the behavior, but he had turned down the volume so that he could not hear me on the laptop, and so he did not hear the requests to remain focused on the test.

Ultimately, I had to call the residential facility and request that a staff member go into the conference room to make Ryan turn up the volume so that audio contact could be restored. Ryan complied and, when the staff left the room again for privacy purposes, I asked him why he had turned down the volume and what he was doing instead of taking the test. He replied that he did not want any distractions so he could "surf the net," while also completing the exam. He reported that he wanted to abscond from the facility and was reviewing various map websites to "plan my escape." I instructed Ryan to remain focused on the test, and he begrudgingly complied. Not surprisingly, the test results were invalid due to significant inconsistency in responding. Since that evaluation, I have shifted to loading the assessment measures on my own computer and using screen share and "mouse" sharing (remote control) capability to ensure that clients remain focused while completing remote testing.

ALTERED USE OF TESTS AND DATA

Finally, perhaps one of the most nuanced and daunting tasks of the psychologist engaging in psychological tele-assessment is the understanding of when test data need to be supplemented, interpreted differently, or deemed unusable, for myriad reasons. The ethical and competent tele-assessor must scrutinize all data that emerge from non-standardized administration procedures to determine how representative they truly are (or are likely to be) of a client's functioning, traits, or abilities. Beyond this, psychologists need to find ways to meet the needs of the client and the assessment at hand if and when they determine that some data are not accurate or usable. Some examples follow of situations that required flexibility and clinical skill on the part of the psychologist in order to adapt to such difficulties.

Michelle Limon Freeman, PsyD
Associate Director and Director of Assessment, Neuropsychologist
Summit Center

"Gina" was a 13-year-old adolescent girl who had a condition that made her immunocompromised. She was precocious, bright, sensitive, and kindhearted. She reportedly had trouble staying focused, estimating how much time it takes to complete her assignments, and following instructions. She was an avid reader, yet she had difficulty getting through academic reading materials. When comfortable, Gina engaged in deep, meaningful conversations about topics of interest. Translating her thoughts into writing was a different story. When asked to write, Gina "drew a blank." She could not formulate her thoughts by way of written expression and became quite upset. Her parents were concerned that there were learning or processing differences that might be hindering Gina's abilities, as well as her related confidence. Gina experienced anxiety and worry to the point of not wanting to go to school on days when she had tests or big assignments due. Gina's parents requested a comprehensive neuropsychological evaluation to gather information about her learning style, neurocognitive functions, related processing, and emotional functioning.

Much of the test administration was completed in person, before this was no longer possible. Her parents and I discussed it, and we decided that the remainder of the testing could feasibly be completed via tele-assessment following best practices. One set of tasks that still needed to be completed was relevant to auditory processing, an important component in reading evaluations. The particular test administered could only be used qualitatively, based on the current guidance specific to this test, as quantitative data could not be yielded. Audio quality during test administration did not appear to be an issue based on my observations and Gina's reports. However, Gina would mishear certain sounds, words, or only capture the gist of what was being said.

This was in line with reports of parents', teachers', and Gina's experiences. Gina often misheard and did not always "get it." These reports and the qualitative data gathered during tele-assessment corroborated my observations during in-person testing as well. Despite the inability to report quantitative scores, I was able to gather enough data to support a recommendation that Gina's auditory processing be further tested by an audiologist, and that auditory processing was contributing to her challenges. Auditory processing was in excess of pure auditory attention issues within Gina's neurocognitive profile, but also in line with her dyslexic processing. In sum, integrating data gathered using both standard and tele-assessment methods resulted in a comprehensive neuropsychological assessment. The goals for the assessment were completely fulfilled without needing to compromise Gina's health because of access to tele-assessment methods and procedures.

Nate Kindig, BS
School Psychology Intern
Assessment Intervention Management, LLC

"Harry" was a trilingual 2nd grade student who was 8 years old. He attended a bilingual (English and another language I will not mention to ensure confidentiality) Pre-K3, Pre-K4, and kindergarten in a non-Western country. Harry spoke his mother's first language and his father's first language, which were two different languages. The common language in the home was English, which was spoken most often, and as such, was considered Harry's primary and dominant language. Language proficiency testing was completed to confirm dominance in the English language before testing cognitive abilities and achievement skills. The referral question surrounded language and reading concerns.

Even though we had followed procedures and protocol to ensure that Harry's environment minimized distractions, he still understood that one of his parents was in the house with him. When certain tasks became difficult, he asked if he could talk to his parent. This problem was particularly apparent on a rebus task, where timing between stimulus exposure and stimulus recall is particularly important. For this task, minimal stimulus interference is important in order to acquire accurate data for a student's associative memory skills within the broad ability of long-term storage and retrieval. In one particular instance, Harry asked if he could talk to his parent, and I redirected him to the task. He then became visibly upset for about 15 seconds, at which point I considered the subtest spoiled and decided to move on to the next subtest. Although his parent was not in the room and was not offering any support (and thus standardization was maintained), the presence of his parent in the house may have caused him to react to difficult tasks in a way that he would not have acted in a quiet room with an evaluator in a school setting.

As an evaluator, I was particularly concerned with Harry's reading fluency skills and long-term storage and retrieval abilities. To get an accurate representation of his long-term storage and retrieval abilities with this spoiled subtest, I decided to examine his meaningful memory and rapid automatic naming abilities. Harry's performance on these tasks indicated deficits for rapid automatic naming, which is highly correlated with reading fluency skills that were of particular concern. The tele-assessment required me to add tasks I likely would not have added in a traditional assessment, and combining these data with all of the other data collected still allowed me to feel confident in making a determination for Harry.

A. Jordan Wright, PhD, ABAP
Faculty and Director, Center for Counseling and Community Wellbeing
New York University

"Audrey" presented for a psychological tele-assessment to evaluate her personality functioning and psychopathology. Specifically, her therapist referred her because she was "a ball of anxiety," and her therapist was beginning to suspect that it may be more personality-driven than a "straightforward anxiety disorder." She opted for a tele-assessment because both she and her therapist felt her tele-therapy was "stalled" at the moment, and she did not want to wait potentially months to "get some answers."

Audrey presented during the tele-assessment as cooperative and friendly, and relating well with me quickly and easily from the beginning. After a thorough clinical interview, I opted to have Audrey fill out three lengthy self-report personality inventories (three of the most widely used ones) as part of the assessment. She did so willingly and seemingly enthusiastically. Throughout the three measures (each completed on a separate day of the tele-assessment), she talked and laughed, both to herself and to me (observing her through the videoconferencing platform while she filled in the respective measures). Unfortunately, all three of the self-report measures had elevated validity scales related to inconsistency (none was invalid, but all noticeably elevated). Each also had elevated anxiety, as well as a host of other elevated scales.

It was extremely unclear if the same thing likely would have happened had Audrey been filling out the measures in my office (it is quite likely) or if her responding was somehow influenced by the tele-assessment methodology, but I decided to "confirm" the data that emerged from the personality inventories in several ways. First, I added a few structured interview modules specifically focused on the areas of elevation that emerged from the inventories. This included anxiety modules, but also some problematic personality traits. Additionally, I added one more brief self-report measure that was developed to look specifically at some of the potential personality pathology that emerged on the larger inventories. Finally, stealing a technique from therapeutic assessment (TA), I presented some of the data that emerged from the inventories back to Audrey to ask for her conceptualization of it (while this did not alter the actual quantitative interpretation of the inventories, it helped me feel more confident in my assertions based on them). It was unclear if the tele-assessment procedure had had an effect on the way she engaged with the tests (and ultimately the data that emerged from them), but I at least entertained the idea that it *might have* had an impact, and proceeded accordingly. Through the addition of data (additional measures and the pseudo-TA technique), I was able to confidently determine Audrey's psychological profile and make specific recommendations to her and her therapist.

Dimitra Robokos, PhD
NYS Licensed Psychologist and Clinical Assistant Professor
Department of Pediatrics
Albert Einstein College of Medicine

Remote tele-assessment was requested for a 22-year-old man, "Roger," residing in a sober living house arrangement. Roger had a history of behavioral challenges in school since preschool and a recent history of depression and substance use. Multiple educational and therapeutic placements were part of his high school years, and he was two classes short of graduating with a high school diploma. The last evaluation on record was from when Roger was 15, and it was conducted by his school district at that time. His scores were very high on intelligence testing, as well as for academic tasks. A previous diagnosis of ADHD was on record from a treating psychiatrist who had worked with Roger. He had also seen a neurologist at the age of 16, and an MRI and EEG yielded normal results. At the sober living house, where he had been residing for a few months, he was receiving individual and group therapy, as well as treatment follow-ups with a psychiatrist.

Roger had observable and significant executive functioning challenges, and this interfered with him keeping all appointments, but he eventually engaged with greater consistency. This easily could have happened similarly with in-person assessment. Multiple neuropsychological and educational standardized tests were administered via remote testing, however I had to revise my normal battery of tests, as several were not available to use in a tele-assessment context. Since processing speed, stamina, and endurance were areas of notable difficulty, I wanted to include more measures of attentional regulation. An internet-developed neuropsychological test was included to evaluate processing speed in particular, as well as attentional control. This test supplemented standardized subtests evaluating fluency of different tasks (able to be adapted to tele-assessment), as well as a number of executive functioning rating forms (more than I typically give), to supplement the information needed on attentional and processing speed issues.

Clinically, the adapted battery of tests and measures administered through tele-assessment yielded sufficient useful data, which provided Roger and his family clarity with diagnosis (confirmed ADHD) and a plan for further treatment options. Enough data were collected that overlapped and confirmed each other that validity of any one measure was not an issue.

CONCLUSION

Psychological tele-assessment requires psychologists to be flexible, creative, and ultimately extremely skilled in multiple areas, many that were not taught to us in graduate school or other assessment training. Introducing distance between the psychologist and client, as well as sometimes-unstable technology, means that more problems can interfere with the data that emerge from tests and measures than is typical of in-person assessment. Psychologists need to think ahead about potential and likely problems that can occur, prepare contingency plans, remain extra vigilant in their observation and monitoring of clients, and ultimately use a great deal of critical thinking and clinical and professional judgment when interpreting data. Although the cases presented in this chapter are non-exhaustive, they illustrate how the common problems that can arise in psychological tele-assessment can impact the process, as well as how they can be creatively and effectively dealt with.

References

Aitken, M., Martinussen, R., & Tannock, R. (2017). Incremental validity of teacher and parent symptom and impairment ratings when screening for mental health difficulties. *Journal of Abnormal Child Psychology, 45*(4), 827–837.

American Educational Research Association, American Psychological Association, National Council on Measurement in Education, Joint Committee on Standards for Educational and Psychological Testing (U.S.). (2014). Standards for educational and psychological testing. Washington, DC: AERA.

American Psychological Association. (2017). *Ethical principles of psychologists and code of conduct*. Washington, DC: APA. Retrieved from https://www.apa.org/ethics/code/index.aspx

American Psychological Association. (2020a). *APA guidelines for education and training in psychological assessment in health service psychology*. Washington, DC: APA. Retrieved from https://www.apa.org/about/policy/guidelines-assessment-health-service.pdf

American Psychological Association. (2020b). *Office and technology checklist for telepsychological services*. Washington, DC: APA. Retrieved from https://www.apa.org/practice/programs/dmhi/research-information/telepsychological-services-checklist

APA Commission on Accreditation. (2017). *Implementing regulations: Profession wide competencies*. Washington, DC: APA. Retrieved from https://www.apa.org/ed/accreditation/section-csoa.pdf

Artiola i Fortuny, L., & Heaton, R. K. (1996). Standard versus computerized administration of the Wisconsin Card Sorting Test. *The Clinical Neuropsychologist, 10*(4), 419–424.

Banks, G. G., & Butcher, C. (2020). *Telehealth testing with children: Important factors to consider*. Washington, DC: APA. Retrieved from https://www.apaservices.org/practice/legal/technology/telehealth-testing-children-covid-19

Barak, A., & English, N. (2002). Prospects and limitation of psychological testing on the internet. *Journal of Technology in Human Services, 19*, 65–89.

Barak, A., Hen, L., Boniel-Nissim, M., & Shapira, N. (2008). A comprehensive review and a metaanalysis of the effectiveness of internet-based psychotherapeutic interventions. *Journal of Technology in Human Services, 26,* 109–160.

Barcellos, L. F., Bellesis, K. H., Shen, L., Shao, X., Chinn, T., Frndak, S., … Benedict, R. H. (2017). Remote assessment of verbal memory in MS patients using the California Verbal Learning Test. *Multiple Sclerosis Journal, 24,* 354–357.

Batastini, A. B., King, C. M., Morgan, R. D., & McDaniel, B. (2016). Telepsychological services with criminal justice and substance abuse clients: A systematic review and meta-analysis. *Psychological Services, 13*(1), 20–30.

Beery, K. E. (2004). Beery VMI: The Beery-Buktenica Developmental Test of Visual-Motor Integration. Minneapolis, MN: Pearson.

Benson, N. F., Floyd, R. G., Kranzler, J. H., Eckert, T. L., Fefer, S. A., & Morgan, G. B. (2019). Test use and assessment practices of school psychologists in the United States: Findings from the 2017 National Survey. *Journal of School Psychology, 72,* 29–48.

Berman, A. I., Haertel, E. H., & Pellegrino, J. W. (2020). Comparability of large-scale educational assessments: Issues and recommendations. Washington, DC: National Academy of Education.

Bessiere, K., Ceaparu, I., Lazar, J., Robinson, J., & Shneiderman, B. (2004). Social and psychological influences on computer user frustration. In E. P. Bucy & J. E. Newhagen (Eds.), *Media access: Social and psychological dimensions of new technology use* (pp. 169–192). Mahwah, NJ: Lawrence Erlbaum Publishers.

Block, A. R., Bradford, A., Butt, Z., & Marek, R. J. (2020). How COVID-19 may affect presurgical psychological evaluations. Washington, DC: APA. Retrieved from https://www.apaservices.org/practice/news/presurgical-psychological-evaluations-covid-19?_ga=2.116775942.169813268.1591026574-1626901323.1573678255

Bolton, A. J., & Dorstyn, D. S. (2015). Telepsychology for posttraumatic stress disorder: A systematic review. *Journal of Telemedicine and Telecare, 21*(5), 254–267.

Bornstein, R. F. (2017). Evidence-based psychological assessment. *Journal of Personality Assessment, 99*(4), 435–445.

Bouchard, S., Payeur, R., Rivard, V., Allard, M., Paquin, B., Renaud, P., & Goyer, L. (2000). Cognitive behavior therapy for panic disorder with agoraphobia in videoconference: Preliminary results. *CyberPsychology & Behavior, 3*(6), 999–1007.

Bracken, B. A., & McCallum, R. S. (2016). Universal Nonverbal Intelligence Test (2nd ed.). Austin, TX: Pro-Ed.

Braden, J. B. (2003). Psychological assessment in school settings. In I. B. Weiner, J. R. Graham, & J. A. Naglieri (Eds.), *Handbook of psychology, vol. 10. Assessment psychology* (pp. 261–290). Hoboken, NJ: John Wiley & Sons.

Brannigan, G. G., & Decker, S. L. (2003). Bender visual-motor gestalt test (2nd ed.). Austin, TX: Pro-Ed.

Brearly, T. W., Shura, R. D., Martindale, S. L., Lazowski, R. A., Luxton, D. D., Shenal, B. V., & Rowland, J. A. (2017). Neuropsychological test administration by videoconference: A systematic review and meta-analysis. *Neuropsychology Review, 27*(2), 174–186.

Brown, K. S., & Bruns, D. L. (2020). Guidance on psychological assessment and management of chronic pain during the COVID-19 crisis. Washington, DC: APA. Retrieved from https://www.apaservices.org/practice/news/chronic-pain-covid-19

Brown, L., Sherbenou, R. J., & Johnsen, S. K. (2010) (2008). Test of Nonverbal Intelligence (4th ed). Austin, TX: Pro-Ed.

Bruchmüller, K., Margraf, J., Suppiger, A., & Schneider, S. (2011). Popular or unpopular? Therapists' use of structured interviews and their estimation of patient acceptance. *Behavior Therapy, 42*(4), 634–643.

Buchanan, T. (2002). Online assessment: Desirable or dangerous? *Professional Psychology: Research and Practice, 33,* 148–154.

Buchanan, T. (2003). Internet-based questionnaire assessment: Appropriate use in clinical contexts. *Cognitive Behaviour Therapy, 32,* 100–109.

Burney, J. P., Celeste, B. L., Johnson, J. D., Klein, N. C., Nordal, K. C., & Portnoy, S. M. (2009). Mentoring professional psychologists: Programs for career development, advocacy, and diversity. *Professional Psychology: Research and Practice, 40*(3), 292–298.

California Commission on Peace Officer Standards and Training. (2020). Compliance with POST selection standards during coronavirus (COVID-19) emergency. West Sacramento, CA: California Commission on Peace Officer Standards and Training. Retrieved from https://post.ca.gov/Portals/0/post_docs/bulletin/2020-18.pdf

Chen, H., Zhang, O., Raiford, S. E., Zhu, J., & Weiss, L. G. (2015). Factor invariance between genders on the Wechsler Intelligence Scale for Children–Fifth Edition. *Personality and Individual Differences, 86,* 1–5.

Chen, H., & Zhu, J. (2012). Measurement invariance of WISC-IV across normative and clinical samples. *Personality and Individual Differences, 52*(2), 161–166.

Cizek, G. J. (1994). In defense of the test. *American Psychologist, 49*(6), 525–526.

Coelho, L. F., Rosário, M. C. D., Mastrorosa, R. S., Miranda, M. C., & Bueno, O. F. A. (2012). Performance of a Brazilian sample on the computerized Wisconsin Card Sorting Test. *Psychology & Neuroscience, 5*(2), 147–156.

CogniFit. (2020). CogniFit Assessment Battery: Validity, tasks and variables description of CogniFit assessments. Yokneam, Israel: CogniFit.

Coleman, R. (2018). *Designing experiments for the social sciences: How to plan, create, and execute research using experiments.* Los Angeles, CA: Sage.

Conners, C. K. (2008). Conners Continuous Performance Test (3rd ed.). Toronto, ON: Multihealth Systems.

Conners, C. K. (2014). Conners Continuous Auditory Test of Attention. Toronto, ON: Multihealth Systems.

Conners, C. K. (2015). Conners Kiddie Continuous Performance Test (2nd ed.). Toronto, ON: Multihealth Systems.

Corey, D. M., & Ben-Porath, Y. S. (2020). Practical guidance on the use of the MMPI instruments in remote psychological testing. *Professional Psychology: Research and Practice, 51*(3), 199–204.

Corona, L., Hine, J., Nicholson, A., Stone, C., Swanson, A., Wade, J., … Warren, Z. (2020). TELE-ASD-PEDS: A telemedicine-based ASD evaluation tool for toddlers and young children. Vanderbilt University Medical Center. Retrieved from https://vkc.vumc.org/vkc/triad/tele-asd-peds

Corona, L. L., Weitlauf, A. S., Hine, J., Berman, A., Miceli, A., Nicholson, A., … Warren, Z. (2020). Parent perceptions of caregiver-mediated telemedicine tools for assessing autism risk in toddlers. *Journal of Autism and Developmental Disorders.* Retrieved from https://link.springer.com/article/10.1007/s10803-020-04554-9?utm_source=Spectrum%20Newsletters

Costantino, G., Dana, R. H., & Malgady, R. G. (2007). TEMAS (Tell-Me-A-Story) assessment in multicultural societies. Mahwah, NJ: Lawrence Erlbaum Associates Publishers.

Council, T. V. (2016). *Eyes overexposed: The digital device dilemma. 2016 digital eye strain report.* Retrieved from https://visionimpactinstitute.org/wp-content/uploads/2016/03/2016EyeStrain_Report_WEB.pdf

COVID-19 Task Force to Support Personality Assessment. (2020). *Tele-assessment of personality and psychopathology.* Falls Church, VA: SPA. Retrieved from https://resources.personality.org/www.personality.org/General/pdf/SPA_Personality_Tele-Assessment-Guidance_6.10.20.pdf

Crisi, A., & Palm, J. A. (2018). *The Crisi-Wartegg System (CWS): Manual for administration, scoring, and interpretation.* New York, NY: Routledge.

Cullum, C. M., Hynan, L. S., Grosch, M., Parikh, M., & Weiner, M. F. (2014). Teleneuropsychology: Evidence for video teleconference-based neuropsychological assessment. *Journal of the International Neuropsychological Society, 20*, 1028–1033.

Cullum, C. M., Weiner, M. F., Gehrmann, H. R., & Hynan, L. S. (2006). Feasibility of telecognitive assessment in dementia. *Assessment, 13*(4), 385–390.

Daniel, M. H. (2012a). Equivalence of Q-interactive administered cognitive tasks: WAIS–IV (Q-interactive Technical Report 1). Bloomington, MN: Pearson. Retrieved from https://www.pearsonassessments.com/content/dam/school/global/clinical/us/assets/q-interactive/007-s-QinteractiveTechnical%20Report%201_WAIS-IV.pdf

Daniel, M. H. (2012b). Equivalence of Q-interactive administered cognitive tasks: WISC–IV (Q-interactive Technical Report 2). Bloomington, MN: Pearson. Retrieved from https://www.pearsonassessments.com/content/dam/school/global/clinical/us/assets/q-interactive/009-s-Technical%20Report%202_WISC-IV_Final.pdf

Daniel, M. H. (2012c). Equivalence of Q-interactive administered cognitive tasks: CVLT®–II and selected D-KEFS® subtests (Q-interactive Technical Report 3). Bloomington, MN: Pearson. Retrieved from https://www.pearsonassessments.com/content/dam/school/global/clinical/us/assets/q-interactive/005-s-Technical%20Report%203_CVLT_DKEFS_final_rev.pdf

Daniel, M. H. (2013a). Equivalence of Q-interactive and paper administrations of cognitive tasks: Selected NEPSY®-II and CMS subtests (Q-interactive Technical Report 4). Bloomington, MN: Pearson. Retrieved from https://www.pearsonassessments.com/content/dam/school/global/clinical/us/assets/q-interactive/006-s-Technical%20Report%204_NEPSY-II_CMS.pdf

Daniel, M. H. (2013b). Equivalence of Q-interactive and paper scoring of academic tasks: Selected WIAT®–III subtests. (Q-interactive Technical Report 5). Bloomington, MN: Pearson.

Daniel, M. H. (2013c). Equivalence of Q-interactive and paper administration of WMS®–IV cognitive tasks (Q-interactive Technical Report 6). Bloomington, MN: Pearson. Retrieved from https://www.pearsonassessments.com/content/dam/school/global/clinical/us/assets/q-interactive/0010-s-Technical_Report_6_WMS-IV.pdf

Daniel, M. H., Wahlstrom, D., & Zhang, O. (2014). Equivalence of Q-interactive and paper administrations of cognitive tasks: WISC®–V (Q-interactive Technical Report 8). Bloomington, MN: Pearson. Retrieved from https://www.pearsonassessments.com/content/dam/

school/global/clinical/us/assets/q-interactive/003-s-Technical-Report_
WISC-V_092514.pdf

De Los Reyes, A., Augenstein, T. M., Wang, M., Thomas, S. A., Drabick, D. A., Burgers, D. E., & Rabinowitz, J. (2015). The validity of the multi-informant approach to assessing child and adolescent mental health. *Psychological Bulletin, 141*(4), 858–900.

de Vet, H. C., Terwee, C. B., Ostelo, R. W., Beckerman, H., Knol, D. L., & Bouter, L. M. (2006). Minimal changes in health status questionnaires: Distinction between minimally detectable change and minimally important change. *Health and Quality of Life Outcomes, 4*(1), 54.

Dekhtyar, M., Braun, E., Billot, A., Foo, L., & Kiran, S. (2020). Videoconference administration of the Western Aphasia Battery–Revised: Feasibility and validity. *American Journal of Speech-Language Pathology, 29*, 673–687.

Delis, D. C., Kaplan, E., & Kramer, J. H. (2001). Delis-Kaplan Executive Function System. Bloomington, MN: Pearson.

Delis, D. C., Kramer, J. H., Kaplan, E., & Ober, B. A. (1994). California Verbal Learning Test Children's Version. Bloomington, MN: Pearson.

Delis, D. C., Kramer, J. H., Kaplan, E., & Ober, B. A. (2017). California Verbal Learning Test (3rd ed.). Bloomington, MN: Pearson.

DePascale, C., & Gong, B. (2020). Comparability of individual students' scores on the "same test". In A. I. Berman, E. H. Haertel, & J. W. Pellegrino (Eds.), Comparability of large-scale educational assessments: Issues and recommendations (pp. 25–48). Washington, DC: National Academy of Education.

Dow, D., Day, T. N., Utta, T. J., Nottke, C., & Wetherby, A. M. (2020). Screening for autism spectrum disorder in a naturalistic home setting using the Systematic Observation of Red Flags (SORF) at 18–24 months. *Autism Research, 13*(1), 122–133.

Dow, D., Guthrie, W., Stronach, S. T., & Wetherby, A. M. (2017). Psychometric analysis of the Systematic Observation of Red Flags for autism spectrum disorder in toddlers. *Autism, 21*(3), 301–309.

Drogin, E. Y. (2020). Forensic mental telehealth assessment (FMTA) in the context of COVID-19. *International Journal of Law and Psychiatry, 71*, 101595.

Drozdick, L. W., Getz, K. G., Raiford, S. E., & Zhang, O. (2016). WPPSI-IV: Equivalence of Q-interactive and paper formats (Q-interactive Technical Report 14). Bloomington, MN: Pearson. Retrieved from https://www.pearsonassessments.com/content/dam/school/global/clinical/us/assets/q-interactive/001-s-WPPSI-Qi-Tech-Report-14-FNL.pdf

Dunn, D. M. (2018). Peabody Picture Vocabulary Test (5th ed.). Bloomington, MN: Pearson.

Ehrler, D. J., & McGhee, R. L. (2008). Primary Test of Nonverbal Intelligence. Austin, TX: Pro-Ed.

Exner, J. E. (2003). *The Rorschach: A comprehensive system; Basic foundations and principles of interpretation* (4th ed.). Hoboken, NJ: John Wiley & Sons, Inc.

Farmer, R. L., McGill, R. J., Dombrowski, S. C., Benson, N. F., Smith-Kellen, S., Lockwood, A. B., ... Stinnett, T. A. (2020). Conducting psychoeducational assessments during the COVID-19 crisis: The danger of good intentions. *Contemporary School Psychology, 1*. Retrieved from https://link.springer.com/article/10.1007/s40688-020-00293-x?fbclid=IwAR1ThsH25Fd1emhLHSVFciBQvDyYPg7A5HAijT5-e7xU5JA4c373DQATOqo

Feldstein, S. N., Keller, F. R., Portman, R. E., Durham, R. L., Klebe, K. J., & Davis, H. P. (1999). A comparison of computerized and standard versions of the Wisconsin Card Sorting Test. *The Clinical Neuropsychologist, 13*(3), 303–313.

Finger, M. S., & Ones, D. S. (1999). Psychometric equivalence of the computer and booklet forms of the MMPI: A meta-analysis. *Psychological Assessment, 11*, 58–66.

Fink, J. W. (2017). Beyond the tests: Record review, interview, and observations in forensic neuropsychology. In S. S. Bush, G. J. Demakis, & M. L. Rohling (Eds.), *APA handbooks in psychology: APA handbook of forensic neuropsychology* (pp. 41–55). Washington, DC: APA.

Finn, S. E., Fischer, C. T., & Handler, L. (2012). *Collaborative/therapeutic assessment: A casebook and guide.* Hoboken, NJ: John Wiley & Sons.

First, M. B., Williams, J. B. W., Karg, R. S., & Spitzer, R. L. (2015). Structured Clinical Interview for DSM-5: Research version. Arlington, VA: American Psychiatric Association.

Folstein, M. F., Folstein, S. E., & McHugh, P. R. (1975). Mini-mental state: A practical method for grading the cognitive state of patients for the clinician. *Journal of Psychiatric Research, 12*, 189–198.

Frick, P. J., Barry, C. T., & Kamphaus, R. W. (2020). Projective techniques. In P. J. Frick, C. T. Barry, & R. W. Kamphaus (Eds.), *Clinical assessment of child and adolescent personality and behavior* (4th ed., pp. 185–207). Cham, Switzerland: Springer.

Frost, K. M., Russell, K. M., & Ingersoll, B. (2020). Using thin-slice ratings to measure social communication in children with autism spectrum disorder. *Research in Autism Spectrum Disorders, 74*, 101550.

Galusha-Glasscock, J. M., Horton, D. K., Weiner, M. F., & Cullum, C. M. (2016). Video teleconference administration of the Repeatable Battery for the

Assessment of Neuropsychological Status. *Archives of Clinical Neuropsychology,* *31*(1), 8–11.

Garb, H. N. (2007). Computer-administered interviews and rating scales. *Psychological Assessment, 19,* 4–13.

Garrison, E. G., DeLeon, P. H., & Smedley, B. D. (2017). Psychology, public policy, and advocacy: Past, present, and future. *American Psychologist, 72*(8), 737–752.

George, C., & West, M. (2012). The Adult Attachment Projective Picture System. New York, NY: The Guilford Press.

Germain, V., Marchand, A., Bouchard, S., Guay, S., & Drouin, M. S. (2010). Assessment of the therapeutic alliance in face-to-face or videoconference treatment for posttraumatic stress disorder. *Cyberpsychology, Behavior, and Social Networking, 13*(1), 29–35.

Golberstein, E., Wen, H., & Miller, B. F. 2020. Coronavirus disease 2019 (COVID-19) and mental health for children and adolescents. *Journal of the American Medical Association Pediatrics.* Retrieved from https://jamanetwork. com/journals/jamapediatrics/article-abstract/2764730

Goodman, W. K., Price, L. H., Rasmussen, S. A., Mazure, C., Fleischmann, R. L., Hill, C. L., ... Charney, D. S. (1989). The Yale-Brown Obsessive-Compulsive Scale: I. Development, use, and reliability. *Archives of General Psychiatry, 46*(11), 1006–1011.

Grady, B., Myers, K. M., Nelson, E.-L., Belz, N., Bennett, L., Carnahan, L., & Voyles, D. (2011). Evidence-based practice for telemental health. *Telemedicine and e-Health, 17,* 131–148.

Grant, D. A., & Berg, E. A. (1948). Wisconsin Card Sorting Test. Lutz, FL: Psychological Assessment Resources.

Grosch, M. C., Weiner, M. F., Hynan, L. S., Shore, J., & Cullum, C. M. (2015). Video teleconference-based neurocognitive screening in geropsychiatry. *Psychiatry Research, 225*(3), 734–735.

Grzadzinski, R., Carr, T., Colombi, C., McGuire, K., Dufek, S., Pickles, A., & Lord, C. (2016). Measuring changes in social communication behaviors: Preliminary development of the Brief Observation of Social Communication Change (BOSCC). *Journal of Autism and Developmental Disorders, 46*(7), 2464–2479.

Gualtieri, C. T., & Johnson, L. G. (2006). Reliability and validity of a computerized neurocognitive test battery, CNS Vital Signs. *Archives of Clinical Neuropsychology, 21*(7), 623–643.

Hall, J. L., & McGraw, D. (2014). For telehealth to succeed, privacy and security risks must be identified and addressed. *Health Affairs, 33*(2), 216–221.

Hammill, D. D., & Larsen, S. C. (2009). Test of Written Language (4th ed.). Austin, TX: Pro-Ed.

Hammill, D. D., Pearson, N. A., & Wiederholt, J. L. (2009). Comprehensive Test of Nonverbal Intelligence (2nd ed.). Austin, TX: Pro-Ed.

Harrell, K. M., Wilkins, S. S., Connor, M. K., & Chodosh, J. (2014). Telemedicine and the evaluation of cognitive impairment: The additive value of neuropsychological assessment. *Journal of the American Medical Directors Association*, *15*(8), 600–606.

Hellman, S. G., Green, M. F., Kern, R. S., & Christenson, C. D. (1992). Comparison of card and computer versions of the Wisconsin Card Sorting Test for psychotic patients. *International Journal of Methods in Psychiatric Research*, *2*, 151–155.

HGAPS/Telepsychology. (2020, August 9). In Wikiversity. Retrieved from https://en.wikiversity.org/wiki/Helping_Give_Away_Psychological_Science/Telepsychology

Hildebrand, R., Chow, H., Williams, C., Nelson, M., & Wass, P. (2004). Feasibility of neuropsychological testing of older adults via videoconference: Implications for assessing the capacity for independent living. *Journal of Telemedicine and Telecare*, *10*(3), 130–134.

Hodge, M. A., Sutherland, R., Jeng, K., Bale, G., Batta, P., Cambridge, A., ... Ganesalingam, K. (2019). Agreement between telehealth and face-to-face assessment of intellectual ability in children with specific learning disorder. *Journal of Telemedicine and Telecare*, *25*(7), 431–437.

Horsley, M., & Walker, R. (2006). Video based classroom observation systems for examining the use and role of textbooks and teaching materials in learning. In E. Bruillard, B. Aamotsbakken, S. V. Knudsen, & M. Horsley (Eds.), *Caught in the web or lost in the textbook?* (pp. 263–268). Caen, France: Proceedings of the English International Conference on Learning and Educational Media.

Hunsley, J., & Mash, E. J. (2007). Evidence-based assessment. *Annual Review of Clinical Psychology*, *3*, 29–51.

Hyler, S. E., Gangure, D. P., & Batchelder, S. T. (2005). Can telepsychiatry replace in-person psychiatric assessments? A review and meta-analysis of comparison studies. *CNS Spectrums*, *10*, 403–413.

Illingworth, D. A., Thomas, R. P., Rozga, A., & Smith, C. J. (2017, September). Cue use in distal autism spectrum assessment: A lens model analysis of the efficacy of telehealth technologies. In *Proceedings of the Human Factors and Ergonomics Society Annual Meeting* (Vol. 61, No. 1, p. 170). Los Angeles, CA: SAGE Publications.

Inter Organizational Practice Committee (2020a). Guidance/recommendations for models of care during the novel coronavirus pandemic. Washington, DC: IOPC. Retrieved from https://static1.squarespace.com/static/50a3e393e4b07025e1a4f0d0/t/5ed7d6c58ec40f3dce143b40/1591203525610/IOPC+Models+of+Care+During+COVID-19+Pandemic.pdf

Inter Organizational Practice Committee. (2020b). Recommendations/guidance for teleneuropsychology (teleNP) in response to the COVID-19 pandemic. Washington, DC: IOPC Retrieved from https://static1.squarespace.com/static/50a3e393e4b07025e1a4f0d0/t/5e8260be9a64587cfd3a9832/1585602750557/Recommendations-Guidance+for+Teleneuropsychology-COVID-19-4.pdf

Jacobsen, S. E., Sprenger, T., Andersson, S., & Krogstad, J.-M. (2003). Neuropsychological assessment and telemedicine: A preliminary study examining the reliability of neuropsychology services performed via telecommunication. *Journal of the International Neuropsychological Society*, 9, 472–478.

Jobes, D. A. (2016). *Managing suicidal risk: A collaborative approach (2nd ed.).* New York, NY: The Guilford Press.

Johnston, C., & Murray, C. (2003). Incremental validity in the psychological assessment of children and adolescents. *Psychological Assessment, 15*(4), 496–507.

Joint Task Force for the Development of Telepsychology Guidelines for Psychologists. (2013). Guidelines for the practice of telepsychology. *American Psychologist, 68*(9), 791–800.

Kaplan, E., Goodglass, H., & Weintraub, S. (1976). Boston Naming Test, Experimental Edition. Boston, MA: Aphasia Research Center, Boston University.

Kaufman, A. S., & Kaufman, N. L. (2004). Kaufman Brief Intelligence Test (2nd ed.). Circle Pines, MN: American Guidance Service, Inc.

Kaufman, A. S., & Kaufman, N. L. (2014). Kaufman Test of Educational Achievement (3rd ed.). Bloomington, MN: Pearson.

Kaufman, A. S., Raiford, S. E., & Coalson, D. L. (2016). Intelligent testing with the WISC-V. Hoboken, NJ: John Wiley & Sons.

Kim, S. H., Grzadzinski, R., Martinez, K., & Lord, C. (2019). Measuring treatment response in children with autism spectrum disorder: Applications of the Brief Observation of Social Communication Change to the Autism Diagnostic Observation Schedule. *Autism, 23*(5), 1176–1185.

Kitzerow, J., Teufel, K., Wilker, C., & Freitag, C. M. (2016). Using the Brief Observation of Social Communication Change (BOSCC) to measure autism-specific development. *Autism Research, 9*(9), 940–950.

Kobak, K. A. (2004). A comparison of face-to-face and videoconference administration of the Hamilton Depression Rating Scale. *Journal of Telemedicine and Telecare, 10*, 231–235.

Kobak, K. A., Williams, J. B., & Engelhardt, N. (2008). A comparison of face-to-face and remote assessment of inter-rater reliability on the Hamilton Depression Rating Scale via videoconferencing. *Psychiatry Research, 158*, 99–103.

Krach, S. K., McCreery, M. P., Dennis, L., Guerard, J., & Harris, E. L. (2020). Independent evaluation of Q-interactive: A paper equivalency comparison using PPVT-4 with preschoolers. *Psychology in the Schools, 57*, 17–30.

Lakens, D. (2017). Equivalence tests: A practical primer for *t* tests, correlations, and meta-analyses. *Social Psychological and Personality Science, 8*, 355–362.

Lexcen, F. J., Hawk, G. L., Herrick, S., & Blank, M. B. (2006). Use of video conferencing for psychiatric and forensic evaluations. *Psychiatric Services, 57*(5), 713–715.

Li, D., Yi, Q., & Harris, D. (2016). Evidence for paper and online ACT comparability: Spring 2014 and 2015 mode comparability studies (ACT Working Paper 2016-02). Iowa City, IA: ACT. Retrieved from https://www.act.org/content/dam/act/unsecured/documents/Working-Paper-2016-02-Evidence-for-Paper-and-Online-ACT-Comparability.pdf

Liang, J. (2015). Live video classroom observation: An effective approach to reducing reactivity in collecting observational information for teacher professional development. *Journal of Education for Teaching, 41*(3), 235–253.

Lilienfeld, S. O., Wood, J. M., & Garb, H. N. (2000). The scientific status of projective techniques. *Psychological Science in the Public Interest, 1*(2), 27–66.

Little, T. (2015). Equivalence testing for comparability. *BioPharm International, 28*(2), 45–48.

Loe, S. A., Kadlubek, R. M., & Marks, W. J. (2007). Administration and scoring errors on the WISC-IV among graduate student examiners. *Journal of Psychoeducational Assessment, 25*, 237–247.

Loh, P. K., Donaldson, M., Flicker, L., Maher, S., & Goldswain, P. (2007). Development of a telemedicine protocol for the diagnosis of Alzheimer's disease. *Journal of Telemedicine and Telecare, 13*, 90–94.

Lohman, D. F., & Hagen, E. P. (2001). Cognitive Abilities Test, Form 6. Itasca, IL: Riverside Publishing.

Lonigan, C. J., Wagner, R. K., Torgesen, J. K., & Rashotte, C. A. (2007). Test of Preschool Early Literacy. Austin, TX: Pro-Ed.

Lord, C., Rutter, M., DiLavore, P., Risi, S., Gotham, K., & Bishop, S. (2012). Autism Diagnostic Observation Schedule–2nd Edition (ADOS-2). Los Angeles, CA: Western Psychological Corporation.

Luxton, D. D., Pruitt, L. D., & Osenbach, J. E. (2014). Best practices for remote psychological assessment via telehealth technologies. *Professional Psychology: Research and Practice, 45*(1), 27–35.

Malhotra, S., Chakrabarti, S., Shah, R., Sharma, M., Sharma, K. P., Malhotra, A., ... Jassal, G. D. (2017). Telepsychiatry clinical decision support system used by non-psychiatrists in remote areas: Validity & reliability of diagnostic module. *The Indian Journal of Medical Research, 146*(2), 196–204.

Manguno-Mire, G. M., Thompson, J. W., Shore, J. H., Croy, C. D., Artecona, J. F., & Pickering, J. W. (2007). The use of telemedicine to evaluate competency to stand trial: A preliminary randomized controlled study. *Journal of the American Academy of Psychiatry and the Law Online, 35*(4), 481–489.

McCaffrey, R. J., Lynch, J. K., Leark, R. A., & Reynolds, C. R. (2019). Pediatric Performance Validity Test Suite. Toronto, ON: Multihealth Systems.

McConaughy, S. H., Harder, V. S., Antshel, K. M., Gordon, M., Eiraldi, R., & Dumenci, L. (2010). Incremental validity of test session and classroom observations in a multimethod assessment of attention deficit/hyperactivity disorder. *Journal of Clinical Child & Adolescent Psychology, 39*(5), 650–666.

Menton, W. H., Crighton, A. H., Tarescavage, A. M., Marek, R. J., Hicks, A. D., & Ben-Porath, Y. S. (2019). Equivalence of laptop and tablet administrations of the Minnesota Multiphasic Personality Inventory-2 Restructured Form. *Assessment, 26*, 661–669.

Meyer, G. J., Finn, S. E., Eyde, L. D., Kay, G. G., Moreland, K. L., Dies, R. R., ... Reed, G. M. (2001). Psychological testing and psychological assessment: A review of evidence and issues. *American Psychologist, 56*(2), 128–165.

Meyer, G. J., Viglione, D. J., Mihura, J. L., Erard, R. E., & Erdberg, P. (2011). *Rorschach Performance Assessment System: Administration, coding, interpretation, and technical manual.* Toledo, OH: Rorschach Performance Assessment System.

Meyer, G. J., Viglione, D. J., Mihura, J. L., Erdberg, P., Bram, A., Giromini, L., ... Vanhoyland, M. (2020). Recommendations concerning remote administration of the Rorschach. Toledo, OH: Rorschach Performance Assessment System. Retrieved from https://rpas.org/Docs/Remote%20Administration%20of%20the%20Rorschach.pdf

Mezure. (n.d.). *MEZURE clinical manual.* New York, NY: Mezure. Retrieved from https://www.studentassessments.com/images/mezureclinicalmanual.pdf

Mihura, J. L., Roy, M., & Graceffo, R. A. (2017). Psychological assessment training in clinical psychology doctoral programs. *Journal of Personality Assessment, 99*(2), 153–164.

Miller, D. N., & Nickerson, A. B. (2007). Projective techniques and the school-based assessment childhood internalizing disorders: A critical analysis. *Journal of Projective Psychology and Mental Health, 14*, 48–58.

Millon, T. (1994). Millon Clinical Multiaxial Inventory, Third Edition (MCMI-III). Minneapolis, MN: National Computer Systems.

Millon, T. (with Grossman, S., & Millon, C.). (2015). *Manual for the Millon Clinical Multiaxial Inventory (4th ed.)*. Bloomington, MN: Pearson.

Monteiro, M. (2018). Monteiro Interview Guidelines for Diagnosing the Autism Spectrum (2nd ed.). Torrance, CA: Psychological Services.

Morgan, R. D., Patrick, A. R., & Magaletta, P. R. (2008). Does the use of telemental health alter the treatment experience? Inmates' perceptions of telemental health versus face-to-face treatment modalities. *Journal of Consulting and Clinical Psychology, 76*(1), 158–162.

Mouzourakis, P. (1996). Videoconferencing: Techniques and challenges. *Interpreting, 1*(1), 21–38.

Naglieri, J. A., Drasgow, F., Schmit, M., Handler, L., Prifitera, A., Margolis, A., & Velasquez, R. (2004). Psychological testing on the internet: New problems, old issues. *American Psychologist, 59*, 150–162.

National Association of School Psychologists. (2017). Guidance for delivery of school psychological telehealth services. Bethesda, MD: NASP. Retrieved from http://www.nasponline.org/assets/documents/Guidance_Telehealth_Virtual_Service_%20Delivery_Final%20(2).pdf

National Association of School Psychologists. (2020a). The professional standards of the National Association of School Psychologists. Bethesda, MD: NASP. Retrieved from https://www.nasponline.org/x55315.xml

National Association of School Psychologists. (2020b). Virtual service delivery in response to COVID-19 disruptions. Bethesda, MD: NASP. Retrieved from https://www.nasponline.org/resources-and-publications/resources-and-podcasts/school-climate-safety-and-crisis/health-crisis-resources/virtual-service-delivery-in-response-to-covid-19-disruptions

National Research Council. (1999). *Uncommon measures: Equivalence and linkage among educational tests*. Washington, DC: The National Academies Press.

Nazneen, N., Rozga, A., Smith, C. J., Oberleitner, R., Abowd, G. D., & Arriaga, R. I. (2015). A novel system for supporting autism diagnosis using home videos: Iterative development and evaluation of system design. *JMIR mHealth and uHealth, 3*(2), e68.

Oak, E., Viezel, K. D., Dumont, R., & Willis, J. O. (2018). Wechsler administration and scoring errors made by graduate students and school psychologists. *Journal of Psychoeducational Assessment, 37*(6), 679–391.

Orbach, Y., & Lamb, M. E. (2001). The relationship between within-interview contradictions and eliciting interviewer utterances. *Child Abuse & Neglect*, *25*(3), 323–333.

Ortiz, S. O. (2018). Ortiz Picture Vocabulary Acquisition Test. Toronto, ON: Multihealth Systems.

Otto, R. K., & Krauss, D. A. (2009). Contemplating the presence of third party observers and facilitators in psychological evaluations. *Assessment*, *16*, 362–372.

Owings-Fonner, N. (2019). Comparing the latest telehealth solutions. Washington, DC: APA. Retrieved from https://www.apaservices.org/practice/business/technology/tech-column/telehealth-solutions

Parmanto, B., Pulantara, I. W., Schutte, J. L., Saptono, A., & McCue, M. P. (2013). An integrated telehealth system for remote administration of an adult autism assessment. *Telemedicine and e-Health*, *19*(2), 88–94.

Pearson. (2020). Wechsler Individual Achievement Test (4th ed.). Bloomington, MN: Pearson.

Pijl, M. K., Rommelse, N. N., Hendriks, M., De Korte, M. W., Buitelaar, J. K., & Oosterling, I. J. (2018). Does the Brief Observation of Social Communication Change help moving forward in measuring change in early autism intervention studies? *Autism*, *22*(2), 216–226.

Prime, H., Wade, M., & Browne, D. T. (2020). Risk and resilience in family well-being during the COVID-19 pandemic. *American Psychologist*. Retrieved from https://psycnet.apa.org/fulltext/2020-34995-001.pdf

Proctor, T. P., Chuah, S. C., Montgomery, M., & Way, W. D. (2019). Comparability of performance on the SAT suite of assessments across pencil-and-paper and computer-based modes of administration: SAT, PSAT™ 10, and PSAT™ 8/9. The College Board. Retrieved from https://collegereadiness.collegeboard.org/pdf/comparing-performance-paper-digital-tests-sat-suite-assessments.pdf

Qiu, W. Q., Dean, M., Liu, T., George, L., Gann, M., Cohen, J., & Bruce, M. L. (2010). Physical and mental health of homebound older adults: An overlooked population. *Journal of the American Geriatrics Society*, *58*(12), 2423–2428.

Rabin, L. A., Paolillo, E., & Barr, W. B. (2016). Stability in test-usage practices of clinical neuropsychologists in the United States and Canada over a 10-year period: A follow-up survey of INS and NAN members. *Archives of Clinical Neuropsychology*, *31*, 206–230.

Raiford, S. E. (2017). *Essentials of WISC-V integrated assessment*. Hoboken, NJ: John Wiley & Sons.

Raiford, S. E., & Coalson, D. L. (2014). *Essentials of WPPSI-IV assessment*. Hoboken, NJ: John Wiley & Sons.

Raiford, S. E., Coalson, D. L., & Engi, M. D. (2014). WPPSI-IV score differences across demographic groups. In S. E. Raiford & D. L. Coalson, (Eds.), *Essentials of WPPSI-IV assessment* (pp. 231–236). Hoboken, NJ: John Wiley & Sons.

Raiford, S. E., Drozdick, L. W., & Zhang, O. (2015). Q-interactive special group studies: The WISC–V and children with autism spectrum disorder and accompanying language impairment or attention-deficit/hyperactivity disorder (Q-interactive Technical Report 11). Bloomington, MN: Pearson. Retrieved from http://images.pearsonclinical.com/images/assets/WISC-V/Q-i-TR11_WISC-V_ADHDAUTL_FNL.pdf

Raiford, S. E., Drozdick, L. W., & Zhang, O. (2016). Q-interactive special group studies: The WISC–V and children with specific learning disorders in reading or mathematics (Q-interactive Technical Report 13). Bloomington, MN: Pearson. Retrieved from https://www.pearsonassessments.com/content/dam/school/global/clinical/us/assets/q-interactive/012-s-Technical_Report_9_WISC-V_Children_with_Intellectual_Giftedness_and_Intellectual_Disability.pdf

Raiford, S. E., Holdnack, J. A., Drozdick, L. W., & Zhang, O. (2014). Q-interactive special group studies: The WISC–V and children with intellectual giftedness and intellectual disability (Q-interactive Technical Report 9). Bloomington, MN: Pearson. Retrieved from http://www.helloq.com/content/dam/ped/ani/us/helloq/media/Technical_Report_9_WISC-V_Children_with_Intellectual_Giftedness_and_Intellectual_Disability.pdf

Rajkumar, R. P. (2020). COVID-19 and mental health: A review of the existing literature. *Asian Journal of Psychiatry*, 102066.

Ramsden, J. (2018). "Are you calling me a liar"? Clinical interviewing more for trust than knowledge with high-risk men with antisocial personality disorder. *International Journal of Forensic Mental Health*, *17*(4), 351–361.

Randolph, C. (1998). Repeatable Battery for the Assessment of Neuropsychological Status. San Antonio, TX: Psychological Corporation.

Randolph, C. (2012). RBANS Update: Repeatable Battery for the Assessment of Neuropsychological Status. San Antonio, TX: Psychological Corporation.

Reese, R. J., Slone, N. C., Soares, N., & Sprang, R. (2015). Using telepsychology to provide a group parenting program: A preliminary evaluation of effectiveness. *Psychological Services*, *12*(3), 274–282.

Reynolds, C. R. (2014). Reynolds Adaptable Intelligence Test. Lutz, FL: Psychological Assessment Resources.

Reynolds, C. R., & Kamphaus, R. W. (2015). Reynolds Intellectual Assessment Scales, Second Edition and the Reynolds Intellectual Screening Test (2nd ed.). Lutz, LF: PAR, Inc.

Reynolds, C. R., Voress, J. K., & Kamphaus, R. W. (2014). Mathematics Fluency and Calculation Tests. Austin, TX: Pro-Ed.

Reynolds, M. R., Keith, T. Z., Ridley, K. P., & Patel, P. G. (2008). Sex differences in latent general and broad cognitive abilities for children and youth: Evidence from higher-order MG-MACS and MIMIC models. *Intelligence, 36*, 236–260.

Riddle, B. C., Byers, C. C., & Grimesey, J. L. (2002). Literature review of research and practice in collaborative assessment. *The Humanistic Psychologist, 30*(1–2), 33–48.

Roid, G. H. (2003). Stanford-Binet Intelligence Scales (5th ed.). Austin, TX: Pro-Ed.

Rollins, K. M., & Raiford, S. E. (2017a). Intelligent WISC-V integrated administration. In S. E. Raiford (Ed.), *Essentials of WISC-V integrated assessment* (pp. 35–89). Hoboken, NJ: John Wiley & Sons.

Rollins, K. M., & Raiford, S. E. (2017b). WISC-V integrated scoring. In S. E. Raiford (Ed.), *Essentials of WISC-V integrated assessment* (pp. 90–122). Hoboken, NJ: John Wiley & Sons.

Roper, B. L., Ben-Porath, Y. S., & Butcher, J. N. (1995). Comparability and validity of computerized adaptive testing with the MMPI-2. *Journal of Personality Assessment, 65*, 358–371.

Ruskin, P. E., Reed, S., Kumar, R., Kling, M. A., Siegel, E., Rosen, M., & Hauser, P. (1998). Reliability and acceptability of psychiatric diagnosis via telecommunication and audiovisual technology. *Psychiatric Services, 49*, 1086–1088.

Sandford, J. A., & Sandford, S. E. (2015). Integrated Visual and Auditory Continuous Performance Test (2nd ed.). North Chesterfield, VA: BrainTrain.

Schopp, L., Johnstone, B., & Merrell, D. (2000). Telehealth and neuropsychological assessment: New opportunities for psychologists. *Professional Psychology: Research and Practice, 31*(2), 179–183.

Schrank, F. A., Mather, N., & McGrew, K. S. (2014). Woodcock-Johnson IV Tests of Achievement. Rolling Meadows, IL: Riverside.

Schrank, F. A., McGrew, K. S., & Mather, N. (2014). WJ IV Tests of Cognitive Abilities. Rolling Meadows, IL: Riverside.

Schrank, F. A., McGrew, K. S., & Mather, N. (2015). Woodcock-Johnson IV Tests of Early Cognitive and Academic Development. Rolling Meadows, IL: Riverside.

Shemmassian, S. K., & Lee, S. S. (2016). Predictive utility of four methods of incorporating parent and teacher symptom ratings of ADHD for longitudinal outcomes. *Journal of Clinical Child & Adolescent Psychology, 45*(2), 176–187.

Shore, J. H., & Manson, S. M. (2004). Telepsychiatric care of American Indian veterans with post-traumatic stress disorder: Bridging gaps in geography, organizations, and culture. *Telemedicine Journal & e-Health, 10*, 64–69.

Shore, J. H., Savin, D., Orton, H., Beals, J., & Manson, S. M. (2007). Diagnostic reliability of telepsychiatry in American Indian veterans. *The American Journal of Psychiatry, 164*, 115–118.

Shriberg, D. (2016). Commentary: School psychologists as advocates for racial justice and social justice: Some proposed steps. *School Psychology Forum, 10*(3), 337–339.

Simpson, S. (2001). The provision of a psychology service to Shetland via teleconferencing: Patient/therapist satisfaction and ability to develop a therapeutic alliance. *Journal of Telemedicine and Telecare, 7*(Suppl. 1), 34–36.

Singh, S. P., Arya, D., & Peters, T. (2007). Accuracy of telepsychiatric assessment of new routine outpatient referrals. *BMC Psychiatry, 7*(1), 55.

Smith, C. J., Rozga, A., Matthews, N., Oberleitner, R., Nazneen, N., & Abowd, G. (2017). Investigating the accuracy of a novel telehealth diagnostic approach for autism spectrum disorder. *Psychological Assessment, 29*(3), 245–252.

Soilevuo Grønnerød, J., & Grønnerød, C. (2012). The Wartegg Zeichen Test: A literature overview and a meta-analysis of reliability and validity. *Psychological Assessment, 24*(2), 476–489.

Stain, H. J., Payne, K., Thienel, R., Michie, P., Vaughan, C., & Kelly, B. (2011). The feasibility of videoconferencing for neuropsychological assessments of rural youth experiencing early psychosis. *Journal of Telemedicine and Telecare, 17*, 328–331.

Stein, M. B., Hilsenroth, M. J., Slavin-Mumford, J., & Pinsker, J. (2011). Social Cognition and Object Relations Scale: Global Rating Method (SCORS-G; 4th ed.). Unpublished manuscript, Massachusetts General Hospital and Harvard Medical School, Boston, MA.

Steinmetz, J., Brunner, M., Loarer, E., & Houssemand, C. (2010). Incomplete psychometric equivalence of scores obtained on the manual and the computer version of the Wisconsin Card Sorting Test? *Psychological Assessment, 22*(1), 199–202.

Sternberg, K. J., Lamb, M. E., Esplin, P. W., Orbach, Y., & Hershkowitz, I. (2002). Using a structure interview protocol to improve the quality of investigative interviews. In M. L. Eisen, J. A. Quas, & G. S. Goodman (Eds.), *Personality and clinical psychology series. Memory and suggestibility in the forensic interview* (pp. 409–436). Mahwah, NJ: Lawrence Erlbaum Associates Publishers.

Stolwyk, R., Hammers, D. B., Harder, L., & Cullum, C. M. (2020). Teleneuropsychology (teleNP) in response to COVID-19 [Webinar]. Salt Lake City, UT: International Neurolopsychological Society. Retrieved from https://event.webinarjam.com/replay/13/pyl2nayhvspsp09

Styck, K. M., & Walsh, S. M. (2016). Evaluating the prevalence and impact of examiner errors on the Wechsler scales of intelligence: A meta-analysis. *Psychological Assessment, 28*, 3–17.

Sutherland, R., Trembath, D., Hodge, A., Drevensek, S., Lee, S., Silove, N., & Roberts, J. (2017). Telehealth language assessments using consumer grade equipment in rural and urban settings: Feasible, reliable and well tolerated. *Journal of Telemedicine and Telecare, 23*(1), 106–115.

Taylor, S. A., & Wright, A. J. (2020). Cognitive and academic tele-assessment: A practical guide. New York, NY: PresenceLearning, Inc. Retrieved from www.presencelearning.com/Cognitive-and-Academic-Tele-Assessment-A-Practical-Guide

Temple, V., Drummond, C., Valiquette, S., & Jozsvai, E. (2010). A comparison of intellectual assessments over video conferencing and in-person for individuals with ID: Preliminary data. *Journal of Intellectual Disability Research, 54*(6), 573–577.

Tharinger, D. J., Finn, S. E., Arora, P., Judd-Glossy, L., Ihorn, S. M., & Wan, J. T. (2012). Therapeutic assessment with children: Intervening with parents "behind the mirror". *Journal of Personality Assessment, 94*(2), 111–123.

Thorndike, E. (1922). On finding equivalent scores in tests of intelligence. *Journal of Applied Psychology, 6*(1), 29–33.

Tolin, D. F., Gilliam, C., Wootton, B. M., Bowe, W., Bragdon, L. B., Davis, E., … Hallion, L. S. (2018). Psychometric properties of a structured diagnostic interview for DSM-5 anxiety, mood, and obsessive-compulsive and related disorders. *Assessment, 25*(1), 3–13.

Tombaugh, T. N. (1996). Test of Memory Malingering. Toronto, ON: Multihealth Systems.

Torgesen, J. K., Wagner, R. K., & Rashotte, C. A. (2012). Test of Word Reading Efficiency (2nd ed.). Austin, TX: Pro-Ed.

TOVA Company. (2020). Test of Variables of Attention. Langley, WA: TOVA Company.

Turkstra, L. S., Quinn-Padron, M., Johnson, J. E., Workinger, M. S., & Antoniotti, N. (2012). In-person versus telehealth assessment of discourse ability in adults with traumatic brain injury. *The Journal of Head Trauma Rehabilitation, 27*(6), 424–432.

Vahia, I. V., Ng, B., Camacho, A., Cardenas, V., Cherner, M., Depp, C. A., … Agha, Z. (2015). Telepsychiatry for neurocognitive testing in older rural Latino adults. *The American Journal of Geriatric Psychiatry, 23*, 666–670.

van Dorn, A., Cooney, R. E., & Sabin, M. L. (2020). COVID-19 exacerbating inequalities in the US. *The Lancet, 395*(10232), 1243–1244.

Varker, T., Brand, R. M., Ward, J., Terhaag, S., & Phelps, A. (2019). Efficacy of synchronous telepsychology interventions for people with anxiety, depression, posttraumatic stress disorder, and adjustment disorder: A rapid evidence assessment. *Psychological Services, 16*(4), 621–635.

Vestal, L., Smith-Olinde, L., Hicks, G., Hutton, T., & Hart, J., Jr. (2006). Efficacy of language assessment in Alzheimer's disease: Comparing in-person examination and telemedicine. *Clinical Interventions in Aging, 1*, 467–471.

Wadsworth, H. E., Dhima, K., Womack, K. B., Hart, J., Jr, Weiner, M. F., Hynan, L. S., & Cullum, C. M. (2018). Validity of teleneuropsychological assessment in older patients with cognitive disorders. *Archives of Clinical Neuropsychology, 33*(8), 1040–1045.

Wagner, G. P., & Trentini, C. M. (2009). Assessing executive functions in older adults: A comparison between the manual and the computer-based versions of the Wisconsin Card Sorting Test. *Psychology & Neuroscience, 2*(2), 195–198.

Wagner, R. K., Torgesen, J. K., Rashotte, C. A., & Pearson, N. A. (1999). Comprehensive Test of Phonological Processing (2nd ed.). Austin, TX: Pro-Ed.

Waite, M., Theodoros, D., Russell, T., & Cahill, L. (2010). Internet-based telehealth assessment of language using the CELF-4. *Language, Speech, and Hearing Services in Schools, 41*, 445–458.

Watzlaf, V. J., Zhou, L., DeAlmeida, D. R., & Hartman, L. M. (2017). A systematic review of research studies examining telehealth privacy and security practices used by healthcare providers. *International Journal of Telerehabilitation, 9*(2), 39–59.

Wechsler, D. (1991). Wechsler Intelligence Scale for Children—Third Edition. New York, NY: Psychological Corporation.

Wechsler, D. (2003). Wechsler Intelligence Scale for Children—Fourth Edition. Bloomington, MN: Pearson.

Wechsler, D. (2008). Wechsler Adult Intelligence Scale—Fourth Edition. San Antonio, TX: Pearson Assessment.

Wechsler, D. (2009). Wechsler Memory Scale (4th ed.). Bloomington, MN: Pearson.

Wechsler, D. (2011). Wechsler Abbreviated Scale of Intelligence (2nd ed.). Bloomington, MN: Pearson.

Wechsler, D. (2012). Wechsler Preschool and Primary Scale of Intelligence (4th ed.). Bloomington, MN: Pearson.

Wechsler, D. (2014). Wechsler Intelligence Scale for Children – Fifth Edition. Bloomington, MN: Pearson.

Wechsler, D., & Kaplan, E. (2015). Wechsler Intelligence Scale for Children Integrated (5th ed.). Bloomington, MN: Pearson.

Westen, D. (1995). Social Cognition and Object Relations Scale: Q-sort for projective stories (SCORS-Q). Unpublished manuscript, Department of Psychiatry, Cambridge Hospital and Harvard Medical School, Boston, MA.

Wiederholt, J. L., & Blalock, G. (2000). Gray Silent Reading Test. Austin, TX: Pro-Ed.

Wiederholt, J. L., & Bryant, B. R. (2012). Gray Oral Reading Tests (5th ed.). Austin, TX: Pro-Ed.

Wiig, E. H., Semel, E., & Secord, W. A. (2013). Clinical Evaluation of Language Fundamentals (5th ed.). Bloomington, MN: Pearson.

Wilkinson, G. S., & Robertson, G. J. (2017). Wide Range Achievement Test (5th ed.). Bloomington, MN: Pearson.

Willard, M., Kroncke, A. P., & Harrison, E. L. R. (2019). Providing a CLEAR answer: Testing a novel scale to assess the accuracy of prediction of autism spectrum disorder diagnosis [unpublished white paper].

Williams, K. T. (2018). Expressive Vocabulary Test (3rd ed.). Bloomington, MN: Pearson.

Wolf, M., & Denckla, M. B. (2005). Rapid Automatized Naming and Rapid Alternating Stimulus Tests. Austin, TX: Pro-Ed.

Woodcock, R. W. (2011). Woodcock Reading Mastery Test (3rd ed.). Bloomington, MN: Pearson.

Wright, A. J. (2018a). Equivalence of remote, online administration and traditional, face-to-face administration of the Reynolds Intellectual Assessment Scales-Second Edition (White paper). Retrieved from https://pages. presencelearning.com/rs/845-NEW-442/images/Content-PresenceLearning-Equivalence-of-Remote-Online-Administration-of-RIAS-2-White-Paper.pdf

Wright, A. J. (2018b). Equivalence of remote, online administration and traditional, face-to-face administration of the Woodcock–Johnson IV cognitive and achievement tests. *Archives of Assessment Psychology, 8*(1), 23–35.

Wright, A. J. (2020a). *Conducting psychological assessment: A guide for practitioners (2nd ed.).* Hoboken, NJ: John Wiley & Sons.

Wright, A. J. (2020b). Equivalence of remote, online administration and traditional, face-to-face administration of the Wechsler Intelligence Test for Children, Fifth Edition (WISC-V). Psychological Assessment.

Wright, A. J., Mihura, J. L., Pade, H., & McCord, D. M. (2020). Guidance on psychological tele-assessment during the COVID-19 crisis. Washington, DC: APA. Retrieved from https://www.apaservices.org/practice/reimbursement/health-codes/testing/tele-assessment-covid-19

Xie, X., Xue, Q., Zhou, Y., Zhu, K., Liu, Q., Zhang, J., & Song, R. (2020). Mental health status among children in home confinement during the coronavirus disease 2019 outbreak in Hubei Province, China. *JAMA Pediatrics.* Retrieved from https://jamanetwork.com/journals/jamapediatrics/article-abstract/2765196

Youngstrom, E. A., Choukas-Bradley, S., Calhoun, C. D., & Jensen-Doss, A. (2015). Clinical guide to the evidence-based assessment approach to diagnosis and treatment. *Cognitive and Behavioral Practice, 22*(1), 20–35.

Yun, K., Lurie, N., & Hyde, P. S. (2010). Moving mental health into the disaster-preparedness spotlight. *New England Journal of Medicine, 363*(13), 1193–1195.

Zhou, X., & Raiford, S. (2011). Using the WASI–II with the WISC®–V: Substituting WASI–II subtest scores when deriving WISC–V composite scores (WASI–II Technical Report #1). Bloomington, MN: Pearson. Retrieved from http://images.pearsonclinical.com/images/CA/Webinars/WASI-II-WISC-IV-Editorial-LR.pdf

Zimmerman, M. (2016). A review of 20 years of research on overdiagnosis and underdiagnosis in the Rhode Island Methods to Improve Diagnostic Assessment and Services (MIDAS) Project. *The Canadian Journal of Psychiatry, 61*(2), 71–79.

Case Study Contributors

Raja M. David, PsyD, ABPP
Licensed Psychologist
Minnesota Center for Collaborative/Therapeutic Assessment

Michelle Limon Freeman, PsyD
Associate Director and Director of Assessment, Neuropsychologist
Summit Center

Lisa Michelle Griffiths, PsyD
Colorado Licensed Psychologist
Center for Valued Living, PLLC (C4VL)

Silva Hassert, PhD
California Licensed Psychologist
Mind Rising Psychological Assessment

Nate Kindig, B. S.
School Psychology Intern
Assessment Intervention Management, LLC

Rebecca MurrayMetzger, PsyD
Licensed Psychologist, Owner
San Francisco Mind Matters

Dimitra Robokos, PhD
NYS Licensed Psychologist and Clinical Assistant Professor
Department of Pediatrics
Albert Einstein College of Medicine

Stephanie Tabashnek, PsyD, JD
Forensic Psychologist
Wellesley, MA

Dustin B. Wygant, PhD
Professor of Psychology
Director of Clinical Training
Eastern Kentucky University

Nancy Corral Ziebert, PhD
Partner, Clinical Psychologist
Positive Developments, LLC

Index

Essentials of Psychological Tele-Assessment, First Edition.
A. Jordan Wright and Susan Engi Raiford
© 2021 John Wiley & Sons, Inc. Published 2021 by John Wiley & Sons, Inc.